HOCKEY HALL OF FAME

TIMELINE OF THE GAME

150 Years of Hockey Stories

12

HOCKEY HALL OF FAME

TIMELINE OF THE GAME

150 Years of Hockey Stories

Don Weekes

FIREFLY BOOKS

Published by Firefly Books Ltd. 2025

2ND PRINTING, 2025

Library of Congress Control Number: 2025935150

Library and Archives Canada Cataloguing in Publication
Title: Timeline of the game : 150 years of hockey stories / Don Weekes.
Other titles: Hockey Hall of Fame
Names: Weekes, Don, author
Description: Includes bibliographical references and index.
Identifiers: Canadiana 20250179598 | ISBN 9780228105756 (softcover)
Subjects: LCSH: Hockey—History—Miscellanea. | LCSH: Hockey—Miscellanea. | LCSH: Hockey players—Miscellanea. | LCSH: National Hockey League—Miscellanea.
Classification: LCC GV846.5 .W44 2025 | DDC 796.96209—dc23

Published in the United States by
Firefly Books (U.S.) Inc.
P.O. Box 1338, Ellicott Station
Buffalo, New York 14205

Published in Canada by
Firefly Books Ltd.
50 Staples Avenue, Unit 1
Richmond Hill, Ontario L4B 0A7

Cover, interior design and colorization of cartoons and illustrations:
Gareth Lind, Lind Design
Typeset in Neue Plak, Unit Slab and Hockeynight Serif

Printed in China | E

We gratefully acknowledge the financial support of the Government of Canada for our publishing program.

Front cover photos credits:

Top row, from left to right: Hockey Hall of Fame (McGimsie), Imperial Oil/Turofsky Collection/ Hockey Hall of Fame (Richard), Macdonald Stewart/Hockey Hall of Fame (Howe), Paul Bereswill/Hockey Hall of Fame (Gretzky), Andre Ringuette/International Ice Hockey Federation (Poulin)

Bottom row, from left to right: Frank Prazak/ Hockey Hall of Fame (Sawchuk), Lewis Portnoy/Hockey Hall of Fame (Orr), Matt Zambonin/International Ice Hockey Federation (Knight), Jeanine Leech/Icon Sportswire (Ovechkin and Crosby)

Back cover photos credits:

Top row, from left to right: McCord Stewart Museum, Gift of the Estate of Mrs. Graham Drinkwater (Montreal Victorias), Andre Ringuette/International Ice Hockey Federation (Team Canada, additional copyright clearances courtesy of Hockey Canada), Graphic Artists/Hockey Hall of Fame (Crozier)

Bottom row, from left to right: Le Studio du Hockey/Hockey Hall of Fame (New York Americans), Dave Sandford/Hockey Hall of Fame (Hasek)

PREVIOUS SPREAD
Team Canada, 2022 Women's World Championship.

OPPOSITE
Toronto Maple Leafs vs. Boston Bruins, 1930–31.

For Danny and Dick and Ron

Connor McDavid scores against Finland's Mikko Koskinen, 2016 World Championship.

Bruins trainer Win Green, Dit Clapper and Jack Beattie in the locker room, Boston Garden, 1930s.

Introduction

The idea of a timeline of hockey history and the pivotal stories that shaped our great game is an outgrowth and culmination of all my writings, both as an author and a television producer of hockey. Each profession brought me a little closer to appreciating how a stick-and-ball game played on millponds and sloughs became an organized major league sport recognized around the world.

The inspiration to tell hockey's story dates to my youth in Île Bigras (on Rivière des Prairies, adjacent to Montreal), where every child learned to swim and skate from the time they learned to walk. There was little in the way of civic resources, but living on a small island forced the rural community to teach its own how to survive on its back rivers in all seasons. I owned a real hockey stick at four years old. Less a shooting or passing tool, it became my prop. I wielded the wooden shaft and blade as support to "run on my skates" across the ice. I got frostbite and near-frozen fingers and toes more times than I can recall. My sister Karen even rescued me once, after I had fallen through the ice near our home. All our hockey was outdoors. For the longest time I thought indoor play only existed for professional players. In fact, my first memory of playing arena hockey was at a failed tryout at 14 years old.

I grew up spoiled, watching the Canadiens win multiple Stanley Cups and attending multiple parades on Sainte-Catherine Street in downtown Montreal. It was a wonderful springtime indulgence few ever know, thanks to the heroics of Jean Béliveau, Ken Dryden, Yvan Cournoyer and Bob Gainey, among others.

When I came to write about hockey decades later, this modest oral history of boyhood dreams and other sporting passions became my wellspring from which to record the everyday mosaic of game competition, as it is lived season to season in NHL and world play.

Among those favorite stories that inspired me occurred during my years in television—one I've never recounted until now. It happened in 1996 during a series of extensive interviews for a television documentary on the Canadiens' historic move from the Montreal Forum. Over three days Montreal sportscaster Ron Reusch interviewed more than two dozen players about hockey's winningest franchise and what playing at the Forum meant to them. The one-on-one sit-downs were conducted in the President's Lounge just steps from the Forum bowl.

Bobby Orr half-chuckled at the time: "All I remember coming in here [Montreal] is speed. The Canadiens had lots of speed." Bobby Hull spoke about respect. He leaned into the camera at one point and recited Lieutenant-Colonel John McCrae's iconic First World War poem, "In Flanders Fields," in particular, the phrase every Canadiens player walks past on the Forum's dressing room wall. "To you from failing hands we throw the torch be yours to hold it high."

On the final day of shooting, several interviews were scheduled, including those with Ted Lindsay and Maurice Richard. During their playing days, these men shared a fierce vehemence typical of the Six Team Era. Back then opponents literally hated each other, refusing to even cross paths during train trips for home-and-away games, to avoid the temptation of inciting a fight. No love lost, Richard and Lindsay were noted as full-on hellfire enemies.

In retirement, when they met on that rare occasion, it was different. They seemed to have buried their bloodied hatchets.

The author (right) and best friend Keith Morse.

Following Reusch's interview with Lindsay in 1996, Lindsay asked me to ask Richard if they could meet and chat. I relished the opportunity of not only bringing these two great adversaries together again, but filming such a reunion, well after their playing days.

It would have been great.

I asked Lindsay to position himself, maybe 10 to 15 feet away from the door of the President's Lounge, which was where Richard and I would have to pass for his interview. After introducing myself to Richard, who by now was exhausted from multiple other interviews, I mentioned that Ted Lindsay was here and wanted to say hello. Would he be amenable?

He shook his head, preferring to only do the interview. I glanced over at Lindsay, now waiting for my signal to approach us. I subtly shook my head in his direction, indicating that any conversation was impossible. Richard and I walked right past Lindsay without a word, stepping into the bright lights of our remote studio shoot to meet Reusch.

I thought about this afterward. Not with regret, but with wonder. Entering the Forum, the house of Maurice Richard, required deference, a greater awe, even for the famed Ted Lindsay, an NHL scoring champion, multiple Stanley Cup winner, fearless organizer of the league's first players' association and, finally, a Hockey Hall of Famer. Both men live on in sport immortality, anointed with the rare praise of namesake NHL trophies. The Maurice "Rocket" Richard Trophy goes to the league's goal-scoring champion. The Ted Lindsay Award is presented to the NHL's MVP as voted by the players themselves.

Lindsay understood the reverence owed to Richard, especially in his own building. The Rocket's greatness was undiminished over time. He still carried all the adventure and aspirations coveted by players and his fandom. The on-ice battles won and lost. The camaraderie shared in rivalry. It was all there in that moment. I was useless to make any difference.

This book is about that kind of stuff, only more on the record, given the timeline's fact-driven storytelling style. It's about bringing an unobstructed picture of game evolution and the true grit and glory of sport. Not only the great scoring feats and acrobatic saves and the championships, but the animal spirits of raw competition.

In its connectedness, the game's timeline becomes part of our own personal timeline. The moments of victory, the disappointment following loss. The highs and lows of fandom do mirror team fortunes through primal and involuntary responses on a vicarious level.

Fans go through their own kind of physical experience of spectating—without getting shiners or bruised. It's why we watch and play and, with any luck, get to touch a small piece of that big league beauty.

—Don Weekes, February 2025

The Early Makings of a Winter Game

In the winter of 1875 a group of sportsmen gathered to play a game of hockey at the Victoria Skating Rink in Montreal. They had practiced for this initial roofed contest the previous two winters, often competing on outdoor ice using sticks, a ball and the rules of British field hockey. None of the events that chilly evening was planned with the intention of creating history. The spectacle of hockey, the passion of many countries, would have to wait another generation or more.

Before the game adopted its proper name and regulations as an organized sport in the late 19th century, its lineage dated to numerous ancestral games of odd names and archaic jargon, each played with a variety of shooting sticks, playing objects, goal markers and wildly confounding rules.

These centuries-old pursuits—the ancient Irish field game of hurley, the English game of field hockey, the Scottish game of shinty, the Indigenous game of baggataway (lacrosse), and other hockey-like play of bandy and shinny—were introduced by military officers and new settlers on Canadian ice, who were inspired through the sporting experiences of their home countries.

Until that time there had only been the occasional reference of "hockey," at least in North America. Its roots as a stick-ball game (played with skates on ice) evolved from the marshy regions of the Fens of eastern England during the mid-1700s, when it was called bandy. The play was eventually picked up and organized more formally by city schools in London.

In Nova Scotia, where ice games were played during the 1800s, there seemed little inclination to standardize play. British garrison members likely fielded a few teams that followed English soccer / field hockey rules. Despite ideal conditions to advance game evolution, play was kept mostly informal and largely undocumented, without any true regulatory body.

"Games were still marginally organized. Garrison officers played rudimentary hockey. Haligonians played their pick-up game of ricket," notes historian Jean-Patrice Martel, concerning two matches played on the same day and sheet of ice on Dartmouth's Oathill Lake in February 1867. Whatever the slapdash play resembled, both contests were emergent forms of hockey. But as *The Halifax Reporter* stated, "Very little science was displayed in either game."

An advertisement by the Starr Manufacturing Company of Dartmouth, Nova Scotia, promotes skates and "Mic-Mac" hockey sticks.

OPPOSITE
Edmund C. Coates, *Indians Playing Lacrosse on the Ice*, 1859.

1825 **"Till the snow fell, the game of hockey, played on the ice, was the morning's sport."**
—British explorer Sir John Franklin, during his second Arctic expedition in search of the Northwest Passage, in one of the earliest references to the game

Mi'kmaq making hockey sticks in Nova Scotia.

▲ 1800s Enthused by lacrosse or a primitive hurley, the Mi'kmaq play games using one-piece wooden sticks and a stone while wearing moccasins or skates. They become master stick carvers, harvesting tree roots and the trunks of hornbeam or yellow birch to produce the best-quality sticks for strength and durability. As hockey's popularity grows during the late-1800s, so too do their handcrafted creations. Widely revered and very heavy, no two sticks are alike. So inspired, the Starr Manufacturing Company brands its product Mic-Mac sticks.

Shubenacadie Canal laborers in Dartmouth, Nova Scotia.

▲ 1826–1861 Halifax/Dartmouth's sheltered harbor and numerous lakes afford ample ice for skating and hockey among British garrison servicemen and Irish and Scottish construction laborers working on the Shubenacadie Canal. Many moonlight at the Starr Manufacturing Company's plant, playing a vital role in hockey's growth, both in assembly shops, making premium skates and sticks, and on the ice in games on Dartmouth's frozen waterways.

Mid-1800s **Hockey isn't confined to Canada.** American references throughout the 1800s confirm *The Gazette*'s assessment in 1875 that hockey is "much in vogue on the ice in New England and other parts of the United States."

▸ 1852 The Quebec City Skating Rink opens as the first purpose-built indoor skating rink in the world.

Victoria Skating Rink, 1862.

1859 **"Ricket is the most exciting game that is played on ice."**

—*The Boston (Saturday) Evening Gazette* describes ricket and hurley play in Nova Scotia. Following his research in 1987, hockey historian J.W. Fitsell insists, "Ricket ... produced the first stickhandlers or puck-hogs."

▲ 1862 The Victoria Skating Rink in Montreal becomes the premier venue of its kind, with a natural ice-surface of 204 feet by 80 feet (62 m × 24 m). Its rink dimensions likely determined the standard 200 feet by 85 feet (61 m × 26 m) for all North American rinks.

▸ 1860s The Starr Manufacturing Company mass-produces and markets Mic-Mac sticks and the Starr Acme Skate. John Forbes' self-fastening all-metal skate uses a "swing lever" mechanism that attaches the skate to the skater's boot, making adjustments and removal easier than the old wood-top metal blades.

John Forbes, inventor of the Starr Acme Spring Skate.

1864 "I should be truly glad to see the police interfere whenever hockey is commenced."

—*Halifax Morning Sun*, in a rant against players, calling them "a disorderly mob, armed with sticks"

1864 Halifax opens Horticultural Gardens, among the first permanent covered skating rinks in Canada. The wooden arched-roof structure measures 180 feet by 60 feet (55 m × 18 m).

1870s Curlers dominate this wintry scene, with a game of ricket in the background.

Lacrosse on skates in Eastern Canada, February 1888.

1870s A pastime played by the Indigenous peoples of eastern North America, their ball game on ice is appropriated by white sportsmen on skates. Unlike lacrosse's field game, which became Canada's first national sport, the ice version is rejected as a winter activity.

1864 By the mid-1850s the word "hockey"—still not a fixture in sporting lexicon—is being used in Nova Scotia. On January 25 the *Halifax Morning Sun* rails about the ice-time debate between players and pleasure skaters: "Hockey, for example, ought to be sternly forbidden, as it is not only annoying (to leisurely skaters on a pond) but dangerous ... It is more than annoying to have the graceful evolutions of a charming quadrille broken up by the interruptions of a disorderly mob, armed with sticks and charging through the circle of skaters and spectators to the imminent danger of all. I should be truly glad to see the police interfere whenever hockey is commenced."

1867 Among some 1,500 skaters on Dartmouth's Oathill Lake in Nova Scotia, two similar games with different names are played. Officers of the British garrison and navy fleet stationed in Halifax play "hockey," modeled after English field hockey, while area locals "took up hurleys [sticks] and followed the ball" in their match of ricket.

1872 Halifax-born engineer James Creighton leaves home to work on the Lachine Canal and introduces his hockey experiences from his native Nova Scotia to the sporting clubs of Montreal and McGill University. During the next few winters Creighton persuades local sportsmen to take up the stick-and-ball game on skates on city ice.

James Creighton

James Creighton held many titles during a lifetime of accomplishments as a skater, scholar, engineer, lawyer and journalist. Nothing in his professional life, however, has stood the rugged test of history like his personal pursuits as an avid sportsman. Most notably, Creighton advanced the ice games played in his hometown of Halifax into the winter sport of hockey.

After arriving in Montreal in 1872, Creighton ordered sticks from Nova Scotia to play stick-and-ball games on ice among members of the Victoria Skating Club and students at McGill University in 1873 and 1874. During winter, "We used to play almost every day in the week and even on Sundays when we could bribe the caretaker of the Victoria rink to let us in," said friend Henry Joseph.

In March 1875, Creighton set the course of hockey, organizing two matches at Montreal's Victoria Skating Rink. They played an onside game with nine men apiece. To prevent injuries to spectators standing on an 8-inch-high (20 cm-high) platform at ice level, instead of a rubber ball, "a flat block of wood was used" that "slid about between the players with great velocity," noted reports.

This "flat block of wood" marks the conception of a distinctive Canadian game. Today, Creighton is recognized as the "father of organized hockey."

BELOW

A game of hockey on the ice, played with the same rules as the British sport of field hockey and using the same hooked sticks and ball as the original fair-weather version.

Our First Home

Hockey's first indoor games were played at "rinks" like the Victoria Skating Rink. As a sporting venue, Victoria Rink wasn't constructed for competitive play, but for the "fancy" skaters, the speed-skating races and the masquerade balls of its members. The two-story brick building in downtown Montreal had an obstacle-free viewing interior for onlookers. A promenade surrounded the boardless natural-ice sheet. Overhead, balconies and graceful wooden arches decorated its ceilings.

HOCKEY.—At the Rink last night a very large audience gathered to witness a novel contest on the ice. The game of hockey, though much in vogue on the ice in New England and other parts of the United States, is not much known here, and in consequence the game of last evening was looked forward to with great interest. Hockey is played usually with a ball, but last night, in order that no accident should happen, a flat block of wood was used, so that it should slide along the ice without rising, and thus going among the spectators to their discomfort. The game is like Lacrosse in one sense—the block having to go through flags

Report of the first organized indoor hockey game. *The Gazette*, March 4, 1875.

OPPOSITE *Hockey Match, Victoria Skating Rink, Montreal*, 1893.

Function defined its form as an ice palace designed for the skating public. Still, it became hockey's first home, accommodating the game's earliest practitioners and the roar and riotous crush of enthusiasts who witnessed hockey in the making. Victoria Rink hosted several historic crownings of the game's original champions. Frederick Arthur Stanley, also known as Lord Stanley of Preston, saw his first hockey match there.

During Stanley's final year as Canada's governor general, photographer William Notman's studios produced *Hockey Match, Victoria Skating Rink, Montreal*. The composite image combines the arts of painting and photography in a fictional action shot of a seven-man game between the Victoria Hockey Club and the Montreal Hockey Club. Montreal HC, sporting the winged wheel crest of the Montreal Amateur Athletic Association (AAA), were the first winners in Stanley Cup play in 1893.

Perhaps, Victoria Rink's greater contribution came from the more "controlled environment" at matches. As author Howard Shubert wrote, "Once enclosed, the sports themselves were transformed." Protected from the inclement elements, indoor games could now be advertised. Leagues could schedule seasons of play to paying customers. To accommodate the crowds, purpose-built hockey arenas were constructed.

For the first time, fans sat on benches and box seats and many more filled standing-room sections three and four deep. This changed the game experience for both player and patron, each seduced by the chaos of play and the mass of spectators that were packed shoulder to shoulder in tiered seating encircling the rink.

1875 The first indoor organized hockey game is played at the Victoria Skating Rink in Montreal on March 3, followed two weeks later by a March 16 contest. Game reports are published in several newspapers, including *The Gazette*. James Creighton plays a prominent role on and off the ice in both matches. Reports note a "block of wood" is used as a scoring object.

PLAYING RULES

FOR THE

GAME OF HOCKEY.

1.—The game shall be commenced, and renewed by a Bully in the centre of the ground. Goals shall be changed after each game.

2.—When a player hits the ball, any one of the same side who at such moment of hitting is nearer to the opponents' goal line is out of play, and may not touch the ball himself, or in any way whatever prevent any other player from doing so, until the ball has been played. A player must always be on his own side of the ball.

3—The ball may be stopped, but not carried or knocked on by any part of the body. No player shall raise his stick above his shoulder. Charging from behind, tripping, collaring, kicking or shinning shall not be allowed.

4.—When the ball is hit behind the goal line by the attacking side, it shall be brought out straight 15 yards, and started again by a Bully; but, if hit behind by any one of the side whose goal line it is, a player of the opposite side shall hit it out from within one yard of the nearest corner, no player of the attacking side at that time shall be within 20 yards of the goal line, and the defenders, with the exception of the goal-keeper, must be behind their goal line.

5.—When the ball goes off at the side, a player of the opposite side to that which hit it out shall roll it out from the point on the boundary line at which it went off at right angles with the boundary line, and it shall not be in play until it has touched the ice, and the 'player rolling it in shall not play it until it has been played by another player, every player being then behind the ball.

6.—On the infringement of any of the above rules, the ball shall be brought back and a Bully shall take place.

7.—All disputes shall be settled by the Umpires, or in the event of their disagreement, by the Referee.

▲ 1876 & 1877 The playing rules of hockey are adopted and first published in February 1877. Apart from minor changes, they faithfully duplicate a subset of the first field hockey rules of England's Hockey Association from 1875.

1876 The first known time the word "puck" is used in print. ***The Gazette's*** **February 7 game report between the Victoria Skating Club and the Montreal Football Club paints a quaint picture of early fandom—before rink boards: "A scramble, the puck is away and glides to the feet of two young ladies, who smilingly watch the sport; a rush for the coveted object and a youth of lengthy proportions stumbles, with the greatest possible awkwardness, into one of the young ladies' laps—shock No. 2—but no casualties to record."**

1877 McGill students form hockey's first organized club, the McGill University Hockey Club. They play two games that winter, a 2-1 win on February 15 and a 1-0 loss on March 19, both against a squad of lacrosse and football players called the Montreal Hockey Club. The teams compete under codified rules and dress in team uniforms. McGill remains the oldest officially formed hockey club in the world.

▼ 1878 Organized hockey spreads beyond Montreal, taking root originally in Quebec City with its first hockey team, the Quebec Hockey Club, in 1880. The team captain is Charles Miller, recognized as "the father of Quebec hockey."

The De La Vergne Machine Company's 220-ton refrigeration machine.

▲ 1879 Artificial ice-making equipment is installed for pleasure skaters at Gilmore's Gardens in New York City—the earliest artificial-ice rink in North America. Water is sprayed over coiled piping to make the ice sheet.

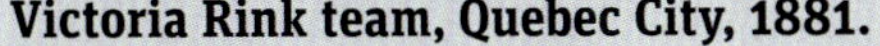

Victoria Rink team, Quebec City, 1881.

Quebec City Skating Rink.

▲ 1881 Quebec (City) Hockey Club play an intercity series against the Victoria Skating Club team of Montreal. Each team wins a game in the original Battle of Quebec.

▲ 1881 A mock face-off by the McGill University Hockey Club is likely the earliest known hockey team photograph. Players in striped jerseys pose with a variety of sticks, skates, pants and hats at Crystal Palace Skating Rink in Montreal.

▸ 1883 The Montreal Winter Carnival. The McGill University Hockey Club win the inaugural Carnival championship. The trophy is the earliest known hockey trophy ever awarded.

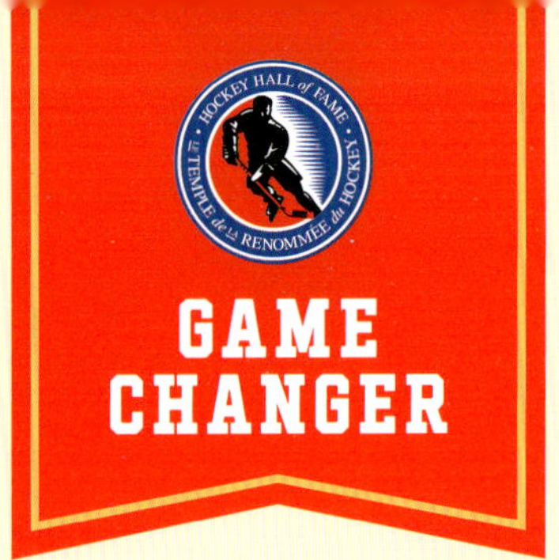

Montreal Winter Carnival

Initiated by city merchants to promote wintertime tourism, Montreal's carnivals ran from 1883 to 1889, a time when, according to period writing, people suffered greatly from the cold extremes but weren't about to be wintered in. When freeze-up halted foreign trade at the port of Montreal, "the frozen river became a bridge, a playground, a crystalline freeway connecting cities and neighbours by lightning-fast sleighs," wrote author Edward Cavell. On that playing field of river ice that linked the Island of Montreal and the city's South Shore, sportsmen made hockey history. Their "*bona fide* hockey clubs" participated in the carnival's round-robin Grand Hockey Tournament, the game's first-ever championship series, in 1883.

McGill University, the Montreal Victorias and Quebec competed in four games over two days for the Carnival Cup that year. As Henry Sandham's illustration below depicts, the initial contests were played outdoors, and in frigid temperatures of -6°F (-21°C). After conditions deteriorated overnight, Crystal Palace Skating Rink hosted the third game and Victoria Rink the final match, an exhibition contest between the Victorias and Quebec that drew 2,000 spectators and closed the carnival. Tied games dominated the competition, but fittingly, McGill, the first organized hockey club in the world, beat the Vics 1-0 to win hockey's first cup title.

Before the carnivals, "Hockey did not elicit much enthusiasm in Montreal or elsewhere," wrote author John Chi-Kit Wong. Winter sports like curling, sleighing and snowshoeing captured the populace's fancy and most of the attention in the press. "Hockey will yet have a great fascination for spectators," reports noted. "It is perhaps to its disadvantage that it has to compete with so many exciting features of the Carnival."

Game popularity climbed steadily during the 1880s and those contests were a major catalyst, said Wong. The competition and social appeal of the event sparked great enthusiasm among locals and tourists, with many visitors taking "the novel game of hockey" back to their communities. Word spread and, in subsequent years, the carnivals attracted new teams from Ottawa and points west.

BELOW
***Hockey*, Henry Sandham's spirited depiction of the seven-man game in *Wide Awake*, December 1883.**

▲ 1884 **A hockey game on an outdoor rink on McGill University's campus is likely the earliest known photograph of actual game play. Mount Royal looms in the background.**

1886 The first recorded international game features the Montreal Hockey Club versus local sportsmen from the Van Ness House, a prominent Burlington, Vermont, hotel. Montreal wins 3-0. The match, part of the Carnival of Winter Sports, is played on Lake Champlain.

► 1886 **The first organized game in Kingston, Ontario.** Queen's University plays the cadets of the Royal Military College under Montreal Rules on Kingston's frozen harbor. Lennox Irvin scores the lone goal in Queen's 1-0 win. *Athletic Life* reports that Irvin's marker is "the first goal of the first authentic match in Ontario." More Queen's-RMC games are staged the following years in what some consider hockey's longest-standing team rivalry. Unprecedented, the matchups represent a cross section of players and rules from Montreal and Halifax. Competitors also come from Quebec City and Ottawa, many taking their skills and love of the game to non-playing markets and regions across North America.

The Royal Military College hockey team, Kingston, 1888.

Wilbur Wright pilots an early glider, 1902.

▲ 1886 Seventeen years before Wilbur and Orville Wright flew their first plane into aviation history, biographers believe Wilbur lost teeth in an ice game of shinny in hometown Dayton, Ohio. During his recovery he read extensively, including several scientific books and journals. "The hockey accident set the stage that led to his intense interest in flight," said historian Dawne Dewey, formerly of Wright State University.

1886 The Amateur Hockey Association of Canada (1887–1898) is established. The five-team circuit of Montreal and Ottawa clubs plays a seven-man, onside game — no attacking player could precede the puck. The league's goal posts are moved 5 feet (1.5 m) out from the rink ends instead of at the rink boundary, as in soccer and field hockey. Historians consider the AHAC "the ancestor of all North American hockey leagues" and, by their estimate, of all ice hockey leagues in the world.

1886 The Montreal Rules are implemented. In a hockey first, a special four-team tournament in Montreal is regulated by 14 rules, including standardizing game time, as well as stick, puck and goal sizes, and, unlike Halifax's rules, players can't pass to players ahead of the puck. The series, with two best-of-three rounds and a playoff, is won by the Montreal Crystals. The prize money is $80. "A new course was charted for hockey," noted historian J.W. Fitsell.

▲ 1887 Montreal AAA goalie Tom Paton, the first Stanley Cup-winning goalie, introduces hockey in Toronto. After rousing friends with stories of hockey "fast becoming the leading game in winter in Montreal," Paton orders sticks, pucks and "a few copies of the rules" to play games on Toronto ice a few nights later.

▲ 1888 The Granite Curling Club beat the Caledonian Curling Club 4-1 at the Granite Club Rink in Toronto's first official hockey contest, on February 16.

▲ 1888–1893 Frederick Arthur Stanley, Lord Stanley of Preston, serves a five-year term as Canada's sixth governor general. During his initial winter in Canada, Lord Stanley attends his first hockey game at the 1889 Montreal Winter Carnival. That same season, Stanley's daughter, Isobel, and three of his sons play casual games on the outdoor rink at Rideau Hall—all four promoting hockey's popularity in Ontario through their active participation.

The earliest known photograph of women playing hockey. Isobel Stanley wears an ankle-length white coat on Rideau Hall's rink, 1890.

▲ 1889 Lord Stanley's daughter, Isobel, becomes an immediate fan and participant of hockey. In March, her Government House team defeats a Rideau women's team on outdoor ice at Rideau Hall in Ottawa. It's considered the first women's hockey match.

The Dartmouth Chebuctos, 1888.

HALIGONIANS AT HOCKEY.

The Montrealers Meet the Visitors at Their Own Game.

◄ 1889 The Halifax-style game comes to Quebec. The first-ever interprovincial hockey series, pitting the Dartmouth Chebuctos against the Montreal Hockey Club and the Montreal Crystals, alternated, half under Halifax rules, which permitted forward passing, and half under Montreal rules, in which passes were only made laterally. Montreal reports said, "The Chebucto Club played a different formation than the home team; no offside, no lifting, etc—well!"

"The goals [posts] consisted of two curling stones, placed at each end *parallel* with the sides, instead of at right angles, it is supposed to prevent a goal from being scored by *lifting*, and the men lined out as in lacrosse." A force among Halifax teams, the Chebuctos lost 6–1 and 4–1.

1888 **"If Montreal hockey clubs attract thousands of spectators to see their games there is no reason whatever why Toronto people should not support this game equally as well."**

—*The Gazette*, February 11, 1888

1890 **The Ontario Hockey Association is formed.** Within a few years hockey clubs outnumber all other athletic clubs and associations in Toronto.

◂ **1889** The Rideau Rebels, Arthur and Edward Stanley's vice-regal exhibition squad of parliamentary officials and friends, broaden hockey's appeal in Ontario with their barnstorming forays into Kingston, Lindsay and Toronto.

The Winnipeg Victorias, 1893.

▴ **1890** **Sportsmen in Winnipeg form the city's first hockey team, the famed Victorias.** Within the year, the Winnipeg Hockey Club begins play as their only opponent. A third team, Fort Osborne's B Squadron of the Royal Canadian Dragoons, joins city league games in 1892.

▴ **1890s** The Starr Manufacturing Company introduces the company's sixth model, the Mic-Mac Hockey Skate — the first skate designed for "hockeyists." Similar to this later ad, Dartmouth's *Atlantic Weekly* dubs it "the fastest skate in the world."

Lord Stanley's Cup

In 1892, Lord Stanley of Preston donated a silver bowl to the "champion hockey team in the Dominion." Engraved with his family's coat of arms and crest, the Dominion Hockey Challenge Cup would make Canada the first nation of hockey, while turning his trophy into an international icon of game supremacy. Nicknamed the Stanley Cup, it was first awarded to the country's amateur champions.

A trophy prize appealed to Stanley's sense of fair gamesmanship. The Ottawa Hockey Club were champions throughout 1891–92, without a loss in six straight games (including four wins against Montreal's two teams). But because the Montreal Hockey Club beat Ottawa 1-0 in the final challenge on March 7, the Montreal-based AHAC awarded that season's final league title to the Montrealers.

This ruling likely displeased Stanley. Soon after, at a banquet honoring the Ottawa team at Russell House Hotel in Ottawa, Stanley, through an aide, announced his new trophy and suggested a different format to decide the next AHAC champion. At December's annual meeting, the Ottawa Hockey Club recommended a "championship series," whereby the club with the most victories in the eight-game season is declared the Cup holders. The idea, while not completely original, was accepted. The next year, Lord Stanley returned to England, never having witnessed a game in competition for his Cup.

Big Money. Tough Men.

The era from Lord Stanley's Cup of 1893 to the beginnings of NHL play in 1917–18 was a period of ambitious rise. Hockey struggled to define its raw self, toying with sporting tradition, embryonic rules and imperfect equipment, while setting standards over money and morality, and, at times, failing miserably.

Billy Barlow's 1893 Stanley Cup championship gold ring.

OPPOSITE
Fred "Cyclone" Taylor, 1900s.

In those short years an ice game of frozen ponds and makeshift rinks became an organized sport, and, grander, a national obsession. It wrestled long with an identity crisis that pitted fanatical amateurs against paid professionals. Opportunity seemed everywhere. And everyone wanted a piece, from northern mining tycoons and newspaper barons down south to arena owners and shifty promoters with get-rich-quick schemes to the homeboys at center ice and between the pipes. A nascent naïve sporting world brought out a rogue's gallery of brilliant game builders and lunatic hatchetmen.

The game gripped the imagination and wonder of supporters. Hockey wasn't remote, like so much of Canada at the time. Devotees watched cheek-to-jowl, intoxicated by the disorder on the ice and pandemonium in the stands. Back then, people really did faint from the intensity of the crowds—in barns barely seating 5,000. The hockey, its sounds as piercing as skates cutting across ice, spoke to fans of every language. They were all immigrants to this new game.

Widespread betting and home-brew at matches were customary for many enthusiasts looking to escape their everyday convention. Electricity charged the air. Fans snuck in game night and hung from the rafters. They shouldered their heroes in victory.

After the Winnipeg Victorias' Dan Bain scored the Stanley Cup overtime winner in 1901, scores of admirers "poured over the sides of the rink and carried the boys to their dressing room," reports noted. Following the Montreal AAA's victory against the same Vics the next season, some 30,000 people massed around Windsor Station and hailed the Cup winners "with lungs of leather and throats of brass," head-lined newspapers.

Carriages were supposed to parade players to club headquarters several blocks away. But when the AAAs exited the downtown railway station, they "were grabbed bodily from the [train] car and carried away half sitting, half lying on the shoulders of their admirers." They were carted off this way to their destination. Because of surging crowds, the short route took almost an hour.

World champion speed skater Jack McCulloch. *Montreal Star*, February 8, 1897.

▲ 1893 The studio of William Notman & Son creates *Hockey Match, Victoria Skating Rink, Montreal*. The mixed media process, which blends photography and painting, produces the general public's first view of arena hockey.

▲ 1893 The first East-West competitions. Manitoba's best amateurs stun hockey's eastern establishment, tallying seven wins in 10 games, outscoring Toronto, Ottawa and Montreal opponents 68–36. Playing mostly to gain experience, their success produces "a wave of hockey that rolled over the North-West like a flood," note reports. Four Winnipeg Victoria players power the western lineup, including Jack McCulloch, a champion speed skater and developer of hockey's tube skate.

▸ 1893 Star center Dr. John "Jock" Harty, Queen's University. This image is among the oldest photographs of an individual hockey player.

The Montreal AAA, 1893 Stanley Cup champions, in their famous blue jerseys with white double-winged wheel crests.

▲ 1893 The Montreal AAA capture the inaugural Stanley Cup as regular-season champions in the five-team AHAC. The AAA finish 7-1-0, claiming the title by edging Ottawa (6-2-0), who ironically hand Montreal its only loss, 4–2, in the season's first game. The Cup is only assured after the AAA's final match on March 10, a 2–1 win against the rival Montreal Crystals. Each AAA player receives a gold ring, a hockey tradition that is only revived by the Toronto dynasty teams of the 1940s.

1894 Teams in Nova Scotia abandon the Halifax rules, a game without offsides, in favor of Montreal's onside game, in which no attacking player can precede the puck.

The St. Mary's College team. Harry Trihey, back row, middle.

▲ 1893–1896 Ontario-born Harry Trihey excels in high school hockey at St. Mary's College, the English sector of Collège Ste-Marie in Montreal. On campus, Trihey and Arthur Farrell tutor their French schoolmates in hockey. They initiate the first organized hockey play among francophones, helping establish collegiate leagues and senior competition in Quebec.

The Quebec Hockey Club, 1893. Goalie Frank Stocking stands on the left.

▲ 1895 The Quebec Hockey Club and the Baltimore Athletic Club (billed as the U.S. champions) stage the first international series played on artificial ice at North Avenue Rink in Baltimore. Quebec HC, led by American-born, Quebec-trained goalie Frank Stocking, win both games, 5–2 and 6–1.

◂ 1895 During hockey's early days, teams could win the Stanley Cup by finishing first in league standings of the current Cup holder or by issuing the defending Cup champions to a "challenge" match. Such is the muddle that Cup trustees find themselves in when both things happen, a day apart. The Montreal Victorias are declared Stanley Cup champions after winning the AHAC regular-season on March 8. But the Cup trustees have already accepted a challenge match on March 9 between the 1894 champion Montreal AAA and Queen's University. The AAA win that Cup challenge 5–1, but the Victorias' first-place AHAC finish takes precedence, and the Vics keep the Stanley Cup.

The Montreal Victorias in a rare action shot, 1895.

The Winnipeg Victorias, 1895–96. Whitey Merritt, seated left.

▲ February 1896 **The first East vs. West Stanley Cup clash.** The Winnipeg Victorias beat the Montreal Victorias 2–0 at the Victoria Rink in Montreal. Winnipeg goalie Whitey Merritt makes history and attracts great attention in his white cricket pads, the first goalie pads in hockey.

OUR VICTORIAS VICTORIOUS.

The Montrealers Re-captured the Stanley Cup.

WAS THE FINEST HOCKEY MATCH EVER PLAYED IN CANADA.

The Victors Won on Their Merits--The Star's Story of the Struggle as Received in Their Bulletin Booth at the Victoria Rink by Direct Wire.

The telegraph brings immediacy to away games for local fans. *Montreal Star*, December 31, 1896.

▲ December 1896 The telegraph becomes the second form of media communication (after newspapers) to promote hockey when "direct wires" are installed at Winnipeg Arena to provide game updates at the Victoria Rink in Montreal. Amid the flags, bunting, lanterns and evergreens that decorate Victoria's ice surface and galleries, the *Montreal Star* erects a bulletin booth with "telegraph equipment" and announcement boards that update the Stanley Cup play between Winnipeg and the Montreal Victorias. It's hockey's original version of today's gatherings by fans who watch out-of-town games on big arena screens. Montreal claims the Cup in a 6–5 win. The match is dubbed "the greatest sporting event in Winnipeg history."

▲ 1896 *Canadian Magazine* publishes H.J. Woodside's *Hockey in the Canadian North-West*, a how-the-west-was-won illustrated chronicle detailing the "dashing attack" of play and the game's quick ascendancy in Manitoba and beyond.

games went to the Dominions.

Montreal Defeat Shamrocks in Baltimore.

Baltimore, Md., March 10.—The Montreal and Shamrock Hockey Teams, of Canada, played a hotly contested game at the North Avenue Ice Rink, last night. The contest sparkled with brilliant playing and wonderful skating. Montreal won by a score of 6 to 5. The line up was as follows:

Shamrocks.	Position.	Montreal.
Drysdale	Goal	Hamilton
Dwyer	Point	Murphy
Stephens	Cover Point	James
Dobby	Forwards	McKerrow
Wall	"	Fernie
Dave Brown	"	Horsfall
Dessie Brown	"	Barlow

Game report, *Montreal Star*, March 10, 1896.

▲ 1896 In an international first, two Canadian teams, Montreal rivals the AAA and the Shamrocks, play a three-city series in Washington, Baltimore and New York. The Shamrocks defeat the AAA 3–1 in the nation's capital and then lose 7–6 in Baltimore. In New York, a fresh sheet of artificial ice is laid down at the 2,500-seat Ice Palace for their contest. *The New York Times* reports it's "the finest exhibition of hockey that New Yorkers have ever seen." Fans are so enthralled with "cheers and applause and shrieks of delight" after the 1–1 tie that an impromptu overtime period is scheduled the next night to decide the series winner. The Shamrocks win 2–1. Hockey becomes "a recognized game in the United States," following the two New York contests.

A HOT TUSSLE.

IN THE GALLERY.

A SPILL.

▲ 1896 Media attention in newspaper game reports entices readers with hockey's earliest action shots.

Montreal Daily Witness, February 15, 1896

Among the earliest organized U.S. leagues, the AAHL featured the New York Athletic Club.

▲► 1896–97 New York City's new four-team American Amateur Hockey League begins play, coinciding with the opening of St. Nicholas Rink, among the first purpose-built, artificial-ice skating rinks in America. The AAHL team rosters are recruited mostly from Ivy League schools like Harvard, Princeton and Yale. Hobey Baker, the first U.S.-born Hockey Hall of Fame member, plays for Princeton.

► 1896 St. Nicholas Rink, New York.

▲ 1897 **Sketches of early Toronto hockey are published in *Toronto Saturday Night*'s column Sporting Comment.**

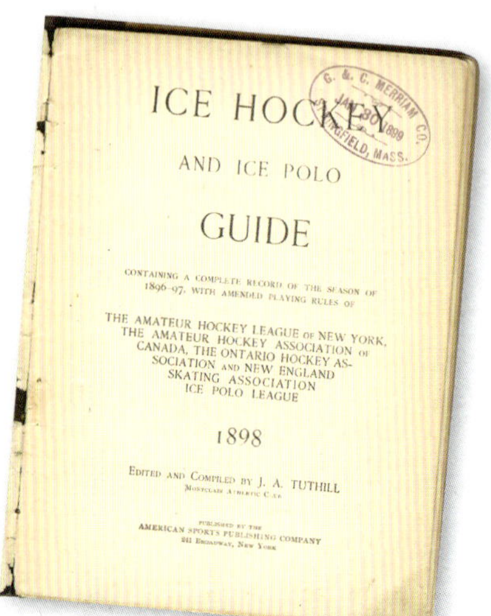
ICE HOCKEY

AND ICE POLO

GUIDE

CONTAINING A COMPLETE RECORD OF THE SEASON OF 1896–97, WITH AMENDED PLAYING RULES OF

THE AMATEUR HOCKEY LEAGUE OF NEW YORK, THE AMATEUR HOCKEY ASSOCIATION OF CANADA, THE ONTARIO HOCKEY ASSOCIATION AND NEW ENGLAND SKATING ASSOCIATION ICE POLO LEAGUE

1898

EDITED AND COMPILED BY J. A. TUTHILL

PUBLISHED BY THE
AMERICAN SPORTS PUBLISHING COMPANY
241 BROADWAY, NEW YORK

▲ 1898 Spalding publishes *Ice Hockey and Ice Polo Guide*, preceded only by Arnold Tebbutt's 1896 British publication *A Handbook of Bandy, Or Hockey on the Ice*—the very first book devoted solely to hockey. Spalding, an American sporting goods manufacturer, produced a vast collection of annual sports and exercise books from 1892 to 1941.

1898 Hockey's top circuit, the AHAC, folds in December amid controversy over promoting a second Ottawa team into league play. Club delegates withdraw from the AHAC and hours later regroup at Montreal's Windsor Hotel to form the Canadian Amateur Hockey League. This development defines the "closed league" structure, which controls franchise accessibility based on unanimous consent among current members.

▲ 1896–97 After completing secondary education in Montreal, Arthur Farrell and Harry Trihey make their senior hockey debut with the Montreal Shamrocks. They soon form a formidable forward line (with the rover position) alongside Fred Scanlan and Jack Brannen.

Trihey initiates the first offensive game strategies rather than relying on improvisation or individual skill and intuition. Unlike the general practice of defensemen flicking the puck over opponents' heads, Trihey carries the puck up ice and passes it when necessary. These innovations are widely adopted and prove crucial in the Shamrocks' Stanley Cups of 1899 and 1900. Trihey leads all scorers in regular-season and playoff play both years.

Harry Trihey

GRAND OPENING of the "ARENA" HOCKEY RINK AND AUDITORIUM,

Corner of ST. CATHERINE ST. and WOOD AVE.

EXCITING TRIPLE EVENT

VICTORIA--SHAMROCK--MONTREAL

Hockey Clubs,

SATURDAY, DECEMBER 31, 1898, (New Year's Eve.)

Play Commences at 8.15 p.m.

BAND OF 30 PIECES.

REFRESHMENT BUFFET WILL BE OPEN.

RUGS CAN DE RENTED AT 10c EACH

LADIES' ORESSING ROOMS WITH ATTENDANCE.

Reserved seats 50c and 35c, admission 25c; boxes containing 6 persons $5.

Sale of seats opens on Wednesday, December 28th, at 9 a.m., at the "Arena";—Club Shoe Store, 2117 St. Catherine street; and Canadian Foreign Music Co., 213 St. James Street.

The Montreal Victorias, 1899, four-time Stanley Cup champions.

▲ 1898–99 The Montreal Victorias, hockey's first dynasty team, claim their fourth consecutive Stanley Cup in February, under bizarre circumstances. Late in Game 2 with Montreal leading 3–2, Bob McDougall injures Winnipeg's Tony Gingras. A two-minute minor penalty is called. Winnipeg protests the light sentence and leaves the ice. Insulted, the referee quits and goes home. Persuaded to return by game organizers (who go to his house), the referee instructs the Winnipeg players to resume play. They refuse and Montreal is awarded the game and the Cup.

▲ 1898–99 The first purpose-designed hockey facility, Westmount Arena in Montreal, opens with tiered seating to accommodate 5,000. Rink boards separate spectators and players. It's the first hockey building named an "arena."

▸ 1899 An 18-year-old Russell Bowie begins his decade-long amateur career in senior hockey, the highest level of play, with the Montreal Victorias. Despite well-paying offers from several teams, Bowie remains an amateur, plying his elite stick-handling and scoring talents to amass 243 goals in 80 games, including multiple six-goal games and a seven-goal and eight-goal game. His only Stanley Cup comes with the Victorias in February 1899.

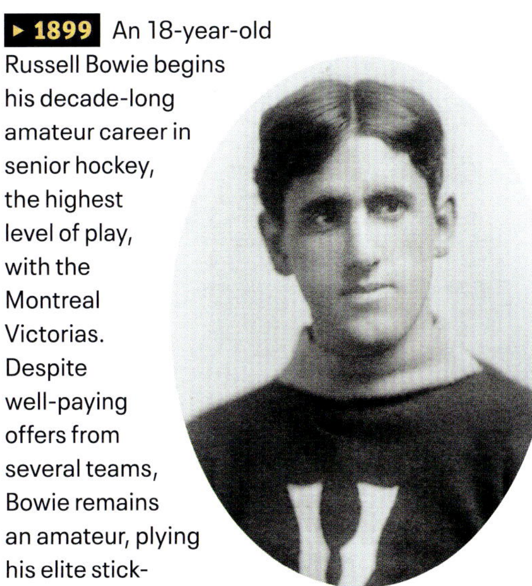

1898–99 **Ottawa goalie Fred Chittick breaks ranks, making some of the earliest public accusations of amateur players being paid.**

Ottawa Citizen, **February 20, 1899**

PROFESSIONALISM IN THE HOCKEY GAME

Fred Chittick Claims that a Member of the Ottawa Executive Offered a Player $100 to Play With that Club This Year

Montrealers Defeated at Hockey and Bowling by the Ottawa Teams—Stanley Cup Game Ends in a Big Wrangle

"YE GUDE OLDE DAYS,"

◂ ▴ **1899** Montreal Shamrocks forward Arthur Farrell writes *Hockey: Canada's Royal Winter Game*—the first book by an elite hockey player. Sketches include a game of pond hockey and hockey's "future," a young woman determined to play.

THE MONTREAL-VICTORIA HOCKEY MATCH—SNAP-SHOTS AT THE ARENA.

▴ **1899–1900** **Goal nets make their big-league appearance.** Replacing two pipes embedded six feet apart in the ice to mark goal limits, hockey now has real posts supported by an iron crossbar and backed with white cotton cord to trap pucks, leaving no dispute over a scored goal. The new contraptions face a rocky start on opening night, January 6, 1900. Montreal AAA goalie Fred Munro struck his head on the crossbar while falling to the ice. Later, a Montreal Victorias player "went sailing into the net in a melee and twisted the whole affair [the net] out of shape." The melee is seen in these game drawings.

MEMBERS OF THE FIRST LADIES' HOCKEY CLUB ORGANIZED IN MONTREAL, AT PRACTICE IN THE ARENA.

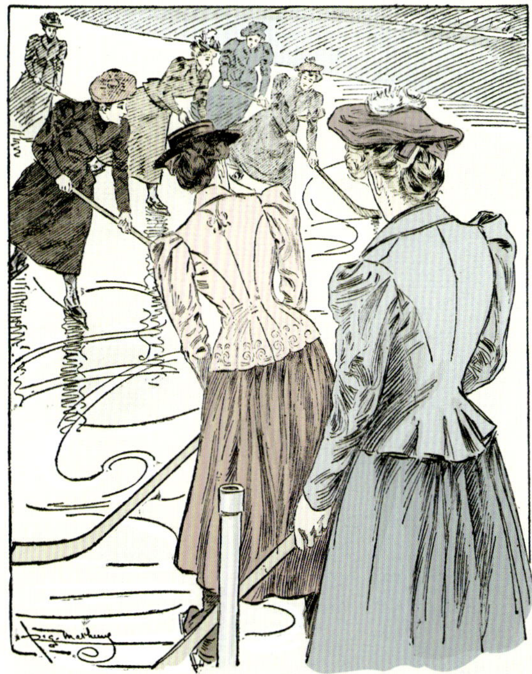

***Montreal Star*, January 27, 1900.**

▲ 1900 The Young Ladies' Hockey Club organize in Montreal. Like several early women's associations that take up hockey, the games are community-driven, earning little publicity or gate receipts. Reports note that their practices are closed affairs to prevent "their graces spied" upon.

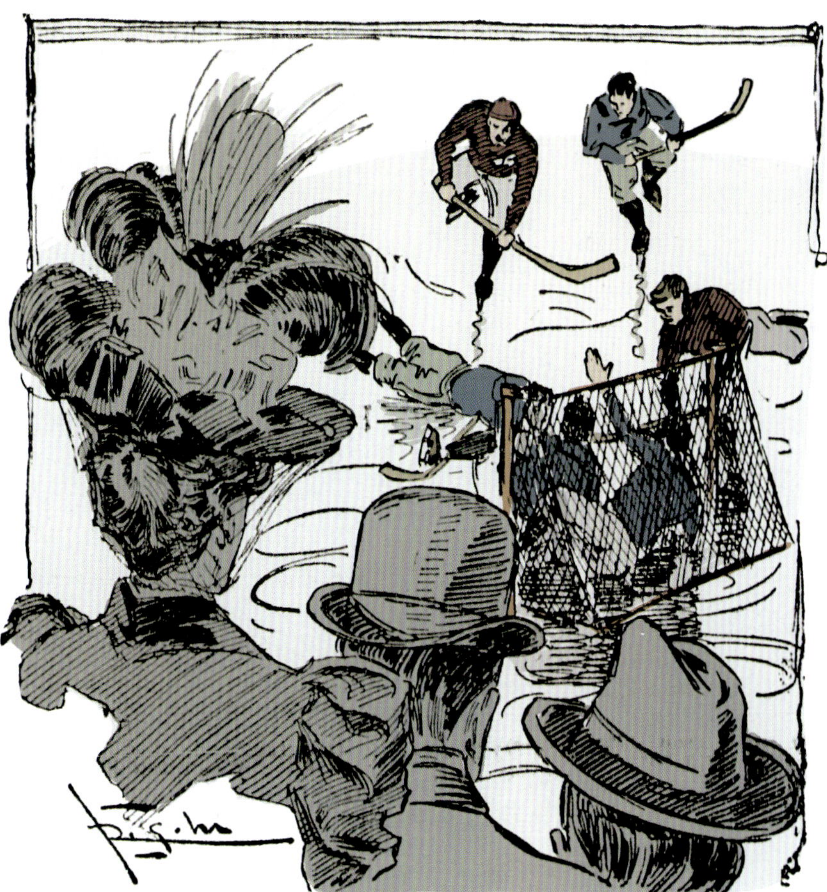

▲ 1900 The Montreal Shamrocks defend their 1899 Stanley Cup title, beating back Cup challenges from the Winnipeg Victorias in February and the Halifax Crescents in March. Captain Harry Trihey shines, notching 12 goals in five games. In the image above, Winnipeg's W.N. Roxborough falls while tying the game 2–2 against the Shamrocks.

▼ 1900s Hockey becomes a national game, arriving in towns like Regina, Calgary, Vancouver and Dawson City (pictured below).

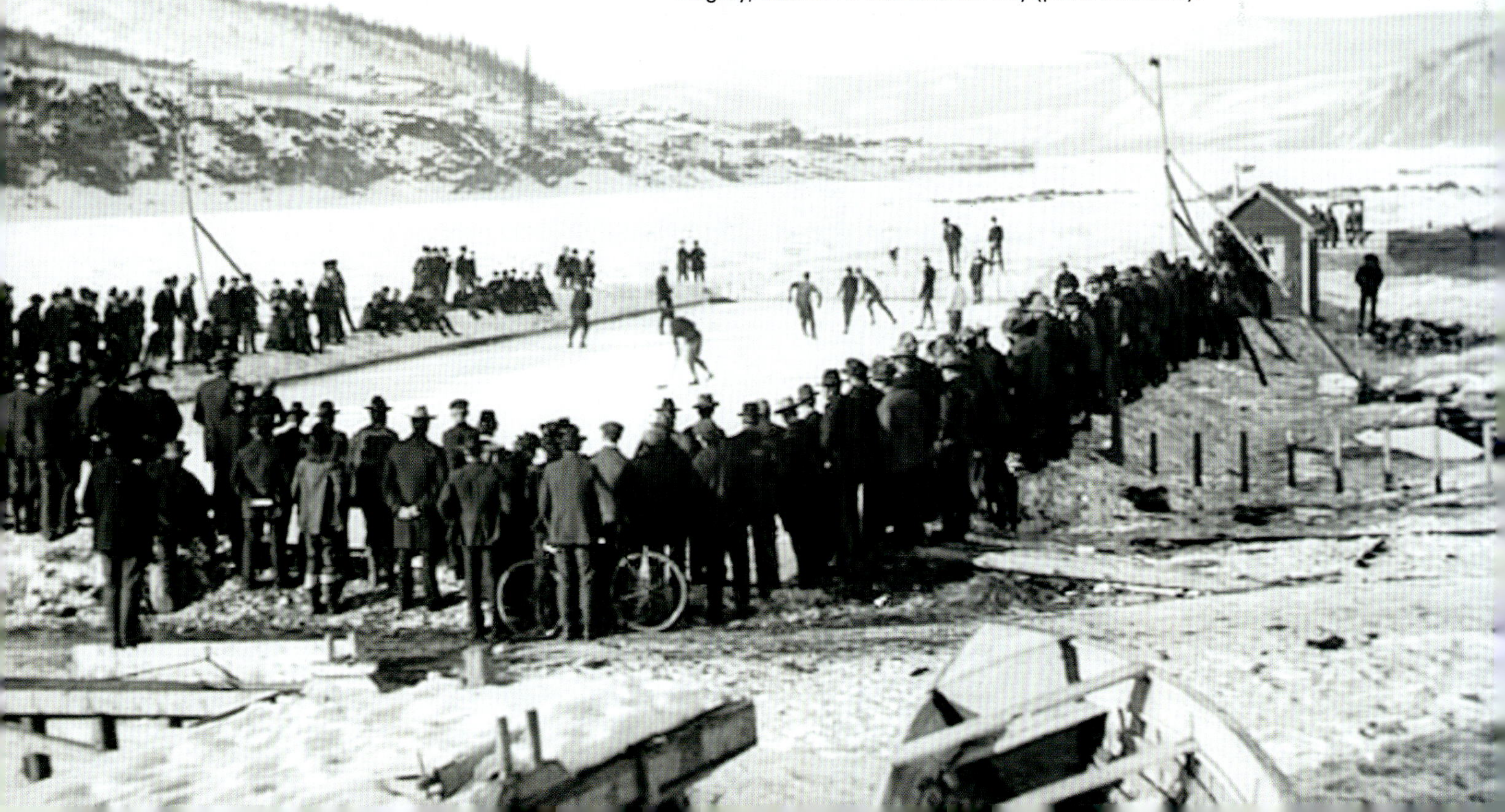

1900 **“The light skates and sticks with which the Winnipegers perform indicate that their forte lies in playing on very hard ice, such as they usually have in Winnipeg.”**

—*Montreal Star*, February 15, 1900

THIS CUP IS OURS!

WINNIPEG VICS
WILL CARRY IT BACK

***Manitoba Free Press*, February 1, 1901.**

▲ 1900–01 After a five-year absence, the Stanley Cup returns to Winnipeg following two wins by the Victorias in their best-of-three series against the Montreal Shamrocks. Vics forward Dan Bain, who wore a mask in Game 1 to protect an eye injury, scores Game 2’s Cup clincher at 4:00 of overtime. Harsh winters with few diversions turn Winnipeg players into hockey innovators. They compete with shorter tube skates and new stick blades that have tapered upper edges, making for improved game skill.

Winnipeg vs. Toronto at Winnipeg Auditorium, January 1902.

The Wellingtons Hockey Club, Ontario Hockey Association Senior Champions, 1900, 1901 and 1902. George McKay, middle row, second from left.

◀ ▲ ▶ 1901–02 Captained by George McKay, the Wellingtons, Toronto’s first “hockeyists” to challenge for Lord Stanley’s prize, lose in January in consecutive 5–3 defeats to the Cup-winning Winnipeg Victorias. In March, the Victorias defend their title, but drop a best-of-three series to the Montreal AAA, who are famously dubbed the Little Men of Iron for fending off Winnipeg in a classic series tiebreaker, winning 2–1.

Toronto captain George McKay of the Wellingtons.

GAME CHANGER

Jack “Doc” Gibson

ABOVE
Doc Gibson.

LEFT
The Portage Lakes Hockey Club, 1903. Doc Gibson, second row, center.

The selling of Canada's game in America began with Ontario-born forward Doc Gibson, who entered hockey's story in 1897, after helping the Berlin (Kitchener) Hockey Club win the provincial intermediate championship. The following season, in a gesture of thanks, Berlin mayor George Rumpel rewarded each player with a $10 gold piece. This bit of remuneration caught the ire of tyrannical bosses of the amateur-pure Ontario Hockey Association. The entire team was charged with professionalism and banned from play. The boys returned the coins and were later reinstated. Gibson, however, never forgot the slight.

He moved to the copper-mining community of Houghton, Michigan, where he practiced dentistry and established the Portage Lakes Hockey Club. In 1903–04, he blew the lid off amateur play, openly paying his recruits, dividing any gate among them.

Gibson's team posted a 23–2 record overall against several clubs, including beating the Montreal Wanderers at the World Pro Championship before 5,000 fans at the Houghton Amphidrome.

Following this commercial success, Doc Gibson helped form the International Hockey League. It attracted stars like Riley Hern and Hod Stuart, while creating an open marketplace for paid players that soon sent the clandestine economy of amateur compensations into chaos in Ontario and Quebec. Amateurs were now gambling on the pro game's viability.

Under threat of banishment, they moved back and forth across amateur-pro ranks, often changing their names to conceal their play with other clubs. Ringers peppered lineups everywhere. In a limited talent pool, it became a seller's market for athletes, as teams outbid rivals and players jumped clubs willy-nilly in what became known as the Athletic Wars.

Within those few pivotal years, the balance of hockey power shifted. The taint of money in the game faded, as the mesmerizing action of pay-for-play hockey became the game's premier attraction.

Today, Doc Gibson is recognized as “the father of professional hockey.”

Fred Waghorne

"Another little incident that impressed the spectators as being an improvement over the eastern style of play was that, in facing the puck ... the referee simply dropped the rubber between their sticks and the game was on the moment it touched the ice."

—*Ottawa Citizen*, March 1, 1904, about a February 26 OHA Arnprior-Renfrew game officiated by referee Fred Waghorne

◂ 1904 Referee Fred Waghorne popularizes the modern face-off. The first puck drop remains a mystery, but historian Eric Zweig suggests it's likely February 1904. Instead of placing the puck between two centers' stick blades and shouting "Play!," Waghorne, without fear or favor, and after smarting from battered shins and feet delivered by flailing sticks, has the players place their blades a foot or so apart and drops the puck between the sticks.

GLORIOUS OPENING OF THE HOCKEY SEASON

Fierce and Fast Is the Contest Between Pittsburg and Portage Lake.

LOCAL TEAM A LOSER, BUT IS NOT DISGRACED.

First Half Ends 4 Goals to Nothing in Favor of the Champions.

***Pittsburgh Daily Post*, December 10, 1904.**

▴ 1904 **The first goal in pro-league hockey.** On December 9, Barney Holden, a tough, punishing Winnipeg cover point (defense) with the IHL Portage Lakes, scores against Pittsburgh goalkeeper James MacKay in a 6-3 road win before nearly 4,000 fans at Pittsburgh's Duquesne Gardens. Right winger Bill Shields assists, after he "secured the rubber, rushed it down the ice, passed it to Holden, who shot, scoring the first goal," confirm reports.

▸ 1903-04 **The Stanley Cup gets dissed.** A war of words wages between Cup trustees and hockey managers over the regular-season scheduling of Cup challenges. Trustees want an amalgamation of leagues to simplify playing schedules. CAHL president Harry Trihey wants a new board of trustees appointed by the leagues. Montreal Victorias president Fred McRobie declares, "The sooner the Cup leaves here never to come back the better." It's a power struggle that goes nowhere. Hockey organizers come to their senses, eventually.

Arthur Racey (cartoonist), *Montreal Star*, April 19, 1904.

DAILY

YUKON WORLD

MORNING

DAWSON, YUKON TERRITORY, SATURDAY, JANUARY 14, 1905.

KLONDIKE HOCKEY TEAM DEFEATED IN EXTREMELY ROUGH GAME IN THE PRESENCE OF THOUSANDS OF PEOPLE

Fights Occur on the Ice Which Cause Both Ottawa and Dawson Men

OTTAWAS CRUSHED KLONDIKE TEAM.

They Defeated Them by Twenty-Three Goals to Two, and Outplayed Them at Every Point.

Special to the Montreal Star.

Ottawa, Ont., January 17.—Many people last night thought the Yukoners would improve on their exhibition of last Friday night and they certainly for the first 15 minutes' of play made

fighting report probably had a good deal to do with filling the rink. The distinctive features of the play necessarily were few when Ottawa won by 23 goals to 2, but the score settled the

1905 Dawson City's Stanley Cup quest. The Klondikers generate national attention during their epic 6,400-kilometer trek from the Yukon to Ottawa. The series, however, is a blowout.

Travel weary, and a month off skates, the seven-man squad of gold prospectors arrive by train just two days before Game 1. Forced to play the Ottawa Silver Seven only 36 hours later, they lose 9-2. The second match is worse, with Dawson City being "played off their feet" in a 23-2 thrashing. Ottawa center Frank McGee mercilessly scores "goal after goal just as soon as he wanted to go in and do so."

Between the pipes is a shell-shocked Albert Forest, Dawson's 17-year-old, 143-pound netminder. Without a shred of sympathy, McGee sets Cup records with 14 tallies on Forest. As for the contest itself, the lopsided score produces little excitement. "The play, while crisp at times, was often monotonous by reason of the Yukoners being practically all the time in the defense ...," note reports.

Despite their legendary Cup collapse, Dawson's Klondikers had already won. They survive the ordeal of the 23-day cross-continent trip and the quick turnaround to play the defending Stanley Cup champions.

Hockey watchers later surmise that had Dawson been victorious the Cup could have been theirs for some time. Considering Cup-holding cities usually hosted, Dawson City (a mere 173 miles from the Arctic Circle) might have been too rigorous a trip for most "southern" clubs in Montreal or Ottawa.

The Dawson City Klondikers, outside Dey's Skating Rink, Ottawa, 1905.

We left Dawson on the 19th [December 1904], some on bicycles, others walking. After a few miles the bicycles broke down and the entire team footed it to White Horse [sic], 320 miles. From 33 to 46 miles were covered daily, a police detachment being made each night. The trip to White Horse occupied nine days, and all of us were very tired. On account of a storm on the White Pass (a narrow-gauge railway between Whitehorse and Skagway, Alaska), we were delayed two days and a further delay of three days followed at Skagway, waiting for the boat (due to an ice buildup). The trip down the coast was extremely rough and all the boys were in such condition that they cared not whether the ship sunk or not. We expect to arrive in Ottawa on the 12th. On account of the delays and hard luck, we will ask [for] a postponement of the first game for three or four days in order to get into condition.

—Dawson rover Randy McLennan's account after his team's trek over rugged winter trails through the Yukon's boreal forest in subarctic winter with only about four or five hours of sunlight each day, to the Klondikers' arrival in Vancouver on January 7, 1905.

Tom Phillips.

▲ 1905 Days after Ottawa wins the Federal Amateur Hockey League regular-season title to retain the Stanley Cup in March, the team faces a best-of-three Cup challenge series from the Rat Portage (Kenora) Thistles. Game 1's 9–3 win by the fleet-footed Thistles features a five-goal effort from Tom Phillips. Overconfident in their first game but now smarting from that thrashing, it's rumored that Ottawa has the ice flooded (or salted) before Game 2 to slow down Rat Portage's fast play on their new thin-bladed tube skates. The match is a "ragged and dirty" affair, providing the Silver Seven with a 4–2 win. Game 3 is tied 4–4, as Phillips notches a hat trick for Rat Portage. Reports note that Ottawa fans call for the ice to be salted or flooded. However, famed Ottawa sniper Frank McGee settles the issue by scoring his third of the game. Ottawa keeps the Cup with its 5–4 win.

GOALKEEPER SCORED.

THIS WAS FEATURE OF LIVELY MATCH AT QUEBEC.

Quebec, February 18.—The champions defeated Westmount in the senior series of the C.A.H.L. tonight by a score of 17 to 5. The features of the game, which the Quebec team won handily, were the number of men penalized in the first half, 15, and the rushes of the goalkeepers, Moran and Brophy, towards the close, Brophy finally scoring. The teams:—

Quebec.		Westmount.
Moran	Goal	Brophy
Leclerc	Point	Burland
R. Power	Cov. point	Patrick
J. Power	Rover	Ross
Jordan	Centre	Church
Morency	Wings	Foulis
Hogan	Wings	Gale

Referee, R. Meldrum; assistant, T. Arnold.

***The Gazette*, February 20, 1905.**

▲ 1905 The first goalie-on-goalie goal is credited to Montreal Westmount goaltender Frank Brophy, who in a penalty-filled February 18 game scores on Quebec netminder Paddy Moran. Quebec beat Westmount 17–5 but the real story was the "erratic rulings" by officials. "There were so few men left on the ice that the two goaltenders began to rush the ice in order to relieve their tired forwards," state reports. Their first attempts to score fail. Then Brophy rushes the length of the ice again and scores the 17th goal (of 22 total goals) of the game. After the Brophy goal, "Moran, as well as all the spectators, were convulsed with laughter." The game, "a roaring farce," is officiated by R. Meldrum and T. Arnold.

Alf Smith, oldest of seven hockey-playing brothers.

▲ 1905–06 Harry and Tommy Smith join their brother, playing-coach Alf Smith, on the Ottawa Silver Seven. "No family more epitomised the brawling, burgeoning days of hockey and its transition from shady amateur and semi-professional to outright professional status than the Smiths of Ottawa," wrote historian J.W. Fitsell. Henry and Anne Smith had four other sons. The seven siblings played in every major league across Canada and in America's first pro leagues.

◂ 1905–06 A well-entrenched cash grab in sports, the 1906 Stanley Cup is rife with accusations of ticket price gouging for the upcoming Montreal-Ottawa Final. Prices double, which has a "general blighting effect ... on amateur sport," note the day's critics. Hockey is "a place where amateur sport has been preyed upon; where amateur players have been taught that there are higher things than the honour of winning in a fair and friendly contest—namely, the money that can be made by their efforts; the pleasures that can be bought by the money they make for their respective clubs."

***Montreal Star*, March 15, 1906.**

The Ottawa Silver Seven, 1905. Standing left to right: Harry Westwick, Mac McGilton, Billy Gilmour, Frank McGee; seated left to right: Dave Finnie, Harvey Pulford, Alf Smith, Arthur Moore.

GAME CHANGER

The Silver Seven

The Ottawa Silver Seven were nothing less than a murderer's row of future Hall of Famers. Led by captain Harvey Pulford, a brute on defense and the heavyweight boxing champion of Eastern Canada over multiple years, the team went undefeated through nine Stanley Cup challenges (sometimes multiples each season) from 1903 to 1906. Ottawa's game reports reveal how they manfully intimidated opponents. But that was just opinion from those unaccustomed to the blunt force of their hockey.

Feared, revered and practically invincible, the true menace of the Silver Seven was an unmatched skill game of speed, adroit passing, defensive discipline and a knack around the net that elevated many on their squads, like Pulford, Harry Westwick, Alf Smith and Frank McGee, to future prominence as Hockey Hall of Fame honorees. In 22 playoff games McGee scored a record 64 goals.

Ottawa's triumphs spurred wealthy team owners into making exorbitant expenditures on hockey talent in their own quest for Stanley Cup glory. Bidding wars over players were simply the cost of doing business. Ringers studded playoff lineups. Rivalries between towns grew where none had existed before. Community leaders and businessmen from small-town Canada regarded a Cup championship as an immediate civic distinction; although only one such town, Kenora, would earn that honor. As author D'Arcy Jenish notes, after the Silver Seven, "hockey quickly became more than a pastime and a private passion once they [civic managers] saw that the game could be used to promote their towns."

1906
Ottawa's unprecedented reign as nine-time Stanley Cup champions ends with its March Cup playoff against the Montreal Wanderers. In the two-game, total-goals series, the Silver Seven lose Game 1, 9–1. In Game 2 the Wanderers' defensive play fails to protect their overall goal lead and surrenders nine goals to Ottawa, with Alf and Harry Smith netting six themselves. Tied 10–10 in total goals (between the two games) with only 10 minutes remaining, pandemonium sweeps through the record crowd of 5,000 at Westmount Arena. In that moment, Lester Patrick, all of 22 years old, makes his reputation as a money player. He scores twice, including the Cup clincher to end the Silver Seven's championship era.

The Kenora Thistles, 1907.

▲ 1906–07 The Manitoba Hockey League becomes the first fully pro circuit in Canada. During the Athletic Wars, when paid players were publicly shamed and amateurs and pros mixed in semipro teams, the MHL Kenora (Rat Portage) Thistles had twice challenged for the Stanley Cup, in 1903 and 1905, and lost.

Their defeats to the not-so-amateur Ottawa squads clearly established money's growing influence in the sport and the Cup's role in professionalizing hockey, as salaries became a stark reality in any pursuit of a championship. In fact, Kenora had fielded and paid the likes of Tom Phillips and Tom Hooper. Because Kenora was judged professional for paying players in those Cup bids, the amateur MHL took the unprecedented step of turning professional. Had it not, the Thistles would have found themselves without a league.

Within months, Kenora wins Lord Stanley's trophy, openly hiring ringers Art Ross and Joe Hall for its January best-of-three tilt against the Cup-champion Montreal Wanderers. The heroes, however, are Phillips and Hooper. Phillips nets all four goals in Kenora's surprising 4–2 win in Game 1. He and Hooper combine to score six times in their Cup-winning game, 8–6. The money pays off. Kenora, a population of 6,000, earns the distinction of being the smallest town to win Lord Stanley's silverware.

Kenora's reign is short-lived. In March's Cup rematch, the Thistles, fielding ringers Alf Smith and Harry Westwick from Ottawa, lose 7–2 in Game 1 and win the second match 6–5, handing the Wanderers the best-of-two, total-goals round, 12–8. Apparently, after the victory, Stanley's bowl is stolen and held for ransom. With no one willing to pay, the thief sheepishly returns the Cup.

◂ 1906–07 Defensive specialist Hod Stuart returns to Canada. Among the earliest stars to publicly criticize the game's violence, Stuart famously quits hockey's first pro circuits in Michigan and Pennsylvania over poor officiating to join the hometown Montreal Wanderers of the Eastern Canada Amateur Hockey Association. Months later, Stuart wins the Stanley Cup of 1907. His triumph is fleeting. That summer he dies tragically in a swimming accident. He was 28.

ARENA
TO-NIGHT
at 8.30
"HOD" STUART
MEMORIAL MATCH
PRICES—Admission 25c and 50c. Reserved Seats 75c. Promenade Seats $1.
V. R. C. BAND IN ATTENDANCE

***Montreal Star*, January 2, 1908.**

Ernie Johnson **Riley Hern**

▲ 1906–07 Hockey's top league, the ECAHA, allows amateurs and professionals to play together, but clubs must file declarations of their players' status and publish them in newspapers. In the December 1906 Stanley Cup challenge against New Glasgow, the Montreal Wanderers play Riley Hern, Frank "Pud" Glass and Ernie Johnson, some of the first pros in Stanley Cup play.

The Dey's Arena, 1908.

▲ 1907–08 Dey's Arena opens in Ottawa, with a natural-ice surface, rink boards and a seating capacity of 4,500 and 2,500 "standee" places.

1907–08 The Ontario Professional Hockey League, better known as the Trolley League, begins play. Sometimes considered the first "entirely pro league" in Canada, the circuit boasts four teams within traveling distance by electric streetcar: Toronto, Berlin (Kitchener), Brantford and Guelph. The OPHL champion Toronto Professionals lose 6–4 in a one-game Stanley Cup challenge versus the Cup-winning Montreal Wanderers.

1907–08 In the days when press members moonlight for the sports clubs they cover, *Ottawa Free Press* sports editor Malcolm Brice signs highly coveted Cyclone Taylor to the Ottawa Senators. On Brice's coup, the *Free Press* crows of being "instrumental in bringing Taylor to the Capital."

▲ 1907–08 Newsy Lalonde plays in his first Stanley Cup challenge. Lalonde, 21, scores twice in the Toronto Professionals' 6–4 loss to the Montreal Wanderers. Remembered as the greatest and most colorful hockey player of his era, Lalonde wins six major league scoring titles during the next 18 seasons in the NHA, PCHA, NHL and WCHL.

1908 Europe's Ligue Internationale de Hockey sur Glace (precursor of the International Ice Hockey Federation) is formed, adopting many of Canada's rules of hockey, such as the momentous change from using a ball to playing with a puck.

1908 **“They don’t seem to appreciate in Toronto that the Montreal public are [*sic*] weary of hockey ... most of us feel inclined to send the Cup to Toronto, and let them have it, and be done with it.”**

—Montreal Wanderers Vice President W. Jennings, following a then-exhaustive 15-game run in 1908, including three Stanley Cup challenges, all between January 8 and March 14

Percy LeSueur, and his goalie stick from 1909’s Stanley Cup–winning Ottawa Senators.

▲ 1908–09 Percy LeSueur wins his second of three Stanley Cups, all backstopping Ottawa. By this time, Ottawa has been nicknamed the Generals, the Capitals, the Silver Seven, the Ottawas and, finally, the Senators. The Senators is the oldest hockey team name still in existence, preceding Montreal’s Canadiens by at least a year and nearly a decade before the founding of the NHL.

1908 **Art Ross opens his sporting goods store Art Ross & Co. on Sainte-Catherine Street in Montreal. Based on old newspaper ads, much of Ross’ merchandise, from his skate blades and boots to his sticks, gloves, padding and uniforms, are his own design—an indication of what hockey could expect from Ross’ resourceful nature and imaginative approach to improving game play.**

1908 In a preseason Stanley Cup challenge against the Montreal Wanderers in December, the Alberta-champion Edmonton Eskimos ice a record number of ringers, including imports Lester Patrick, Tom Phillips and Didier Pitre. Only rover Fred Whitcroft is a regular on the star-studded seven-man squad. Edmonton still falls 7–3 to Montreal. In the second match of the total-goals series, two Edmonton regulars return to the lineup and beat Montreal 7–6, but lose the Cup on goals scored, 13–10.

1908–09 **Hockey’s top league, the ECAHA, drops “Amateur” from its title to become the all-pro ECHA, a long overdue admission of inevitability regarding the arrival of professional play in Canada. Montreal’s two remaining amateur teams, the AAA and the Victorias, quit the league.**

▲ 1909–10 **Renfrew owner Ambrose O’Brien signs Lester and Frank Patrick, Newsy Lalonde and Cyclone Taylor (all in center of frame) to his Millionaires. Taylor receives a reported $5,250, making him the highest-paid team athlete on a per game basis in North America. Despite Renfrew’s elite talent, the Montreal Wanderers win the Stanley Cup.**

1909–10 The National Hockey Association, the predecessor of the NHL, is founded and begins professional play with teams in Ontario and Quebec. Ottawa wins two Stanley Cup challenges in January but finishes second to the Montreal Wanderers in NHA regular-season play, which concedes the Cup to Montreal. In their one-game Cup challenge against OPHL champion Berlin (Kitchener) in March, Montreal’s Ernie Russell and Harry Hyland score all seven goals, winning the famed Wanderers their last Stanley Cup.

Ottawas Won Stanley Cup From Wanderers by Brilliant Play

Better Organized and Using Greater Skill They Simply Overwhelmed the Montreal Team in the Second Half---Crowd Enthusiastic and Very Friendly---Ice and Officials Fine

Kerr, the Boy With the Dimples, One of the Coming Men---Too Many Men on the Wanderer Side Off at One Time and This Left Riley Hern Unprotected---Vair Replaced by Johnson for the Second Period

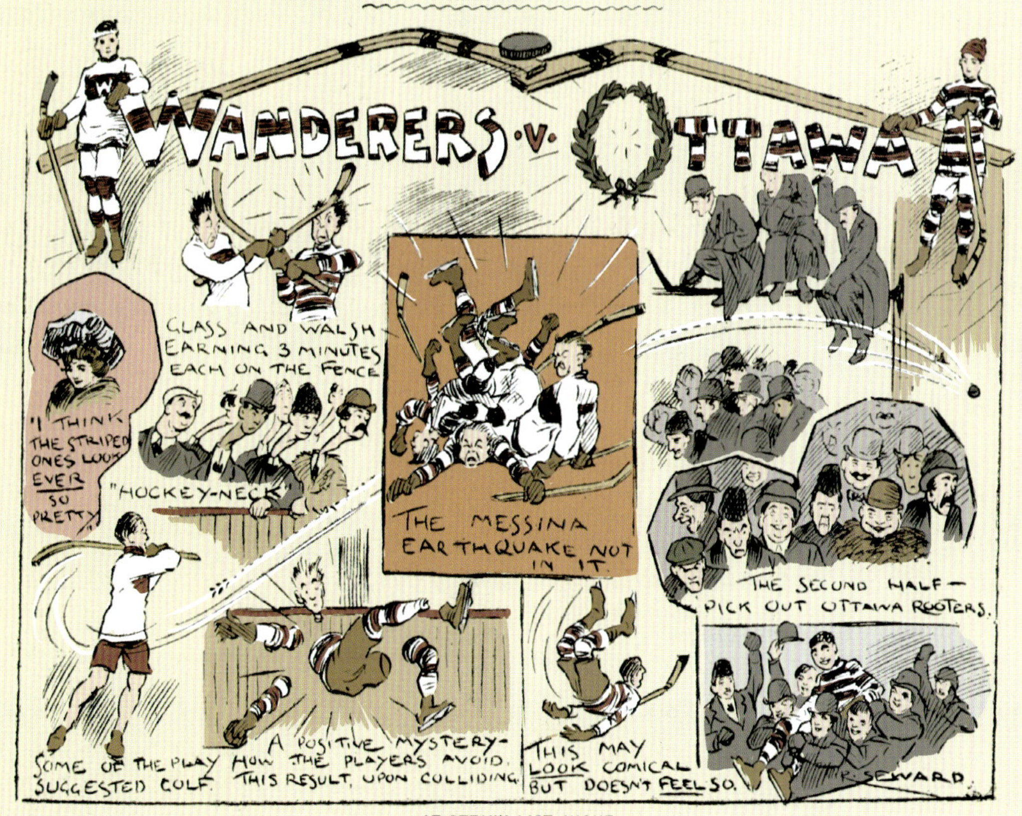

A "game cartoon" of Montreal vs. Ottawa highlights, *Montreal Star*, March 4, 1909.

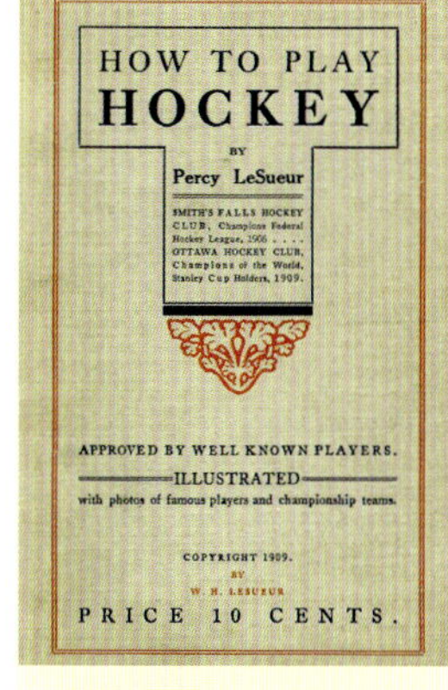

▲ 1909 Goalie pioneer Percy LeSueur writes *How to Play Hockey*, a 48-page handbook that breaks down offensive and defensive strategies in game play. A student of the game, LeSueur held numerous jobs at all levels, from coach to radio commentator and columnist. He is credited with introducing the gauntlet-type glove to shield a goalie's forearm and advancing ideas like the afternoon game and "shots on goal" statistics in box scores.

▲ 1909 The Stanley Cup is decided in a climactic late regular-season match between the Ottawa Senators and the archrival Montreal Wanderers. Both teams, now fully professional, have nine wins. A 3–3 tie ends the game's first half. Scoring leader Marty Walsh takes over and pots a hat trick in the second half. Ottawa's 8–3 victory secures a first-place ECHA finish and the Cup championship. Due to the lateness of the season, no Cup challenge is held.

▶ 1909 Shipping magnate Sir Montagu Allan donates the Allan Cup, emblematic of the amateur championship of Canada. His trophy replaces the Stanley Cup, which had become a professional competition. Until the 1960s, Allan Cup champions like the Toronto Granites, Penticton Vees and Trail Smoke Eaters represented Canada at the IIHF World Championship and Olympics.

Sir Montagu Allan.

1910 **International hockey officially begins play at the European Championship in Les Avants, Switzerland.** Participants include Germany, Belgium, Switzerland and Great Britain, which claims the first gold medal in hockey. This tournament evolves into the World Championship in 1930.

1910–11 Hockey's first salary cap, set at $5,000 per team, is introduced in NHA play. Players threaten to form their own league, before yielding when they can't secure ice time from arena owners.

LA PRESSE

LA SAISON DE HOCKEY Elle s'Ouvrira Samedi Prochain et la Première Rencontre Aura lieu Entre les Canadiens et les Ottawas

The Montreal Canadiens' second NHA season, *La Presse*, December 24, 1910.

▲ 1909–10 **The Montreal Canadiens' inaugural season.** Defenseman Jack Laviolette is appointed player-manager. His first hire is rearguard Didier Pitre. The defensive pair possesses such speed and agility that sports writers dub them the Flying Frenchmen, a nickname that soon becomes synonymous with the freewheeling Canadiens when Pitre and Laviolette are moved up as wingers with center Newsy Lalonde. The trio leads Montreal to its first Stanley Cup in 1916.

1910–11 Game formats change from two 30-minute periods to three 20-minute periods.

A women's hockey team in Alberta, 1910s.

1909–10 The Stanley Cup trustees take action against the number of "ringers" imported by Cup participants, ruling that only players who skated with their teams in regular-season play are eligible for Cup competition.

▲ 1910–11 Imperial Tobacco issues the first cataloged hockey cards. Each card in the 36-card set comes in cigarette packages and features color images of players like Cyclone Taylor, Newsy Lalonde and Georges Vézina on the front and a brief bio on the back.

Hobey Baker.

◀ 1910–11 **Hobey Baker enrolls at Princeton University.** Remembered today by his namesake trophy that honors the U.S. college hockey player of the year, Baker starred in every sport he entered. Football and hockey were his fields of choice. Equal parts legend, myth and hero, while skating in the NCAA from 1911 to 1914, he captained Princeton to two intercollegiate championships. Baker played for the love of the game. He never turned pro.

▲ 1911–12
Sprague and Odie Cleghorn join the Montreal Wanderers. Mean and tough, the Cleghorn brothers play six seasons with the Wanderers and multiple seasons with the Canadiens during the 1920s. Odie scores over 200 career goals, a feat in early hockey. But it's Sprague's rink-long rushes that make him an idol in Montreal. After winning two Stanley Cups with Ottawa in 1920 and 1921, he's reunited with Odie to claim the Canadiens' 1924 Cup championship.

1911
The Beaches Hockey League is founded. The Toronto-area loop, with five teams and 99 players, evolves into the Metro Toronto Hockey League and is known today as the Greater Toronto Hockey League, probably the largest minor hockey organization in the world.

The Denman Street Arena, Vancouver.

▲ 1911–12 Frank and Lester Patrick form the Pacific Coast Hockey Association and sign 23 players, pinching 16 from NHA rosters. The three-team western circuit plays seven-man hockey on Canada's first artificial-ice rinks at Denman Street Arena in Vancouver and Victoria Arena in Victoria. In the first pro game on artificial ice in Canada, the New Westminster Royals beat the Victoria Senators 8-3 at Victoria Arena on January 2.

The Quebec Bulldogs, 1912–13.

▲ 1911–12 A first-place finish and the Stanley Cup are again settled in the NHA's final regular-season game. A riveting 6-5 overtime victory by the Quebec Bulldogs against the Ottawa Senators forces Ottawa into a must-win final contest against the Montreal Wanderers. The Senators, however, lose 5-2 versus Montreal. Quebec's 10-8-0 record secures a first-place finish and the Cup. They defend their title by whipping the Moncton Victorias 9-3 and 8-0 in their best-of-three Cup challenge.

Rover Fred "Steamer" Maxwell, MHL Winnipeg Monarchs.

▲ 1911–12
The NHA drops the rover position, introducing six-man hockey that fields a goalie, two defensemen and three forwards. Typically, the best two-way player on a seven-man team, the rover was the extra attacker and extra defender on the ice. To identify teams more easily, uniforms become more distinctive in color and design. Player numbers are added to armbands on sweaters.

GAME CHANGER

Lester and Frank Patrick

The Patricks transformed early hockey, not only as elite players but as team managers and owners and major league founders. Most notably, they were sport innovators, each a guiding visionary who advanced the course of pro hockey through technical upgrades in game play and on organization levels that brought hockey's best skilled and the Stanley Cup to Western Canada and America.

Lester and Frank were born in Drummondville, Quebec. They starred in amateur play as Stanley Cup champions, and, at the pro level, competed in the NHA before moving to British Columbia. Their family's lumber interests in BC afforded them the opportunity to create the PCHA, which heralded pro hockey's first consequential expansion west.

During its existence from 1912 to 1924, the PCHA iced franchises in Vancouver, Victoria and New Westminster but also in first-time U.S.-based franchise cities Portland, Seattle and Spokane. Playing in the "syndicate hockey" league they founded and administered, the Patricks were forever experimenting with various ideas and tactics to make hockey more exciting and competitive.

Decades ahead of their time, they built Canada's first arenas equipped with artificial-ice rinks, instituted the forward pass, painted the first blue lines for offside calls and introduced the penalty shot. Their best tinkering may have been Frank's idea of a playoff series between the top regular-season finishers.

The brainwave struck him in 1918 as a means to spur attendance. While the idea had already been percolating out there, Patrick's version determined playoff participants differently, over the entire season. His vision has produced an untold fortune for pro sports ever since.

Lester Patrick, Seattle Metropolitans, 1917–18.

Frank Patrick, Vancouver Millionaires, 1911–12.

Frank Patrick, Renfrew Creamery Kings, 1909–10.

RIGHT
Lester Patrick's New York Rangers, 1928.

1912–13 After seven seasons on eastern teams, including a Stanley Cup with Ottawa in 1909, Cyclone Taylor joins the PCHA Vancouver Millionaires, where over the next 10 seasons he wins multiple scoring titles and another Cup in 1915. It was said that Taylor could skate faster backward than any player could skate forward.

RULE CHANGE

1913–14 The PCHA introduces the forward passing rule and new blue lines. Limited to center ice, the forward pass forever changes the tactics and traditions of hockey's onside game. With players having to skate harder and faster to receive a pass, the play speeds up. There are fewer whistles and players tire more quickly. The Vancouver and Seattle Stanley Cup titles in 1915 and 1917 guarantee the forward pass its future in hockey. Author Craig Bowlsby writes, it was "akin to introducing gunpowder to a medieval battlefield."

The Toronto Blueshirts, 1914.

▲ 1914 **Toronto wins its inaugural Stanley Cup.** In the first playoff-styled round between the top contending NHA teams, the Blueshirts defeat the Montreal Canadiens 6–2 in goals in the two-game, total-goals series to win the NHA championship. Eight days later, Toronto sweeps the PCHA Victoria Aristocrats in a best-of-five Stanley Cup Final, as Frank Foyston pots three goals, including the Cup winner. It's the first of 13 consecutive East–West Cup Finals, ending in 1926.

A junior squad of the 228th Battalion, 1916–17. Hockey's most famous military team fielded NHA stars who were enlisted to fight overseas, including Art Duncan, Duke Keats and Captain Howard McNamara (standing in as coach, back row, center).

▲ 1914–1918 The First World War scatters players to several fronts, from working civilian jobs at war plants to soldiering on foreign shores. Among those who lose their lives are Frank McGee, Hobey Baker and Scotty Davidson. Howard McNamara joins the 228th Battalion, a team of soldier athletes that play in NHA action in 1916–17 and are shipped overseas in February.

Dick Irvin of the Portland Rosebuds, the first American team to play in the Stanley Cup.

▲ 1915–16 After capturing the NHA championship, the Montreal Canadiens play the PCHA-champion Portland Rosebuds in a best-of-five Stanley Cup series. In a Cup first, the title comes down to a fifth and deciding game. Montreal prevails in a 2–1 match when George "Goldie" Prodgers beats Portland goalie Tommy Murray. Montreal's Georges Vézina registers a 2.60 goals-against average, awarding the Canadiens their first championship.

The Vancouver Millionaires, 1915.

▲ 1914–15 **The PCHA Vancouver Millionaires win the Stanley Cup in the first Cup series played west of Winnipeg.** Vancouver pummels Ottawa in the best-of-five round, 6–2, 8–3 and 12–3, establishing the ascendancy of the Patricks' western league. Cyclone Taylor leads all scorers with seven goals in the three matches. Before the next season the Patricks raid the Toronto Blueshirts, poaching five regulars — Harry Holmes, Ed Carpenter, Jack Walker, Cully Wilson and Frank Foyston — for the Seattle Metropolitans.

▸ 1917 The Seattle Metropolitans are the first American-based Stanley Cup winners, the first U.S. team to host the Cup Final and the first to break one of Lord Stanley's original conditions to win his silver bowl — the trophy must be held by the champions of the Dominion of Canada. In the best-of-five Cup Final the defending-champion Montreal Canadiens are favored. They take Game 1 in an 8–4 rout, suggesting the critics were right about it being a fast series. However, Game 2's convincing 6–1 score by Seattle, settles the Mets down. Montreal barely gets on the scoreboard again, losing Games 3 and 4, 4–1 and 9–1. Regina-born Bernie Morris stars for Seattle, scoring a series-high 14 goals, six in the Cup-winning game.

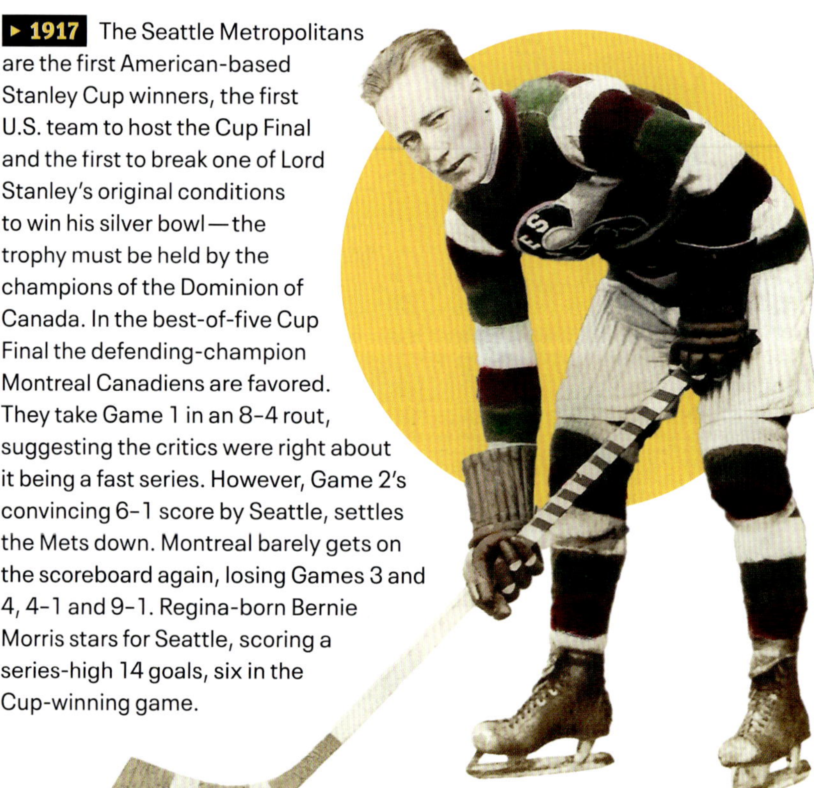

Bernie Morris, Seattle Metropolitans.

NHL President Frank Calder, 1930s.

Frank Calder and the NHL

The NHL game was built on the business acumen and savvy of Frank Calder. He was the league's first president, from 1917 to 1943, an old-time era when fighting, drinking and betting among fans were commonplace and often overshadowed the on-ice fisticuffs. A lawlessness swept through the rinks on game night. Players dodged fan debris of every kind, even a lucky horseshoe for hometown heroes. In NHL-expansion Boston, firecrackers and hardware rained down, including a steamfitter's pipe which, according to longtime Bruin Eddie Shore, once forced Calder to wear a hard hat in his Garden's box seat.

Calder was that kind of boss. Tough and resolute. Some observers called him out for unfair play and crushing the spirit of the greater game. He seemed, however, to possess exactly what the fledgling NHL would need competitively as an international hockey circuit in the budding American sports landscape of the Roaring Twenties.

To create a better product and business model, Calder would modify rules, bring about organizational reforms among owner members, set controls on salaries and create new revenue streams to bridge a binational league of divergent cultures and economies. His governance would turn competing leagues into player-supply circuits that mechanized the talent pipeline through the feeder ranks to NHL play.

At the same time, Calder's capitalist instincts never recognized the historical significance or sentimental value of small hockey markets, anywhere. Wielding his authority, like an "autocrat" some said, to establish NHL supremacy, Calder set market-stability standards that gutted a litany of cities of their franchises. Vancouver, Calgary, Portland, St. Louis, Ottawa and Hamilton. None would survive. The game's power base swung from north to south and from west to east, concentrating—and boxing in—hockey's major pro league in that geographic domain for another half century.

R

The NHL: Keeper of the Cup

Few eras have been more profoundly marked by one individual than the NHL times under Frank Calder. A case can be made for commissioner Gary Bettman's reign, whose overhaul of the league remains unprecedented in organized team sport history.

Less similar were the challenges facing each man. Unlike Bettman, Calder was establishing a sustainable league enterprise. His fledgling four-team circuit had a talent pool of only 39 players in 1917–18. A weak Quebec City franchise would suspend operations. Then, weeks after opening night, fire destroyed the Montreal Wanderers' arena. The club was forced to disband, leaving Calder with three teams and an unbalanced schedule.

The next season, an influenza epidemic canceled the 1919 Stanley Cup. Shortly after, the failed Quebec team was transferred to Hamilton. Still, the NHL dominated the western-rival PCHA, winning five straight East vs. West Cup Finals.

Faced with the frailties of a small all-Canadian league and the ever-present specter of a rival American pro circuit forming, Calder chased what sport entrepreneurs had been long seeking, "a big international hockey league." America had large city populations. Its ambitious wealthy investors could build bigger arenas, fill more seats and make more money.

Under Calder, U.S. expansion became the goal. Boston came aboard first in 1924–25. Then, the Hamilton Tigers' player strike happened. Without any resolution, their stock of players, the top squad that year, became available—just when New York was eyeing pro hockey as an import investment. Charting a course for hockey's future, Calder quickly established a fallback for failing franchises north of the 49th: southern relocation. The Tigers morphed into the New York Americans.

Fortunately, Calder had Howie Morenz, the generational player of his day. Morenz's explosive up-ice rushes brought fans to their feet and U.S. financiers out of the woodwork. Western leagues struggled to compete against the player salary dollars of eastern American moneymen. The 1926 exodus of elite western talent filled NHL expansion clubs in New York, Detroit and Chicago. Calder's "dream of hockey's manifest destiny" had come true. The NHL claimed sole possession of the Stanley Cup.

Howie Morenz: "his name means speed."

OPPOSITE
The Vancouver Millionaires play to a packed house at Seattle Arena, 1921.

> **"We didn't throw Eddie Livingstone out ... That would have been illegal and unfair ... We just resigned, and wished him a fine future with his National [Hockey] Association franchise."**
> —Montreal Wanderers owner Sam Lichtenhein, on why the NHL was formed in 1917

Eddie Livingstone.

▲ 1917 The NHA's eight-season run as pro hockey's top circuit ends, folding into the new National Hockey League. Frank Calder is elected president. The four-team league changes the game forever—all thanks to one individual. Toronto Blueshirts cantankerous owner Eddie Livingstone was such a major pain to the other NHA club owners, in order to rid themselves of him, they form the NHL.

ARENA FIRE MAY CAUSE TOTAL BREAK UP OF PRO. HOCKEY SEASON

Officials of the Wande[illegible] Hockey Club announce that owing to the Arena fire [illegible]e will be no National Hockey League match tonight, although no doubt arrange-.nents could have been made with the Jubilee Rink people.

Judging from the unofficial talk of certain prominent professional hockey men, it should not be at all surprising if the fire may result in the entire National Hockey League series being broken up, to remain unfinished.

The Westmount Arena fire, 1918.

▲ 1917–18 Frank Calder's NHL faces early setbacks that raise concerns about its inaugural season, following the departures of the Quebec team and the Montreal Wanderers, who withdraw after four games when fire razes Westmount Arena. As a result, one Wanderers' game is forfeited to Toronto and another to the Montreal Canadiens. Toronto proceeds with the "game" anyway to ensure its two points in the standings and to pursue legal matters. On January 5, at 8:15 pm, six Toronto players line up against no opponent for NHL referee Lou Marsh's opening face-off at Toronto's Arena Gardens. Cy Denneny skates down the ice and shoots the puck into an empty net. Toronto claims the 1-0 forfeit.

RULE CHANGE

1917–18 **Goalies are permitted to fall to make saves.** NHA rover Art Ross had long complained about forcing goalies to always stand, but it's Clint Benedict's deceptive methods that make a mockery of the rule, becoming an expert at "accidently" losing his balance and falling to smother a puck. It brings the first major rule change in NHL history.

◂▸ 1917–18 Cyclone Taylor and Joe Malone lead the PCHA and the NHL in goal scoring. Malone nets 44 goals in 20 games to set an unbroken NHL standard until Maurice Richard scores 50 in 50 in 1944–45. Malone is the only NHLer ever to average two-plus goals per game, 2.20, in a season.

Joe Malone.

Highest Goals per Game, One Season (Min. 20 Goals)*

Rank	Player	Team	Season	GP	G	G/GP
1	Joe Malone	Montreal	1917-18	20	44	2.20
2	Cy Denneny	Ottawa	1917-18	21	36	1.71
3	Newsy Lalonde	Montreal	1917-18	14	23	1.64
18	Wayne Gretzky	Edmonton	1983-84	74	87	1.18
19	Odie Cleghorn	Montreal	1918-19	18	21	1.17
20	Mario Lemieux	Pittsburgh	1992-93	60	69	1.15

*Current to 2024-25

▲ 1917–18 **The Toronto Arenas win the first Stanley Cup in NHL play.** Toronto's best-of-five Cup Final series against the Vancouver Millionaires goes to Game 5, with alternating games played under eastern and western rules. Each team loses when playing under its opponent's rules. Game 5, under eastern rules, favors Toronto in a 2–1 Cup win at Arena Gardens.

Reg Noble.

▲ 1919 The Toronto Arenas' NHL franchise is purchased and renamed the St. Patricks. Hurt by the NHL-PCHA bidding wars and Quebec's return to NHL play, the Arenas lose five players. Only regulars Reg Noble, Ken Randall and Corbett Denneny return.

►▼ 1918–19 Scrappy defenseman Joe Hall amasses 130 penalty minutes—in just 16 games. Almost 38 years old, Hall still holds a century-old mark as the NHL's oldest single-season penalty leader.

Oldest NHL Penalty Minute Leaders, One Season

Player	Team	Season	GP	PIM	Age
Joe Hall	Montreal	1918–19	16	130	37 yrs / 9 mos
Joe Hall	Montreal	1917–18	21	100	36 yrs / 9 mos
Pat Maroon	Tampa Bay	2022–23	80	150	35 yrs / 0 mos
Red Dutton	NY Americans	1931–32	47	111	34 yrs / 8 mos
Ted Lindsay*	Detroit	1958–59	70	184	33 yrs / 8 mos

*In 1964–65, Lindsay, 39, collected 173 PIM, only four minutes behind Carl Brewer's league-leading total.

1918–19 The Art Ross puck debuts, replacing the standard Spalding puck as the official disk of the NHL. Instead of Spalding's "sharp edges" on its upper and lower surfaces, Ross' puck has beveled edges, which allows for better puck control and reduces injuries to players.

RULE CHANGE

1918–19 To reduce disruptive behavior the NHL implements no substitutions for penalized players. Players must serve immediate box time. The NHL introduces two blue lines painted 20 feet (6.1 m) from center ice. First used in the PCHA, the innovation creates three playing zones and a 40-foot (12.2 m) neutral zone where forward passing is permitted.

The Seattle Metropolitans, 1919.

Tuesday, April 8 at 8 o'clock.

WORLD'S HOCKEY SERIES CANCELLED

Seven of the Canadiens and Owner George Kennedy Stricken With "Flu"

Seattle, April 1.—Definite and final announcement was made by the Arena management at 2.30 p.m. that there will be no more world series games here this year. At noon to-day workmen started tearing up the Arena ice floor preparatory to converting the building into a roller skating rink.

▲◄ 1918–19 An influenza epidemic halts Stanley Cup Final play after five games, with Montreal and Seattle knotted 2-2-1 (including a 0–0 tied game). Several Canadien players are hospitalized with the deadly flu. Montreal's Joe Hall dies days later at Seattle's Columbus Sanitarium. It's the first of only two occasions the Cup has not been awarded since 1893.

Best Scoring Percentage—Joe Malone vs. Pavel Bure

Player	Team	Season	G	Team	%
Joe Malone	Quebec	1919–20	39	91	42.9
Pavel Bure	Florida	2000–01	59	200	29.5

▲ 1919–20 After two years of dormancy, Quebec returns to NHL play. The Bulldogs are so bad, Joe Malone, the club's only saving grace, has a Pavel Bure–Florida Panthers-type season, setting an all-time NHL mark for highest percentage of a team's total goals. Malone nets an NHL-record seven goals against Toronto's Ivan Mitchell in Quebec's 10–6 win versus the St. Pats on January 31. In unheated barns like Quebec's Arena, where comfort is practically nonexistent, temperatures are little warmer than outdoors. In this Toronto–Quebec contest, the mercury fell to −33°F (−36°C) outside. Corbett Denneny quits the game with a "badly frozen" hand, note reports.

game away for them.

Joe Malone had a big night, scoring seven out of Quebec's ten goals, while Carey, Ritchie and Carpenter were the other scorers. The cold was so intense that Corbett Denneny, Toronto's centre player, had his right hand badly frozen during the match and was compelled to retire in the third period.

Quebec started out with a rush, and Malone nearly scored from the face-

▼ 1920–21 Olympic star Frank Fredrickson signs with the PCHA Victoria Aristocrats. Fredrickson, who scored 12 goals in three games in Canada's gold medal romp at the 1920 Games, is the first Olympian to join major league pro hockey. He tallies 20 goals in 21 games with Victoria, finishing third in league scoring.

The Olympic champion Winnipeg Falcons.

▲ 1920 The birth of world hockey. North America's game comes to Europe as an official sport at the 1920 (Summer) Olympics. Six countries participate. Canada wins gold as the Winnipeg Falcons, a team of Icelanders from Manitoba, make history and become the first world champions. Audiences are thrilled. The Games bring greater acceptance to the sport and launch international play.

Jack Darragh.

▲ 1920–21 The Ottawa Senators capture consecutive Stanley Cups — an NHL first. Jack Darragh plays clutch again. After scoring Ottawa's Cup winner in 1920, he pots both Senators' goals in 1921's Game 5 2–1 victory against the Vancouver Millionaires. Darragh's Cup winner almost never happened. Ottawa Mayor Frank Plant interceded on Darragh's behalf when his employers, the Ottawa Dairy Company, initially refused him the time off.

▲ 1921 Sports entrepreneurs Léo Dandurand, Joseph Cattarinich and Louis Létourneau purchase the Montreal Canadiens for $11,000, following the death of owner George Kennedy in October. Under their ownership and coach Cecil Hart, the Canadiens win Stanley Cups in 1924, 1930 and 1931.

1920 The NHL's first team transfer. Hamilton interests buy the Quebec City franchise and form the Tigers. To bring competitive balance, NHL boss Frank Calder unilaterally awards Hamilton the rights to Ottawa's Harry "Punch" Broadbent and Sprague Cleghorn. Both players refuse to report and return to Ottawa. Even with scoring champion Joe Malone in their lineup, the Tigers finish last.

TIGERS

The Edmonton Arena, 1924–25.

▲ 1921 The Western Canada Hockey League is formed, creating a third major league that impacts player dispersal, salary escalation and a new playoff structure, whereby the western champions of the WCHL and the PCHA face off for the right to meet the NHL champions for the Stanley Cup. The WCHL has four teams, in Calgary, Edmonton, Regina and Saskatoon.

RULE CHANGE

1921–22 **Minor penalties are reduced from three to two minutes. Goalies are allowed to pass the puck forward up to their blue line.**

▲ **1921–22** Jake Forbes snubs hockey's "option clause," which gives clubs first rights to re-sign players. He seeks a $2,500 salary. Instead, Forbes earns the league's first season-long benching in an NHL contract dispute. His rights are sold to the Hamilton Tigers.

▶ **1922**

Ernie "Moose" Johnson retires. Johnson earns the nickname "Moose" from playing through injuries that would sideline most players. His proneness to injury coupled with his physical play and any ensuing retaliation bring a litany of breaks, rips, tears, stitches and bruises during a 19-year career. He rarely misses a game.

◀ **1921–22** Cecil "Babe" Dye pots a Stanley Cup–record nine of the Toronto St. Pats' 16 goals in Cup Final play. Two goals are game clinchers. Dye has a chance to top both Cyclone Taylor and Frank Foyston's PCHA marks of nine goals in Game 3 on March 20, when he is awarded a "free shot"—the first penalty shot in playoff history. Under western rules, Dye stands 36 feet out to shoot. His shot sails over the net of Vancouver's Hugh Lehman.

Cecil "Babe" Dye.

Punch Broadbent.

1921–22 The last pro hockey game with seven men aside. The Toronto-Vancouver Stanley Cup Final is played with alternating NHL-PCHA rules. Game 4 of the best-of-five series is played under western PCHA rules—its final season of employing the rover position in seven-man hockey. The Toronto St. Pats beat the Vancouver Millionaires 3-0 on March 23.

◀ **1921–22** Ottawa ace Punch Broadbent sets the all-time NHL record for goal streaks, tallying goals in 16 straight games between December 24 and February 15. He wins the NHL scoring title with 32 goals and 46 points.

▲ **1922–23**

The NHL's earliest known guide, *The Hockey Hour*, is published. The 3 inch by 5 inch (8 cm × 13 cm) guidebooks include team and player bios and stats, photos, rules and advertising.

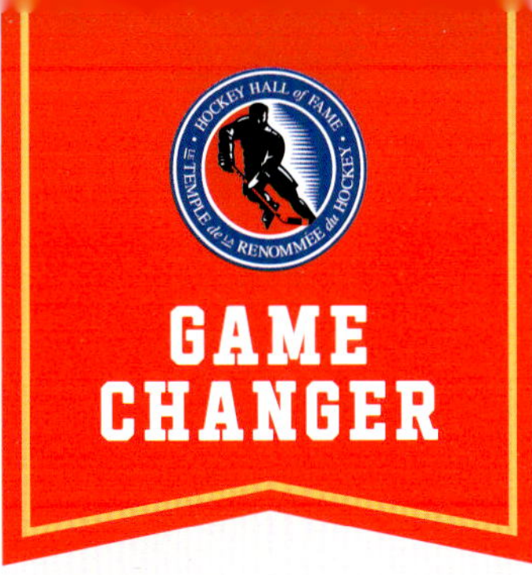

GAME CHANGER

Radio

FOSTER HEWITT

The first radio broadcast of hockey came on February 8, 1923, with Norman Albert huddled in "a little hut about the size of a coffee table" near the penalty timekeeper's stall, calling the third period of an OHA North Toronto-Midland match on radio station CFCA. Albert was on air again on February 14 for the Toronto St. Pats' 6–4 win against the Ottawa Senators. It's the first broadcast of an NHL game, albeit, again, only of third period play. Two nights later, Foster Hewitt calls his first match on CFCA in a 3–3 tie between the Toronto Argonauts and the Kitchener Greenshirts.

Some believe that Pete Parker of CKCK in Regina gave the first ever complete 60-minute game account. His March 14 broadcast of the WCHL Edmonton-Regina match however is bested by Winnipeg radio station CJCG's full-game broadcast between Winnipeg and Port Arthur (4-1) on February 22.

The dawn of radio has many suitors, chief among them is Foster Hewitt (seen here at CKFH Radio, Toronto), whose chilling vibrato announcements from his famous gondola at Maple Leaf Gardens made household names of hockey's greatest stars while connecting urban centers and country life across Canada. His ubiquitous "He shoots, he scores" became a play-by-play standard—and radio a news-communicator that, through its immediacy and intimacy, changed how sports fans experienced game play. Hewitt was the voice of Canadian hockey for the next half century.

Howie Morenz, Aurèle Joliat and Johnny Gagnon, 1936.

▲ 1922 In a much-criticized move in September, Montreal trades team captain and scoring champion Newsy Lalonde to the WCHL Saskatoon Crescents for $3,500 and untested amateur Aurèle Joliat. In what may be early hockey's greatest steal, Joliat is soon teamed with Howie Morenz and Billy Boucher, the NHL's first scoring line of historic importance. Joliat plays the next 16 years with the Canadiens.

"Forget 'em kid ... You're here to stay."

—Montreal co-owner Léo Dandurand, reassuring rookie Howie Morenz, 22, that the goals would come after he fails to score in his first two NHL games. In his 14-year career, Morenz nets 472 points in 550 games, and wins multiple MVP awards and scoring titles and three Stanley Cups.

▸ 1923–24

Frank Nighbor: the inaugural NHL MVP.

Despite finishing ninth in league scoring, Nighbor's all-round talents as a great scorer, playmaker and defensive center, combined with his clean play and sportsmanlike conduct, earn him the first Hart Trophy. On January 12, Nighbor scores his 100th career goal in Ottawa's 3–2 win against Hamilton.

Frank Nighbor, in his hometown team uniform, Pembroke, Ontario.

Eddie Gerard.

▲ 1922–23

Defensive great Eddie Gerard wins his fourth consecutive Stanley Cup—three captaining Ottawa in 1920, 1921 and 1923 and another with Toronto in 1922. Gerard also claimed a Cup coaching the Montreal Maroons in 1926. All told, he netted five championships on three different teams in a seven-year span.

King Clancy.

▲ 1922–23 Ottawa's King Clancy plays all six positions against the Edmonton Eskimos in the Stanley Cup Final. In Game 1 Clancy, 18, subs for Ottawa's injured defensive stars George Boucher (cut foot) and Eddie Gerard (dislocated shoulder), left-winger Cy Denneny (bruised leg), fatigued center Frank Nighbor and right-winger Punch Broadbent. In Game 2 of the best-of-three series, Senators goalie Clint Benedict draws a slashing penalty and, as is the custom, serves two minutes in box time. Who gets the call? Out skates Clancy, stepping between the pipes to help preserve the 1–0 shutout. Benedict returns and Ottawa goes on to win the 1923 Stanley Cup.

Howie Morenz

In July 1923, Howie Morenz inked a two-year contact that paid the speedy amateur and railway machinist apprentice $1,600 per season plus bonuses. Morenz soon had a change of heart. He told Montreal Canadiens manager Léo Dandurand "I am too light and the league is too tough ... I don't believe I'm good enough ..." Morenz pleaded that his livelihood and amateur standing would suffer. "My whole life would be ruined."

Dandurand was sympathetic yet held his ground. Late that year, the "Stratford Streak" packed his steamer trunk for the Canadiens camp in Grimsby, Ontario. *The Gazette* noted, "He showed sufficient speed and carries enough weight to warrant him making a bold bid for a berth."

Following the 24-game NHL season, Montreal played the Calgary Tigers in a best-of-three Stanley Cup Final. The Canadiens star line of Morenz, Aurèle Joliat and Billy Boucher scored five times in Game 1's 6–1 win. Morenz got a hat trick. In Game 2 Morenz scored first, which brought out Cully Wilson and Herb Gardiner, both of whom sidelined Morenz with torn shoulder ligaments, a dislocated collarbone and cuts to the head. Morenz's goal prevailed as the Cup winner in Montreal's 3–0 victory.

In eight months that changed hockey history, Morenz went from "contract remorse" to Stanley Cup champion. The Canadiens' No. 7 became the NHL's first superstar and its biggest box-office attraction to sell Canadian hockey in America. In only a few seasons the fledgling four-team circuit ballooned to a 10-team international league.

1924 **"The shots rattled off Vézina like a hail of machine-gun fire. He kicked them out, battled them like a ball-player, caught them in his hands, took them on his pads, legs and chest."**

—Elmer Ferguson, on Georges Vézina's Stanley Cup heroics. Vézina's skates are pictured at left.

Georges Vézina.

1924 **"Well ... where *is* this Stanley Cup you've been talking about?"**

—Emilie Dandurand, wife of Montreal Canadiens owner Léo Dandurand, asking to see the famed Cup at their Westmount home, after the Canadiens win in March 1924. The Cup, however, had been abandoned on snowy Côte St. Antoine Road when their Model T Ford stalled and its occupants, Dandurand, Georges Vézina, Sylvio Mantha and Sprague Cleghorn (who was holding the Cup), all jumped out to push the vehicle up the hill. Still sitting on the curb, the Cup was retrieved by Dandurand and Cleghorn almost an hour later.

▲ 1923–24 The Montreal Canadiens win their first NHL Stanley Cup. Rookie Howie Morenz notches seven goals in six games in Montreal's unbeaten streak through three series against Ottawa, Vancouver and Calgary, but *The Gazette* calls goalie Georges Vézina "the real hero of the Canadiens victory" after his "cool, yet spectacular play," during Montreal's 3–0 shutout Cup win against Calgary.

Charles Adams.

◂ 1924–25 Grocery store magnate Charles Adams' $13,000 ante for an NHL franchise in Boston pays off as the Bruins become the first American-based NHL team. Amateurs and old professionals fill out the roster. Adams hires legendary star Art Ross as vice president, manager and coach. Boston is home to Ross for the next 30 years, until his retirement in 1954.

Boston Arena hosts the inaugural NHL game in America. Smokey Harris pots the game winner as the Bruins beat their freshman-rival Montreal Maroons 2–1 on December 1. It's a good start, but Boston loses its next 11 straight.

◂ 1923–24 Harry Watson is remembered as Canada's "finest example of a 'purely' amateur player." After racking up 37 goals in five games (as Canada amassed a goal-count margin of 110-3) at the 1924 Olympics, Watson refuses to be tainted by signing a pro contract, unlike teammates Hooley Smith and Dunc Munro. While he played against inferior European clubs during hockey's formative years, Watson proved that not all the best players played professionally.

NHL EXPANSION

1924–25 **The NHL introduces a 30-game regular-season schedule. Following promoter Thomas Duggan's request for franchise options in Boston and New York, the Bruins (Boston) and the Maroons (Montreal) begin league play. The next year, Duggan's New York bid, the Americans, becomes the second U.S.-based NHL club.**

The Montreal Forum, under construction, September 1924.

▲ 1924–25 The Montreal Forum opens its doors as the home rink of the first-year Maroons. Due to warm weather, the hometown Canadiens are first to play on Forum ice on November 29 in a 7–1 victory against the Toronto St. Pats.

▸ 1924–25 **Lady Evelyn, the wife of Canada's 12th governor general, Baron Byng of Vimy, donates a trophy for the most gentlemanly player in NHL play.**

1924–25 Victoria Cougars' Harry "Hap" Holmes wins his fourth Stanley Cup in his 17-year career. No journeyman, Holmes is the only goalie to hoist the Cup with four different franchises. In an era when teams from several leagues compete for the Cup, each of Holmes' clubs represented a different top-tier league in existence between 1912 and 1928.

▲ 1924–25 **The WCHL Victoria Cougars: the last non-NHL Stanley Cup winners.** Innovations like the forward pass in the attacking zone and line changes on the fly (using a second line) by the Cougars during the Cup Final mitigate the blazing speed of the Montreal Canadiens' attack. "Who could stop Morenz, Joliat and Boucher?" Victoria manager Lester Patrick asked. "Who could score on the great Vézina? But I knew we'd win because our second line would just tire them out, and it did."

It was the west's last Cup for another 59 years until Edmonton in 1984, and the last by a West Coast club until Anaheim in 2007. More significantly, Victoria's 3–1 defeat of Montreal in the best-of-five Cup Final soon spelled the end of the proud era of the 60-minute man, when teams generally played with one unit most games.

▲ 1924–25 Prior to the playoffs, the Hamilton Tigers strike over pay issues of $200. "The boys are unanimous in what they consider their just dues, hence the reason for the stand we have taken," states captain Shorty Green. League boss Frank Calder suspends the team. Hamilton loses its NHL franchise. The entire roster is sold for $75,000. Months later, Green and his teammates become the New York Americans of 1925–26.

1924–25 Montreal fans once again have rival French and English teams. To challenge the Canadiens, the Maroons acquire veterans Clint Benedict and Punch Broadbent from Ottawa for cash. The following season Benedict and Broadbent are key to the sophomore Maroons' 1926 Stanley Cup.

▼ 1920s "Some of your [Canadian] owners are narrow and small ... They are against every suggestion to widen the game, particularly as concerns the United States."

—New York promoter Tex Rickard, on NHL expansion into America

NHL EXPANSION

◂ 1925–26 NHL expansion in America swells the league from four to seven franchises in two years. Canada adds the Montreal Maroons and loses Hamilton. The U.S. adds Boston, New York and Pittsburgh. Salaries skyrocket league-wide. Pittsburgh's Lionel Conacher and the Maroons' Dunc Munro reportedly earn $7,500. Billy Burch, Joe Simpson and Hap Day make about $6,000.

◂ 1925–26 Nels Stewart racks up multiple NHL rookie scoring records and wins the Hart Trophy. Unprecedented for a freshman, Stewart leads the league in goals (34) and points (42) while scoring six of 10 goals for the Montreal Maroons in 1926's Stanley Cup Final. Stewart's 34-goal rookie standard wouldn't be broken until Gilbert Perreault's 36 goals in 1970–71's 78 games.

The New York Americans' inaugural training camp, 1924–25. Promoter Tex Rickard, middle row, third from left.

▴ 1925–26 **The NHL debuts in New York.** Impresario Tex Rickard's Madison Square Garden is all pomp and circumstance for the Montreal Canadiens–New York Americans tilt on December 15. The largest hockey crowd ever attends—about 17,000 people. "I can make bigger money with less worry and fewer risks out of hockey than I have been getting out of boxing," says Rickard. Montreal beats New York 3–1.

RULE CHANGE

1925–26 The NHL introduces delayed penalty rules. Only team captains are allowed to talk to referees. Goalie leg pads are limited to 12 inches. Team salary caps are $35,000.

1925–26 Montreal goalie Georges Vézina dies of tuberculosis just months after collapsing in his net on November 28. Vézina never missed a match during 15 years of play, a streak of 367 consecutive starts.

Odie Cleghorn Only Manager Who Has Been Able to Use Two Full Forward Lines

Odie Cleghorn's Pirate reserves are about the best in the National Hockey league, and if the belief that a team is no stronger than its substitutes counts for anything, then the Pittsburgh sextet is second

Playing-coach Odie Cleghorn, Pittsburgh Pirates.

▲ 1925–26 **The two forward lines system debuts.** At a time when NHL teams generally played with one set threesome, Pittsburgh playing-coach Odie Cleghorn takes advantage of the new rule of dressing 14 players instead of 12 and regularly alternates two forward lines. The first line plays until "the half time mark is reached in each period," note reports. "The second line of offense usually remains on the ice for six or eight minutes and then the first line goes out to finish the period." The tactic helps earn the freshman Pirates an unexpected third-place finish.

New York's Bread Line: Bill Cook, Frank Boucher and Bun Cook.

▲ 1926–27 The western pro WHL folds, supplying players to new NHL clubs in New York, Chicago and Detroit. In three short years NHL expansion turns Canada's home game into a cartel-league of eastern millionaire owners and promoters, with six of 10 franchises residing in America. In the process, major pro hockey is shuttered in western regions of both Canada and the U.S. Players coming east include former Saskatoon Crescents forward Bill Cook, who won the NHL's scoring title.

THE NATURAL

Lionel Conacher

At hockey's pinnacle is the generational player. Someone so skilled they redefine greatness in their time. A few like Wayne Gretzky, Bobby Orr and Maurice Richard have transcendent careers. They live in the public's mind outside the sporting context. Their personal identity is universal, while attaining some mythic quality.

Then, there is the natural—that individual who excels in almost every facet on their fields of play, but not necessarily as the best statistically. In the case of Lionel Conacher, he wasn't even the best hockey player in his family. He only strapped on blades at age 16. A mission-first, mentally tough competitor, "He could do anything and do it hard and rough and surprisingly well," wrote sports writer Trent Frayne. His drive for success and athletic prowess earned him Canada's Athlete of the Half Century in 1950.

Conacher didn't join pro play until late, at 25 years old. He only played because hockey paid better. It was neither his best sport nor his first obsession. He accomplished much outside the game: a Canadian light-heavyweight boxing title; a 27-0 record as an amateur wrestler; a 1921 Grey Cup in Canadian football; a Triple-A baseball championship in 1926; and an Ontario senior title in lacrosse in 1927. By his own words, "You learn things in other sports which come in mighty handy in hockey."

Conacher has been inducted into five different sports halls of fame.

NEW OWNERS TAKE OVER THE ST. PATRICKS CLUB

Henceforth Pro. Hockey Team Will Be Known as Maple Leafs of Toronto

▲1927 Conn Smythe's ownership group buys the Toronto St. Pats on February 14.

▲1926–27 Ottawa's Alec Connell records the NHL's longest shutout sequence. Connell's shutout mark of 460 minutes and 49 seconds comes during the dead-puck era, an offense-limiting time before full forward passing was allowed in 1929. Still, he notches six straight blanks, three of them in consecutive scoreless ties, which include overtimes. Chicago's Duke Keats finally puts a puck past him in the seventh game, a 3–2 win on February 22. Connell posts 15 shutouts with eight wins and seven scoreless ties during the 44-game schedule.

▲1926–27 In honor of Georges Vézina, the NHL establishes the Vezina Trophy, given to the league's leading netminder. Vézina is the first player to have an NHL award named in his honor. The first recipient is Montreal Canadiens goalie George Hainsworth.

RULE CHANGE

1926–27 The neutral zone is enlarged with the blue lines repositioned 60 feet (18.3 m) from each goal line. Uniform goal nets are adopted league-wide and are securely fastened to the ice.

▼1926–27 Veteran western league goalie Hugh Lehman joins the Chicago Black Hawks and, at age 41, becomes the NHL's oldest "rookie" ever. Recognized as a hockey visionary, his skating and stickhandling abilities likely make Lehman hockey's first "third defenseman," years before Jacques Plante and Martin Brodeur modernized the position with their own wandering and puck-passing skills. *The Manitoba Free Press* said, Lehman "was as valuable to his team as almost any two of his teammates."

Hugh Lehman.

▼1926–27 The NHL takes control of Lord Stanley's Cup. What was once a challenge trophy competed for by amateur and, later, pro teams from multiple leagues across Canada is now in the sole possession of the NHL and exclusively awarded to its franchises.

The demise of the western leagues creates the first ever all-NHL Cup Final as the American Division champion Boston Bruins meet the Canadian Division champion Ottawa Senators. Ottawa ousts Boston to score its fourth championship in eight years and its last title to date. Cy Denneny scores four of Ottawa's seven goals, including both game winners. The series records two overtime draws—the last ties ever in Cup Final play.

Cy Denneny.

GAME CHANGER

The Old-Time Manager

Toronto GM and owner Conn Smythe.

The era between 1928 and 1942 had some of hockey's most colorful coaches, managers and owners — many as well-known as their star players. They exhibited a brand of showmanship that lit up a dark time of miserable economies and wartime worries, while providing players the opportunity to make real money instead of the pennies-per-hour wages offered in factory jobs. For every Eddie Shore and Howie Morenz thrilling fans, working upstairs were Conn Smythe in Toronto, Lester Patrick in New York, Jack Adams in Detroit, Art Ross in Boston and Tommy Gorman in Chicago. Behind the scenes they competed just as intensely for Lord Stanley's prize. Like their players, the bosses who wanted it more usually won.

Smythe was no mere manager, but more of a sport maker. After rescuing the talent-thin St. Pats in 1927 and rebranding them the Maple Leafs in the blue and white colors of his alma mater, the University of Toronto, Smythe hired Frank Selke to run things. They established feeder teams in the Toronto Marlboros and St. Michael's College, which yielded his future offensive core. Players like Syl Apps, Red Horner, King Clancy and the Kid Line of Charlie Conacher, Busher Jackson and Joe Primeau became hockey heroes and celebrities across the country. Smythe then built Maple Leaf Gardens. He defied his era's compromising times to create the model NHL franchise, instilling a new level of class into Canadian hockey. The cathedral-like Gardens acquired sports shrine fame and propelled the Leafs to unique prominence as Canada's favorite team, in any sport. Their popularity also spiked NHL fortunes, helping bolster the struggling pro circuit and transform it into the most prominent organization on ice.

1927 "Never saw anything like it. Those fellows wanted to kill one another. Thank God I'm in baseball. It's so peaceful and quiet."

—Babe Ruth, told to a companion after witnessing his first hockey game, Chicago vs. Boston, November 15, 1927

New York Rangers coach Lester Patrick.

▲ 1926–27 Coach Lester Patrick replaces injured goalie Lorne Chabot. Retired 19-year career defenseman, Patrick, 44, defies age and fate by gallantly stepping into the breach mid-game to inspire a 2–1 overtime victory for the New York Rangers in Game 2 of the Stanley Cup Final.

The Montreal Maroons are ahead a game and the Rangers down a regular goalie. The players watch Patrick for instructions and hang closely on his every move in the nets, note reports. His rearguards respond, "We'll hold them out, or kill them." Patrick allows one goal on 17 shots, including three in overtime.

Game 3 swings the deadlocked series in Montreal's favor. The Maroons win 2–0, in a fast, rough contest against New York, who uses reject netminder Joe Miller, the sub for the injured Chabot.

But the Rangers rally 1–0 in Game 4 and then gut out the climactic 2–1 Cup winner. After 35 years of Stanley Cup play, the Rangers become only the second U.S.-based Cup champions.

The Art Ross net. Detroit Cougars vs. New York Americans, 1940.

▲ 1927–28 The Art Ross goal net is adopted as the official net of the NHL. Ross' distinctive B-shape design and angled-back support bar cut down on rebounds and disputes on disallowed goals. Almost all nets follow his design until 1983–84. Today's nets are reworks of Ross' original model.

◄ 1928 Multi-sport athlete Fanny "Bobbie" Rosenfeld of the Toronto Patterson Pats becomes a household name in Canada after sprinting to Olympic gold and silver in 1928. After her playing days, Rosenfeld distinguishes herself in the advocacy of women's competition by covering women's sports in the press. Later, she is named Canada's Female Athlete of the Half Century.

RULE CHANGE

1927–28 Forward passing is permitted in defending and neutral zones. Goalie pads are reduced in width from 12 inches to 10 inches (30.5 cm to 25.4 cm). Three 20-minute periods and two 10-minute intermissions become standard.

Canada at the 1928 Olympics.

▲ 1928 Without any serious competition, Canada's representatives, the University of Toronto Grads, win Olympic gold, beating Sweden 11–0, Great Britain 14–0 and Switzerland 13–0 in the medal round. The United States is absent from these Olympics.

Goalies George Hainsworth and Roy Worters.

▲ 1928–29 In the final NHL season before forward passing is permitted in all three zones, the 44-game schedule features some great goalie records. George Hainsworth nets zeroes in 50 percent of Montreal's games, setting an all-time standard of 22 shutouts. Only 16 are wins, as six more are scoreless draws. In 44 matches Hainsworth gives up 43 goals for an unbreakable record .921 goals-against average.

RULE CHANGE

1929–30 The rules are again amended to allow forward passing inside all three zones but not across either blue line. Then, in December, after goal counts double, a further amendment is adopted. Similar to the modern offside rule, no attacking player is allowed to precede the play when entering the opposing zone.

▲ 1928 **The first hockey game at Boston Garden.** Three nights after the Garden's official opening on November 17, the Bruins host Montreal. By game time 17,000 fans — 2,500 above capacity — are jammed into the new arena, with hundreds of late arrivals still demanding entrance. Fights erupt between police and the surging crowds, who break windows and doors. The Canadiens blank Boston 1–0.

1928–29 The NHL's first All-American Stanley Cup Final. Boston sweeps the New York Rangers in 2–0 and 2–1 wins in the best-of-three Cup Final to claim its first championship. Bruin veteran Cy Denneny is credited twice on the Cup, as a player and as a coach. Denneny is the last playing-coach of a Cup winner.

◂ 1930 "I saw it at the last split second and lunged ... Wham, I was out like a light and woke up in the hospital."

—Montreal Maroons goalie Clint Benedict, on the Howie Morenz shot that forced him to briefly wear a mask

Clint Benedict and his leather mask.

◂ 1929–30 **Clint Benedict is (probably) hockey's first masked man.** After being struck in the nose and cheekbone by a Howie Morenz shot on January 7, Benedict sports the game's first (regularly-worn) facial protector, a crude leather mask he wears for five games. Then, on March 4 against Ottawa, following a goal-mouth scramble, the mask cracks and caves into his face, breaking his nose again. Benedict's 17-year NHL career is over.

▸▾ 1929–30 Boston records the highest points percentage in NHL play, with an all-time regular-season mark of .875 and a 38-5-1 record. Backstopped by Tiny Thompson, the Bruins don't lose two games in a row all season—until the Stanley Cup playoffs against Montreal, who had finished 26 points back of Boston and lost all four regular-season matches against the Bruins. But the speed of Howie Morenz and the surprise element of the underdog Canadiens sweep the Bruins in the best-of-three Cup Final two straight, 2-0 and 4-3. Boston's shocking defeat prompts the league to extend all Cup Finals to a best-of-five series.

The Dynamite Line: Dit Clapper, Cooney Weiland and Dutch Gainor.

Highest Points Percentage, One Season

Team	Season	GP	W	L	T	Pts	P%
Boston	1929-30	44	38	5	1	77	.875
Montreal	1943-44	50	38	5	7	83	.830
Montreal	1976-77	80	60	8	12	132	.825
Boston	2022-23	82	65	12	5	135	.823

▴ 1929–30 Boston's Ralph "Cooney" Weiland shatters Howie Morenz's scoring record. Weiland takes full advantage of the new forward passing rule, scoring 73 points, 22 better than Morenz's old mark of 51. The record held for another 12 seasons until Chicago's Doug Bentley matched it in 1942–43 and Boston's Herb Cain registered 82 points in 1943–44.

◂ 1930–31 The NHL's inaugural All-Star Team concept is launched. A legendary lineup of players and coaches forms the original First and Second All-Star squads. It's a promising beginning. All 14 members from both teams, including Eddie Shore, Dick Irvin and Bill Cook, are eventually elected to the Hockey Hall of Fame.

New York Rangers defenseman Ivan "Ching" Johnson, member of the 1930–31 Second All-Star Team.

1930–31 Roy Worters is the only NHL goalie to lead in goals-against average with a non-playoff team. In the 44-game schedule, Worters ices an NHL-best 1.61 average with the New York Americans. He allows only 74 goals. But New York's offense musters only 76 goals to finish seventh in a 10-league circuit. Of some comfort, Worters does win the Vezina Trophy.

The 1932 Stanley Cup champion Toronto Maple Leafs.

▲ 1931–32 Against great odds during the Depression, Conn Smythe builds Maple Leaf Gardens at a cost of $1.5 million. When construction bids roll in, Smythe is short $300,000 of the original price tag of $1.3 million. Near bust, the project gets new life when manager Frank Selke convinces the 24 member-unions to take a wage cut and receive the balance of their usual pay in stock shares. With the unions on board, the Canadian Bank of Commerce picks up the difference. Smythe predicts that a new arena might bring a championship. The Maple Leafs come through, breaking in the Gardens with the Stanley Cup of 1932.

1932–33
Canada's vulnerability in world play emerges at the 1933 IIHF World Championship, when Toronto's National Sea Fleas meet USA in a gold medal overtime match. Six minutes into the 10-minute extra frame, John Garrison scores, beating Canadian goalie Ron Geddes for the historic U.S. win.

1931–32
Boston owner Charles Adams demands an icing rule in NHL play. In a New York Americans-Boston Bruins game on December 8, New York ices the puck 61 times to hold onto their 3-2 lead. Adams petitions NHL boss Frank Calder, calling for a face-off in the defending team's zone when that team shoots the puck out to stem an offensive threat. The idea is rejected. Adams makes a mockery of the rematch in New York on January 3, ordering his Bruins to play the same style. Boston ices the puck 87 times in the scoreless draw. Calder doesn't adopt Adams' icing rule until 1937-38.

▲ 1930–31 Conn Smythe gambles on Rare Jewel and trades for King Clancy. In "hockey's greatest money deal," Smythe bets on his filly Rare Jewel at Coronation Stakes in 1930, earning the Maple Leafs' owner $214.40 for a $2 ticket—a 100-to-1 long shot that nets $9,372 plus the purse. Three weeks later, Smythe deals Art Smith and Eric Pettinger and $35,000 for Ottawa defenseman King Clancy. Like Rare Jewel, Clancy pays off immediately. In his first five matches, between November 13 and 22, Toronto runs a perfect five-game shutout streak, the all-time NHL record for consecutive zeroes for a season start. Clancy becomes a Maple Leaf mainstay for the next six decades.

▲ 1931–32 Maple Leaf Gardens installs the first suspended time clock. Hung above center ice, the four-sided Art Deco clock displayed the time remaining, the period and the score. Sometimes known as the "Player's Please" clock, due to its prominent cigarette ad, this once-technical marvel was replaced in 1967.

1932 Don Munro, of Burlington, Ontario, devises the first tabletop hockey game. Munro builds his prototype of materials found around his home. Eaton's department store likes the idea enough to sell it in Toronto in 1932. Munro's "mechanical table" becomes an immediate success. It survives, with modifications, until the 1950s when the Eagle Toy Company, among others, develops a better game with painted tin players and metal rods that move them up and down the rink and twirl them 360 degrees.

The Edmonton Rustlers.

▲ 1933 The Dominion Women's Amateur Hockey Association is founded and oversees a national playoff among the top women's hockey teams across Canada. In the first Dominion Championship, the western champion Edmonton Rustlers, led by Eleanor and Rosemary Tufford, surprise the Ontario champion Preston Rivulettes with 3–2 and 1–0 victories to become the first ever Canadian women's hockey national champions.

PRESTON LADIES ARE CHAMPIONS

▲ 1930s The Preston Rivulettes are the women's game's most famous dynasty, competing in organized exhibition and league games in Ontario and barnstorming tours across Canada. Skilled forwards like Hilda Ranscombe and Marm Schmuck and goalie Nellie Ranscombe lead the Rivulettes through a reported 350 matches, losing or tying just five during their decade of domination. This includes 10 regional championships and six national titles. They receive little more than athletic distinction and are frequently targeted by the pearl-clutchers. Like so much of hockey during and following the Second World War, the team soon scatters like seeds in the wind, making way for a greater self-determination and gamesmanship that will only take root generations later in women's play.

▼ 1932–33 New York Rangers captain Bill Cook wins the NHL scoring race with 50 points in 48 games to become the all-time oldest scoring champion—until Martin St. Louis. Ironically, because of 2012-13's lockout-shortened season, both men played a 48-game schedule.

The NHL's Oldest Scoring Champions*

Player	Age	Year	GP	G	A	P
Martin St. Louis	37/1	2012-13	48	17	43	60
Bill Cook	36/5	1932-33	48	28	22	50
Gordie Howe	34/11	1962-63	70	38	48	86
Wayne Gretzky	33/2	1993-94	81	38	92	130

*Current to 2024-25

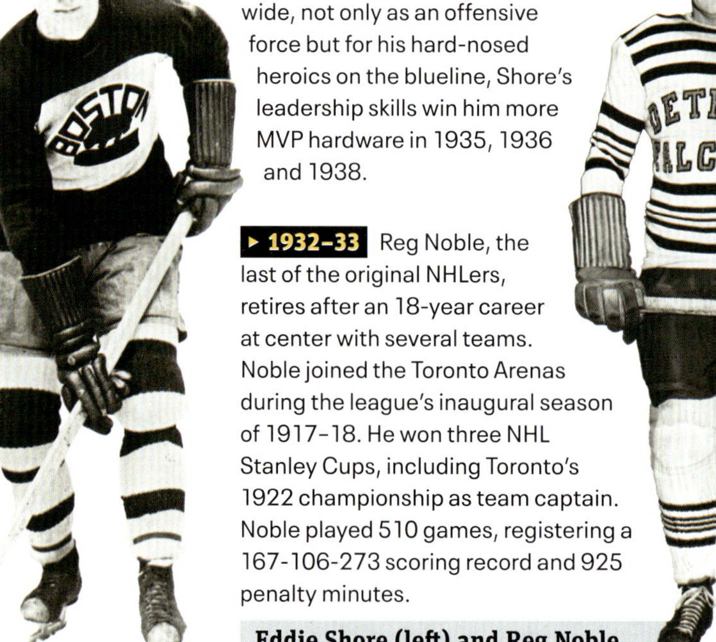

◀ 1932–33 Boston defenseman Eddie Shore earns his first Hart Trophy, scoring a career-high 35 points. Respected league-wide, not only as an offensive force but for his hard-nosed heroics on the blueline, Shore's leadership skills win him more MVP hardware in 1935, 1936 and 1938.

▶ 1932–33 Reg Noble, the last of the original NHLers, retires after an 18-year career at center with several teams. Noble joined the Toronto Arenas during the league's inaugural season of 1917–18. He won three NHL Stanley Cups, including Toronto's 1922 championship as team captain. Noble played 510 games, registering a 167-106-273 scoring record and 925 penalty minutes.

Eddie Shore (left) and Reg Noble.

The Eddie Shore–Ace Bailey melee, Boston Garden, 1933.

▲ 1933-34 Eddie Shore blindsides Ace Bailey. Regarded as the most appalling event in NHL play, Shore's hit from behind on December 12 sends Bailey crashing to the ice. In retaliation, Red Horner punches Shore, knocking him out cold. Bailey suffers a fractured skull and hovers near death for several days in a Boston hospital. After two delicate operations Bailey makes a miraculous recovery, though he never plays again. Shore receives a 16-game suspension. Two months later, the two men meet and shake hands at the Ace Bailey Benefit Game between the Maple Leafs and the NHL All-Stars at Maple Leaf Gardens.

1934-35
After years without an official safe space, netminders finally have an actual crease, 8 feet wide by 5 feet deep (1.5 m × 2.4 m) and painted on the ice. Skaters are forbidden from interfering with netminders in this 40-square-foot (3.7 m²) area.

1934-35 **Ottawa loses the Senators.** An Original Four NHL franchise dating to 1917-18, the small-town Senators can't keep financial pace in Frank Calder's America-centric NHL. Market size finally jettisons the team after several attempts to stay solvent and three last-place finishes. The Sens land in St. Louis as the Eagles. Missouri is no better, and the team folds after one season.

1934-35 **The Howie Morenz trade.** On October 3, a surprising six-player deal between Montreal and Chicago includes Howie Morenz, a three-time Stanley Cup winner with the Canadiens and the NHL's career scoring leader. The Great Depression brought a hard team cap of $62,500, and Morenz, among several aging veterans with diminished skills, is dealt. He only averages seven goals per season in Chicago and New York before returning to Montreal in 1936.

Toronto's Ace Bailey and a helmeted Eddie Shore of Boston. After his crushing hit ended Bailey's career, Shore cut his penalty minutes per game from 2.60 to 1.07 minutes.

"No other player will ever use this number on the Maple Leafs hockey team."

—Conn Smythe, on Ace Bailey's No. 6, the first number retired in hockey history

Charlie Gardiner.

▲ 1933-34 **Chicago wins the Stanley Cup.** Goalie (and captain) Charlie Gardiner carries an average Black Hawk team through three rounds, allowing one goal or fewer in five of eight games. In the Cup Final against Detroit, Gardiner wins two double overtimes, including the dramatic 1-0 Cup clincher after 30 minutes of OT on April 10. Two months later, he dies unexpectedly at age 29.

"When I was playing in this league, I worried about my job. Even the stars worried. If you went sour for five games, maybe even a couple, down you went ..." —Coach Toe Blake, on NHL hockey during the 1930s and '40s

Normie Smith and Mud Bruneteau (inset).

▲ 1935–36 **The longest game in Stanley Cup history.** Almost six hours after puck drop, Detroit rookie Mud Bruneteau finally ends hockey's epic 176-minute, 30-second endurance test by beating Montreal Maroons goalie Lorne Chabot. Reports note it's "a flukey goal" by Bruneteau, who "batted a rolling puck" past a bone-weary Chabot. "The ice was churned and cut." Chabot has no chance on the winner. It comes at 2:25 a.m. of Game 1 in the Red Wings-Maroons Cup semifinal. Detroit goalie Normie Smith records the league's longest overtime shutout (116:30) and blocks roughly 90 shots to Chabot's 68 in the 1-0 win. Determined more than ever, Detroit goes on to win its first ever Stanley Cup.

Toe Blake against Mike Karakas, 1944.

▲ 1935–36 **The Toe Blake trade.** The deal between Montreal-rivals the Maroons and the Canadiens that brings Blake to the Canadiens for veteran goalie Lorne Chabot changes hockey history in Montreal. Chabot, 35, is a two-time Stanley Cup champion and the most recent Vezina Trophy winner. Blake, a 24-year-old promising left winger, has only played eight games for the Maroons. After the trade in February, Chabot plays 16 games and is sold to New York. Blake becomes a lifelong Canadien. He plays 13 seasons, wins the 1938–39 scoring title and joins the Punch Line alongside Maurice Richard and Elmer Lach. The trio revitalizes the sagging franchise with Stanley Cups in 1944 and 1946. Blake coaches Montreal to eight more championships between 1956 and 1968.

◂ 1936

Great Britain defeats Canada for Olympic gold, based on a ruling that states that any team that has beaten another in a previous round doesn't have to meet them in the medal round. Effectively, Canada couldn't avenge the earlier 2-1 loss to a British team stocked mostly with British-born Canadian players. Canada loses the gold medal on a technicality.

Great Britain.

Howie Morenz memorial service, Montreal Forum, 1937.

▲ 1937 Howie Morenz's death shocks the hockey world. During a January 28 game at the Montreal Forum, Morenz falls awkwardly into the boards after a check by Chicago's Earl Seibert. Seibert then falls on Morenz. The Canadiens star is hospitalized with broken bones in his left leg and ankle. According to the coroner's report, Morenz dies of cardiac deficiency on March 8. Days later, the public funeral for Morenz at the Montreal Forum draws 15,000 mourners, while another 250,000 jam streets outside the arena. The following season, on November 2, the Howie Morenz Benefit Game raises $20,000 for the family of the deceased Montreal star. Morenz's No. 7 is retired, as the NHL All-Stars beat a combined Canadiens-Maroons team 6-5 at the Forum.

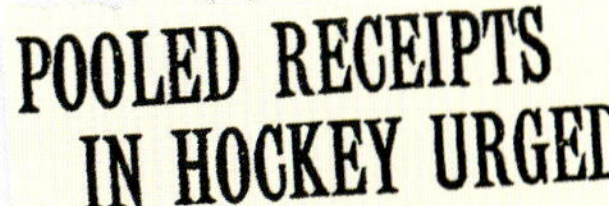

POOLED RECEIPTS IN HOCKEY URGED

Gorman Predicts Collapse of National League Unless U. S. Income Is Shared.

▲ 1937 Montreal Maroons manager Tommy Gorman advocates pooling gate receipts with American clubs, citing "economically unfair" conditions between U.S. and Canadian clubs. Gorman predicts the demise of franchises in Canada and the "ultimate collapse" of the NHL. The following season the Maroons fold after 14 seasons.

1937 "That Colville, he dekes me ... You know. Makes me take the first move then makes a sucker of me."

—Toronto goalie Turk Broda, using "deke" for the first known time in hockey, to describe the adroit play of New York forward Neil Colville

◂ 1936-37 Hardscrabble Maple Leafs defenseman Red Horner racks up the first 1,000 career minutes while leading the NHL in box time each year from 1932-33 to 1939-40, except 1937-38. Horner held the title seven times in his 12-year career, compiling 1,254 penalty minutes in 490 games. Toronto manager Conn Smythe called Horner "the inspirational force behind the Leaf teams of the 1930s."

1936-37 Hockey's first minor pro loops, the International Hockey League and the Canadian-American Hockey League, interlock schedules and form the International-American Hockey League in 1938. Before 1940-41, the IAHL drops the word "International" to officially become the American Hockey League, now a feeder league to the NHL.

▲ 1937-38 The Chicago Black Hawks win their second Stanley Cup, sporting a 14-25-9 regular season, a Russian-born captain in Johnny Gottselig, a bench with eight U.S.-born regulars and a Major League Baseball umpire in Massachusetts-native and coach Bill Stewart. Chicago scores the fewest goals and allows the second most, finishing with a .385 regular-season win percentage—the worst by a Cup winner in NHL history. Despite the championship, Stewart is fired 21 games into the next season.

▲ **1938** After a 1935 Stanley Cup, the cash-strapped Montreal Maroons suspend operations following a 12-30-6 last-place finish and leave Montreal's rabid fan base to the rival Canadiens. With only seven clubs, the NHL reverts to one division for the first time since 1925–26.

RULE CHANGE

1938–39 The penalty shot is modified to allow the puck carrier to skate in before shooting.

The Detroit Red Wings at a railway station for an NHL first, a nine-game exhibition series against the Montreal Canadiens in Europe.

▲ **1938** **The first NHL teams play in Europe.** Montreal and Detroit tour England and France in exhibition play in April and May. In the first match between NHL teams outside North America, Montreal wins 5–4 before a London crowd of 8,000, many shouting, "Come on Canada," presumably for the Canadiens. They take the series 5-3-1.

Boston goalie Frank Brimsek, 1948.

▲ **1938–39** Frank Brimsek ousts Tiny Thompson in Boston nets. Talented and popular with Bruin fans, Thompson is sold for $15,000 to Detroit to make room for the 25-year-old Brimsek. One of manager Art Ross' biggest gambles, the unheralded Brimsek quickly makes Boston fans forget Thompson. The native of Eveleth, Minnesota, notches six shutouts in his first eight games to attain everlasting fame as "Mr. Zero." The Bruins finish in first place. Brimsek nets a league-high 33 victories. His fairytale debut only gets better. He earns the Calder and Vezina Trophies and posts a 1.25 goals-against average, backstopping Boston to its first Stanley Cup in a decade.

▲ **1938–39** Rookie Mel Hill emerges from the shadows following a 10-goal regular season to be immortalized as Mel "Sudden Death" Hill after firing six goals in 12 playoff games for Boston, including three overtime deciders in its Stanley Cup semifinal against the Rangers. Two goals come in triple OT, one is Game 7's series winner. Hill never scores another overtime goal. His record stands today.

▲ 1939 *The Hot Stove League* premieres on CBC Radio. Canada's first sports talk show becomes a program fixture on *Hockey Night in Canada* and establishes subject standards, such as hockey's best players, trade rumors, game strategies and Stanley Cup predictions. Sponsored by Imperial Oil, the program advertises Esso 3 Star gasoline, which inspired the three-star selection. Old-time greats like Elmer Ferguson and Bobby Hewitson broadcast from a small studio between periods.

▲ 1939–40 The Kraut Line finishes 1-2-3 in the NHL scoring race. Boston's potent trio of Milt Schmidt (52 points), Woody Dumart (43) and Bobby Bauer (43) is the first line to sweep the top scoring spots. The line's nickname refers to their Germanic hometown of Berlin (Kitchener), Ontario.

(Left to right) Syl Apps, Hank Goldup, Gaye Stewart, Bob Davidson, Sweeney Schriner, Turk Broda, Lorne Carr and Reg Hamilton, 1942.

▲ 1939–40 **The Sweeney Schriner trade.** In one of hockey's biggest deals, the New York Americans trade Schriner, their two-time NHL scoring leader, for Toronto's Busher Jackson, Murray Armstrong, Doc Romnes and Buzz Boll (and an option on Jimmy Fowler). Jackson, Armstrong, Romnes and Boll play a combined nine seasons in New York. Schriner has six seasons with the Maple Leafs, winning two Stanley Cups and scoring twice in Game 7 of 1942's famous comeback championship.

Boston Rains 83 Shots on Lo Presti to Gain 3-2 Win

1940–41 Chicago's Sam LoPresti faces a firing squad of 83 shots in Boston on March 4—and yet only loses 3-2 to the Bruins. How bad is it? A tireless LoPresti kicks out 41 shots before Roy Conacher scores Boston's first goal early in the second period. Milt Schmidt clicks on the 55th shot and Eddie Wiseman fires home the winner with 2:31 left. LoPresti doesn't get the W, but he's still a trivia favorite today after breaking the NHL's 80-saves mark.

1939–40 The Art Ross-Eddie Shore feuds. The long-running acrimony between Bruins boss Art Ross and multiple Hart Trophy-winner Eddie Shore peaks when Shore purchases the AHL Springfield Indians. Ross initially agrees to Shore, 37, splitting his duties between Boston and Springfield. Instead, after 14 seasons as a Bruin fan favorite, Shore is traded mid-season to the New York Americans, where he plays 10 of 16 games and three playoff matches before quitting the NHL to run his Springfield franchise.

◂ 1941 **"He was good alright ... if he hadn't been good he wouldn't be alive now."**

—Boston defenseman Jack Crawford, on whether Chicago goalie Sam LoPresti was good or lucky after facing 83 shots on March 4

Maurice Richard and coach Dick Irvin, 1940s.

◂ **1940–41** Dick Irvin signs with Montreal. Coach Irvin was quick to turn his teams into Stanley Cup contenders. He did it in Chicago, as Cup finalists in 1930–31. Then, in Toronto, when the Maple Leafs won the 1932 championship. And, again, behind the bench with Montreal in 1944, the Canadiens' first Cup in 13 years. Irvin, however, couldn't sustain any of that success. His Leafs went to the Cup Final six more times without another title. That, in part, led to his dismissal and availability to Montreal in 1940. The Irvin-coached Canadiens did become the league dynamo, reaching the Cup Final eight times, winning three championships.

1940 A hockey broadcast first, on February 25, NBC in New York sets up experimental television station W2XBS and airs Montreal's 6-2 win against the Rangers to a small viewing audience.

Bill Cowley and Dit Clapper.

◂▾ **1940–41** Bill Cowley becomes the first player to total more regular-season assists than any other player's point total, with his record-setting 45 assists. He tops five runners-up by one point—a feat Wayne Gretzky achieved three times, twice by much greater margins.

Bill Cowley's Assist Total Tops Points Total, 1940–41

Player	Team	GP	G	A	Pts	PIM
Bill Cowley	Boston	46	17	45	62	16
Bryan Hextall	NYR	48	26	18	44	16
Gordie Drillon	Toronto	42	23	21	44	2

Several more players have 44 points

▴ **1941–42** Tom Anderson wins the Hart Trophy, leading the Brooklyn Americans in scoring with 41 points. Brooklyn, however, ices the worst record in the seven-team NHL, making Anderson the first MVP on a last-place team.

Detroit Red Wings Vanquished Before Record Gardens Crowd

▸ **1941–42** **The NHL's greatest comeback.** On the brink and down 3-0 in the Stanley Cup Final against a buoyant Detroit squad, before Game 4 Toronto coach Hap Day benches veterans Gordie Drillon and Bucko McDonald for subs Don Metz and Ernie Dickens. He, also, reportedly reads a letter to the players from a 14-year-old girl who believes the team will recover from the deficit. Inspired, their backs against the wall, the Leafs stave off elimination and take Game 4, 4-3. After the loss, an apoplectic Jack Adams (Detroit's coach) is suspended indefinitely for accosting referee Mel Hardwood. The Red Wings never recover, as Toronto ties the series 3-3. A Canadian record crowd of 16,218 witnesses hockey history in Game 7 at Maple Leaf Gardens. The Leafs win 3-1 to clinch their comeback championship.

A career Maple Leaf player, coach Hap Day dresses in uniform to celebrate his first Stanley Cup behind the bench.

Boston coach and GM Art Ross, with Milt Schmidt and Frank Mario, 1941.

Art Ross

Art Ross was a player, coach, manager and hockey inventor. He approached the game from a wide-eyed perspective, advancing the potential of hockey's true genius during its most important growth phase, shepherding it from a raw outdoor game to a regulated arena sport. For everything he did to further play strategies and technologies, he reached sports immortality through the Art Ross Trophy, awarded to the NHL's scoring leader.

Ross was Ontario-born and grew up in Montreal, the incubator city of organized hockey. He played on its back streets and neighborhood rinks, moved up to city leagues and, at 22, made "ringer" status on the Stanley Cup-winning Kenora Thistles. His time and place on ice came before the NHL. Ross is credited with one career NHL goal in 1917-18, an irony given the criterion for his namesake trophy.

While Ross is recognized as a founding father of the Boston Bruins, his enterprise brought the game the B-shape goal net and a puck redesign that allowed it to slide more smoothly. In 1940-41, the Art Ross puck, adorned with an orange label bearing his name, became the official puck of the NHL.

Ross was the first NHL coach to pull his goalie for an extra attacker. He, along with Lester Patrick, helped devise the league's new forward passing rules in 1929-30. Reports noted that the Ross-coached Bruins "would be the first to master the new game," when his team responded with a 14-game winning streak.

The Six Team Era

With the Second World War raging overseas and the NHL depleted of 80 regulars serving in the armed services by the early 1940s, the league was seriously considering suspending operations. The player shortage had affected every team and the overall quality of professional play.

League boss Frank Calder seized on the full weight of the complexities of another world war. Was this a time for pro sport? Calder leaned in and issued, "that in the interest of public morale, the league should carry on."

Hockey did continue. The cost, however, was the demise of another NHL franchise, the Americans in New York. By 1942–43, hockey's premier league had devolved into a six-team operation. Now, only 12 pro teams existed between the NHL and AHL. Senior amateur hockey kept awarding the Allan Cup. But international hockey and the women's game had all but disappeared.

Following the war years the next generation of players would raise the sport's profile to produce some of its greatest stars, bitterest rivalries and most memorable moments of what became the Six Team Era. The hockey was uncomplicated. No megabuck contracts, rink-board advertising, league lockouts or electronic scoreboards. Without social media, the internet or even television (for some years), "the closest thing we kids had to an interactive experience," noted broadcaster Ron MacLean, was that young fan's rite of passage: the hockey card. Back then, memorabilia was personal not profitable. Fans treasured autographs for the signature rather than their market value.

The most prized card might be of Gordie Howe or Maurice Richard. Throughout their mid-century dominance, Howe and Richard set standards by which today's greatest players are measured. Fans and sports experts argued endlessly who was better, Richard, the pure goal scorer, or Howe, the game's most complete player.

New players, rules and equipment altered the dynamics of play during the six-team years, but nothing revolutionized the sport quite like television. For the first time millions of fans could watch the game live in the comfort of their homes. It eclipsed radio to become the primary medium of hockey and the fantasy-creator for thousands of kids everywhere.

Gordie Howe.

OPPOSITE
Jacques Plante at Madison Square Garden, 1957.

Bep Guidolin.

▲ 1942–43

The youngest NHL goal-scorer. Too young to go to war, but not to play major league, 16-year-old Bep Guidolin pots his first NHL goal in his second game as a wartime replacement with Boston on November 24. On a youth kick, the Bruins form the Sprout Line, matching Guidolin with Don Gallinger (17) and Bill Shill (19).

RULE CHANGE

1942 Wartime restrictions on train scheduling halt regular-season overtime.

1943 NHL president Frank Calder passes away on February 4 after suffering a heart attack during a league meeting. Red Dutton takes over as president. Calder was 65.

The Brooklyn (New York) Americans in their final season, 1941–42.

▲ 1942 Limited on-ice success, financial challenges and a highly competitive field of local sports teams, including the hometown rival New York Rangers, the Brooklyn (New York) Americans are forced to fold after 17 NHL seasons, leaving the league a six-team, 84-player circuit.

Lester Patrick and Frank Boucher.

"We've got no hockey players."

—New York GM Lester Patrick's blunt evaluation of his war-ravaged Rangers, who lost a league-high 28 players due to military call-ups from 1941-42 to 1943-44. Only six regulars return in 1943-44 from the previous season. Coach Frank Boucher, 43, activates himself to fill the bench, as New York records the NHL's worst season start, going 0-14-1.

◄ 1942–43

Ken "Tubby" McAuley. A minor-league war addition, McAuley might have considered serving overseas rather than between the pipes. The 22-year-old backstopped all 50 New York Ranger games and won only six, giving up an all-time record 310 goals. His worst outing was a 58-shot, 15-0 shellacking by Detroit on January 23. Edmonton-born, McAuley set several humiliating NHL marks: the only goalie to lose 10 consecutive starts from a season start; the most consecutive goals allowed in one game; the most losses (39) by a rookie goalie in one season. To name a very few.

Bill Mosienko against Ken McAuley, January 13, 1944.

LEAFS AND HAWKS IN SCORELESS TIE

First Period.
No scoring.
No penalties.
Second Period.
No scoring.
No penalties.
Third Period.
No scoring.
No penalties.

▲ 1943–44 **The only scoreless, penalty-free NHL game.** Toronto and Chicago squander a night of hockey before a sellout crowd at raucous Chicago Stadium. Nothing really happens. Nobody scores. Nobody gets riled enough for a whistle from referee Bill Chadwick. Chicago forward Fido Purpur does try, but his high-stick goal is called back in the two-hour match on February 20. Goalies Mike Karakas and Paul Bibeault salvage some athletic pride, as both record shutouts in the scoreless tie.

Tommy Gorman and Charlie Gardiner, 1934.

▲ 1943–44 Everywhere Tommy Gorman went he won. Between 1920 and 1946, Gorman built seven Stanley Cup champions with four different franchises. Under Gorman, Ottawa becomes the NHL's first dynasty team in the early 1920s. He popularizes hockey in New York with the city's first NHL club, the Americans. Then, Gorman wins consecutive titles, managing and coaching the 1934 Chicago Black Hawks and the 1935 Montreal Maroons. His fourth Cup-winning club is the Dick Irvin–coached Montreal Canadiens, with championships in 1944 and 1946.

Ted Kennedy (No. 9) against Bill Durnan.

▲ 1943 **The Ted Kennedy trade.** During a stellar OHA junior year with Port Colborne, Kennedy is traded by Montreal to Toronto for defenseman Frank Eddols. Kennedy, 17 and fresh out of high school, plays two games in 1942–43. The next season he finishes second in goal scoring and will become one of the Maple Leafs' greatest stars for 12 more seasons, winning five Stanley Cups in seven years, two as captain. Kennedy is the last Leaf player to win the Hart Trophy (1955) as league MVP until Auston Matthews in 2022.

Bill Durnan against an unknown skater.

▲ 1943–44 An avid amateur, Bill Durnan finally acquiesces and turns pro at 27 years old. Backstopping Montreal, the ambidextrous Durnan wins the Vezina Trophy with a sterling 38-5-7 record and First All-Star Team honors, beginning an unprecedented stretch of six top goalie awards and All-Star appearances over the next seven seasons. Durnan wore identical gloves on each hand, able to switch his stick and glove hand depending on the attack. He would switch back and forth just to psych out shooters.

1945 "The caliber of play is going to make the fans forget the war years."

—NHL president Red Dutton, on the player returnees from the Second World War, including many like Milt Schmidt, Max Bentley and Sid Abel

RULE CHANGE

1943–44 The red line at center ice is introduced to speed up play and reduce offside infractions common under rules that once forced defenders to carry the puck over their blue lines. Players can now pass the puck from their zone to center ice, transforming counterattack mobility. This advance is considered the beginning of hockey's Modern Era.

◂ 1943–44 Maurice Richard is named all three stars. After a 3–1 loss to Toronto in Game 1 of the Stanley Cup semifinal, where Maple Leaf defender Bob Davidson successfully shadows Richard pointless, Montreal coach Dick Irvin goes with four defensemen and only eight forwards plus Richard in Game 2. Irvin plays Richard on multiple lines, so half the time when Richard is out there, Davidson is sitting on the bench. Before Montreal's frenzied faithful, Richard pots all five goals and all three stars in the Canadiens' 5–1 win. Montreal doesn't lose again, bouncing Toronto four straight and Chicago four straight in the Cup Final. Hockey witnesses its next great scoring star, as Richard tallies a record 12 goals and leads the Canadiens to their first Cup in 13 years.

The Punch Line: Maurice Richard, Elmer Lach and Toe Blake.

▴ 1944–45 Hockey's first milestone man. Maurice Richard sets the definitive benchmark for snipers, firing 50 goals in the 50-game schedule. His 50th on March 18 is the first of hockey's most revered standards: the 50-goal, 100-point, 500-goal, 1,000-point and 1,000-game plateaus. Linemates Elmer Lach, Richard and Toe Blake finish 1-2-3 in the scoring race.

Sweeney Schriner and goalie Frank McCool, following Game 1's 1–0 win against Detroit. Schriner got the game's lone goal and McCool his first of three shutouts in their 1945 Stanley Cup–winning series.

▴ 1944–45 Toronto engineers a Stanley Cup upset, eliminating the defending Cup-champion Canadiens in a grueling six-game semifinal series and pulling off a seven-game heart-stopper against the Red Wings in Cup Final play. Ted Kennedy scores four in Toronto's meager nine-goal output, as Maple Leaf rookie Frank McCool blanks Detroit 1–0, 2–0 and 1–0. The Red Wings storm back to tie the series, but McCool and the Leafs eke out a 2–1 Cup winner before unruly fans at Detroit's Olympia.

Flash Hollett.

▲ 1944–45 Detroit's Flash Hollett stages the NHL's first 20-goal performance by a defenseman. No stay-at-home blueliner, Hollett learned his rushing and puck management skills from Bruin greats Eddie Shore and Dit Clapper. After a record-high pair of 19-goal seasons, Hollett is traded to the Red Wings, where he is partnered with Earl Seibert and hits his 20-goal target—a mark that stands for 24 years until Bobby Orr's 21 goals in 1968-69.

Hall of Famer Harvey Pulford.

▲ 1945
The Hockey Hall of Fame is born. Nine players and two builders are inaugural inductees, including former NHL stars Charlie Gardiner, Eddie Gerard, Howie Morenz and Georges Vézina and pre-NHLers Hobey Baker, Frank McGee, Tom Phillips, Harvey Pulford and Hod Stuart. The first builders honored are Sir Montagu Allan and Lord Stanley of Preston.

Charlie Rayner and "Sugar" Jim Henry.

▲ 1945–46 New York coach Frank Boucher experiments with a two-goalie system, rotating Charlie Rayner (41 games) and Sugar Jim Henry (10), sometimes within games and even within periods as the first alternating goalie tandem.

1945–46 Andy Clovechok scores 103 points with the Vancouver Canucks of the Pacific Coast Hockey League to become pro hockey's first 100-point player—almost a quarter-century before Phil Esposito's NHL landmark 126-point season in 1968-69.

PREJUDICIAL CONDUCT LAW KAYOES BIG 'BABE' PRATT

HE IGNORED WARNINGS AGAINST BETTING

▲ 1945–46 **Babe Pratt's lifetime banishment.** Nine months after becoming the first NHL rearguard to score a Stanley Cup–winning goal in Toronto's 1945 championship, the Maple Leafs' star rushing defender is expelled for "conduct prejudicial to the welfare of hockey" on January 29. Pratt had bet on hockey and allegedly on his Maple Leafs. His confession and promise to quit gambling pays off. He's reinstated after only 16 days, or five lost games. The stain, however, is permanent. That summer Pratt is dealt to Boston and then demoted to the AHL.

◀ 1945–46 **The newly formed IHL honors Joe Turner.** Turner's NHL career lasts a single game as a war fill-in for Detroit goalie Johnny Mowers in February 1942. Soon after, the Canadian-born Turner joins the U.S. Army during the Second World War. He's killed in action in January 1945. In tribute, the IHL chooses to venerate him with the Turner Cup, which is presented annually to the IHL champions until the league folds in 2001.

New NHL chief Clarence Campbell and outgoing league boss Red Dutton, 1946.

▲ 1946 Clarence Campbell is named NHL president. A Rhodes scholar, lawyer and, fittingly, former NHL referee, Campbell meets all prerequisites as a future league boss to replace president Red Dutton. He even prosecuted war crimes on the world stage following the Second World War. Campbell serves as the third NHL president, from 1946 to 1977.

"'What size?' he asked. I said, 'I don't know.' He said, 'What position do you play?' I said, 'All of 'em.' He said, 'You a smart ass?' I said, 'No sir, I'm not a smart ass. I have no idea what they drafted me for.'"

— Gordie Howe, 15, questioned by a New York Rangers equipment manager at their Winnipeg training camp in 1943. Howe had never worn proper equipment before and he once played goalie.

◂ **1946–47** **A rookie named Gordie Howe.** After rejecting a New York Rangers rights contract at their Winnipeg training camp in 1943, Howe, a shy and homesick 15-year-old, returns home to Saskatoon. The following season, he attends Detroit's camp in Windsor and signs a "C" form granting them his NHL rights. Howe is soon promoted to the USHL Omaha Knights, where, at 17, he scores 48 points in 51 games in 1945–46. In his Red Wings' debut, the kid from Floral, Saskatchewan, proves himself a gifted stickhandler, passer and shooter, with a battler's readiness to fight. On October 16, he scores his first NHL goal, against Toronto's Turk Broda and scraps with tough guy Bill Ezinicki. Howe wears No. 17 before his switch to No. 9, the jersey number he dons for the next five decades, an incomprehensible 32 hockey seasons, until his 1980 retirement.

Dit Clapper.

▴ **1946–47** Dit Clapper becomes the first 20-year NHLer. Clapper played from 1927–28 to 1946–47, originally as a right winger, then on defense and as a playing-coach during his last two seasons, all with Boston. He retires mid-season on February 12 and is inducted into the Hockey Hall of Fame that same day. In an on-ice ceremony Clapper is presented with a Hall admission scroll and a sterling silver tea set.

Toronto wins the 1947 Stanley Cup.

▴ **1946–47** Toronto manager Conn Smythe's major team rebuild pays off immediately after shedding six veterans, including Sweeney Schriner and Babe Pratt. Smythe signs eight additions, among them Harry Watson and Howie Meeker. Six rookies crack the revamped lineup. In an all-Canadian Stanley Cup Final against Montreal, Maurice Richard leads the playoffs in scoring and penalty minutes. Toronto, however, prevails in six games to win the title. Ted Kennedy, 21, becomes the youngest NHLer to score a Cup-winning goal.

The Hockey News

THE INTERNATIONAL HOCKEY WEEKLY

VOLUME 1, NUMBER 1 — MONTREAL, OCTOBER 1, 1947 — PRICE: TEN CENTS

Pro Teams In Swing Of Pre-Season Drills

Training Camp Tune-Ups

THOSE N.H.L. CHAMPS, THE MONTREAL CANADIENS, ARE IN TRAINING IN THEIR HOME TOWN, MONTREAL. COACH DICK IRVIN IS WELL PLEASED WITH HIS PROSPECTS AND HOPES THEY WILL TAKE THE CHAMPIONSHIP AGAIN THIS YEAR.

HOW AM I DOING, COACH?

... AND THE STANLEY CUP WINNERS, THE TORONTO MAPLE LEAFS, ARE GETTING THEIR LEG MUSCLES TUNED UP AT ST. CATHARINES IN ONTARIO!

THOSE RESOUNDING BODY CHECKS YOU HEAR THESE DAYS ARE THE NEW YORK RANGERS. THEY ARE UP THERE GETTING A PRE-SEASON WORKOUT UNDER THE WATCHFUL EYE OF... COACH FRANK BOUCHER!!!

HERSHEY, PA. IS THE SCENE ... BOSTON ARE OUT OF HIBERNATION AND RARING TO GO!

DETROIT IS HAVING A TOUGH TIME DECIDING WHICH OF HER BOYS ARE THE BETTER. THE RED WINGS TRAINED AT SASKATOON, SASK. AND WATERLOO, ONT. THE PICK OF BOTH GOING TO DETROIT TO FINISH THE TRAINING GRIND!

THE CHICAGO BLACK HAWKS ARE PREPARING TO GO ON THE WARPATH AND ARE GETTING THEIR EXERCISING DONE AT REGINA, SASKATCHEWAN!

ME GETTUM OUT OF LAST PLACE THIS YEAR!

Bumper Crop Of Veterans And Rookies Fighting For Starting Posts

Hockey For Cuba?

Proposal Advanced For N.H.L. Teams To Play Spring Exhibitions In Havana

RULE CHANGE

1946–47
A system of signals by officials to indicate infractions is introduced.

1947–48 Led by Doug Bentley and Roy Conacher, Chicago fires a league-high 195 goals and, thanks to a porous defense, allows a league-worst 225 goals against — only the third time an NHL team manages to lead in both goals for and against in one season. Those same Black Hawks did it 21 years earlier in 1926–27, as did Toronto in 1925–26.

The 1948 Olympics in St. Moritz, Switzerland.

▲ 1948 Canada's representatives, the RCAF Flyers, win Olympic gold based on the goals-for/goals-against ratio for Canada (13.80) versus silver medal winner Czechoslovakia (4.44). Both teams had 7-1-0 records and 15 points.

▲ 1947
On October 1, *The Hockey News* debuts as the first hockey-only publication. Price: 10 cents.

Larry Kwong of the QSHL Valleyfield Braves, 1950–51.

▲ 1947–48
Larry Kwong's New York minute. Kwong is the first NHLer of Asian ancestry. Unfortunately, his stay lasts only one shift with the New York Rangers against Montreal on March 13. The Vernon, British Columbia–born Kwong later thrives in the Quebec Senior Hockey League, playing for coach Toe Blake's Valleyfield Braves, where he wins the league's MVP award in 1950–51 and leads the senior club to the league title.

MAX BENTLEY GOES TO LEAFS FOR 5 PLAYERS

Doug and Max Bentley after Max's trade to Toronto.

▲ 1947–48 **The Max Bentley trade.** Once the biggest deal in NHL history, Bentley, a two-time scoring champion with Chicago, is sent with Cy Thomas to Toronto for a five-player unit of Bob Goldham, Gaye Stewart, Bud Poile, Gus Bodnar and Ernie Dickens. The move pays full dividends for Conn Smythe's Maple Leafs. They repeat as Stanley Cup champions, sweeping Detroit in Toronto captain Syl Apps' last campaign. Gordie Howe plays his first Cup Final.

Bill Durnan, the last goalie captain, and Turk Broda.

▲ 1947–48 Few netminders have captained NHL teams. The last is Bill Durnan, after Montreal captain Toe Blake suffers a career-ending leg injury on January 10. Durnan does such a good job of questioning the referees that opposing teams object, believing he deliberately slows the game for strategic breaks. After that, the NHL prohibits goalies from serving as captains.

1949 **Hockey's most lopsided score.** At the 1949 World Championship, Canada beats Denmark 47–0, scoring 13 goals in the first period, 16 in the second and 18 in the third. All 11 Canadian players get at least a hat trick. The Danes rarely pass the center red line all game. Denmark doesn't enter elite play again for another half-century, until the 2003 Worlds.

Bill Quackenbush against Harry Lumley, 1954.

▲ 1948–49 The first defenseman to win the Lady Byng Trophy. Detroit's Bill Quackenbush played a disciplined, positional game with a pokecheck rather than a bodycheck. His zero-penalty season was part of a 131-game penalty-free streak from March 1948 to January 1950.

The Toronto Maple Leafs battle the New York Rangers, late 1940s.

▲ 1948–49 Toronto's third-straight Stanley Cup. After stumbling into fourth place with a modest 22-25-13 regular-season record, the Maple Leafs dump Boston in five games and sweep Detroit in the Cup Final to set an NHL mark for most consecutive championships. Gordie Howe, 21, becomes the youngest top point-earner in Stanley Cup history, scoring 11 points in 11 games.

1950 Prior to boarding a plane en route to defend their title at the 1950 World Championship in London in March, members of the Czechoslovak national team are accused of attempting to defect and jailed on trumped-up charges of treason by the Stalinist Czechoslovak government. Months later they appear in court and 12 players are found guilty. Their sentences range from eight months to 15 years. Gutted of talent and spirit, the Czechs take years to rebuild their hockey system.

RULE CHANGE

1948–49 NHL ice surfaces are painted white. Clubs are allowed to dress 17 players, besides goalies.

The Production Line: Gordie Howe, Sid Abel and Ted Lindsay.

▲ 1949–50 The Production Line of Ted Lindsay, Sid Abel and Gordie Howe finish 1-2-3 in the NHL scoring race, giving notice to Detroit's ascendancy as a league powerhouse. The trio's formidable skills, chemistry and toughness fire the Red Wings to seven-straight regular-season championships and four Stanley Cups. Alongside Abel and Lindsay, Howe wins four consecutive scoring titles.

◂ 1950 **"I knew who paid our salaries. It wasn't the owners; it was the people. This is what we dream about, maybe from the time we're born — to be recognized as the best in the world. I just wanted to share it with the fans."**

— Ted Lindsay, said later, on taking the Stanley Cup for the first on-ice victory lap after Detroit's win on home ice in 1950

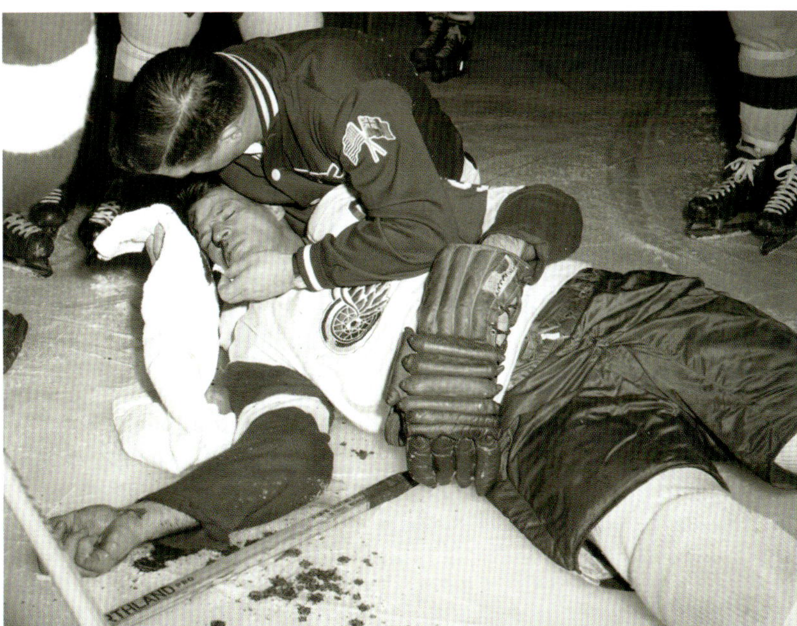

Gordie Howe suffers a near-fatal on-ice injury, 1950.

▴ 1949–50 **Gordie Howe almost dies.** Without game footage, it's unclear what caused Howe's near-fatal crash during Game 1 of the Detroit–Toronto Stanley Cup semifinal. But an up-ice rush to catch Ted Kennedy leads to Howe losing his footing in mid-stride and crash headfirst into the boards. "Just as I threw the check at Kennedy, he suddenly dumped the puck ahead and stopped," said Howe. "People tell me — people at the game — that Kennedy butt-ended me in the face just as we collided, causing me to lose my balance ... I just remember hitting the boards." Howe sustains facial fractures, a lacerated right eyeball, a concussion and possible brain damage. He is sidelined the rest of the playoffs.

More determined than ever, the Howe-less Red Wings capture the semifinal against Toronto and then the Stanley Cup against New York in a sudden-death overtime showdown in Game 7. At 8:31 of the second OT, Pete Babando scores for Detroit. No other team in NHL history (except Detroit again in 1954) has claimed a championship in Game 7 overtime. Howe, in civvies, comes onto the ice to celebrate with his teammates.

RULE CHANGE

1950–51 Each NHL team's home rink is required to provide an emergency goalie with full equipment at each game for use by either team.

▸ 1950 The stresses of tending goal in a maskless era without any of today's netminding basics finally catches up with future Hockey Hall of Fame goalie Bill Durnan. He walks away mid-playoffs.

▴ 1950–51 **Terry Sawchuk wins the Calder Trophy.** After top rookie honors with both Omaha (USHL) and Indianapolis (AHL), Sawchuk claims his third freshman title, with Detroit, in a four-year span. Sawchuk leads the NHL in record wins (44), shutouts (11) and goals-against average (1.97). His rookie 44-win mark has never been broken.

Gordie Howe against Cesare Maniago, 1961.

▲ 1950–51 Gordie Howe's triumphant return. Following a severe head injury during the 1950 NHL playoffs, a helmeted Howe notches 43 goals and 43 assists to set a league record 86 points—a first in all three scoring categories since Howie Morenz in 1927–28. Howe's scoring spree powers Detroit to a league first, breaking triple digits with a 101-point season—an unbroken mark until Montreal's 103-point year in 1968–69's expanded 76-game schedule.

Bill Barilko in mid-flight, scoring Toronto's 1951 Stanley Cup winner.

▲ 1950–51 **The Bill Barilko goal.** In the only Stanley Cup Final where every game ends in overtime, Toronto eliminates Montreal, with the Cup winner coming at 2:53 of extra play in Game 5 off the stick of Barilko—the unlikely hero-turned-tragic-figure who dies in a plane crash on a Northern Quebec fishing trip later that summer. His remains and those of pilot Dr. Henry Hudson aren't found until 1962, the year the Maple Leafs win their next Stanley Cup. Toronto is the only team to win Lord Stanley's prize by scoring four overtime goals in Cup Final action. By that measure, the only team to lose the Cup while allowing four overtime goals is Montreal.

1951–52
NHL home teams wear white uniforms; visitors wear colored uniforms. Goal creases are enlarged to 4 feet by 8 feet (1.2 m × 2.4 m). Face-off circles are enlarged from 20 feet to 30 feet (6 m to 9 m) in diameter.

Bill Mosienko.

▲ 1951–52 **The fastest hat trick in NHL history.** Behind 6–2 versus New York in the third period on March 23, Chicago's Bill Mosienko snaps a low-wrister past rookie goalie Lorne Anderson at 6:09. The Black Hawks' top line of center Gus Bodnar and wingers George Gee and Mosienko take the next face-off. Bodnar wins it and passes to Mosienko, who dashes by Ranger blueliner Hy Buller and buries another past Anderson at 6:20. Chicago coach Ebbie Goodfellow sticks with his red-hot line. Bodnar wins the face-off again, passes to Gee, who dishes to Mosienko, who dekes left and blasts his third goal against Anderson at 6:30. Twenty-one seconds. The deflated Rangers lose 7–6.

Anderson, the victim of Bill Mosienko's famous hat trick and owner of the second-fastest three goals allowed, never plays another NHL game.

Turk Broda, 1947.

◀ 1951–52
Turk Broda retires. Among hockey's best all-time money goalies, Broda ends his 14-season NHL career with Toronto following his 101st playoff game on March 29. Two nights earlier, he became the first NHL goalie to appear in 100 playoff games in a 1–0 loss to Detroit. Broda led the Maple Leafs to five Stanley Cups.

Terry Sawchuk and teammate Marcel Pronovost (in crease) against Milt Schmidt, 1951–52.

▲ 1951–52 Detroit sweeps Toronto and Montreal in eight games in Stanley Cup play. Terry Sawchuk is a wall. He notches four straight shutouts on home ice, allowing only five goals all playoffs. His save percentage is .978, stopping 224 of 229 shots. Meanwhile, brothers Jerry and Pete Cusimano create a sensation in Game 4's 3–0 Cup-winning game when they fling an eight-tentacled mollusk onto the ice in anticipation of the Red Wings' eighth-straight win. The octopus toss becomes a long-standing Detroit ritual at playoff time.

The Edmonton Mercurys, 1952.

1952 The Edmonton Mercurys win Olympic gold and become Canada's last top-place finisher for the next half century until the Salt Lake City Games in 2002. Why the 50-year absence from gold? While Canada was still sending amateur-level players into world competition, the Europeans were leveling the playing field, developing hockey programs and leagues to stock their national teams with top talent.

Forum Rafters Shake as Rocket Bags Record Goal

Maurice Richard and his 324th goal puck.

▲ 1952–53 Maurice Richard dethrones Nels Stewart as NHL goal-scoring leader. Richard breaks Stewart's record of 324 goals with his 325th on November 8—10 years to the day after Richard's first NHL goal in 1942. Like his first, the record-setter comes backhanded, this time a trickler through Chicago goalie Al Rollins.

Gump Worsley against Bill Gadsby, 1958.

▲ 1952–53 Gump Worsley wins the Calder Trophy. Worsley's major league break comes after New York's Charlie Rayner suffers an NHL career-ending injury. Backstopping the feeble Rangers, he nets a 13-29-8 record for the last 50 games and achieves top rookie status. Seeking a $500 raise, Worsley is demoted to the WHL Vancouver Canucks, where he wins the league's MVP award. The Rangers bring him up for good in 1954–55.

▶ 1952–53 The first televised NHL games in Canada. René Lecavalier calls the play-by-play on *La soirée du hockey*, the inaugural French TV broadcast, as Montreal beats Detroit 2–1 on October 11. Three weeks later, on November 1, English viewers watch *Hockey Night in Canada*'s first broadcast, with Foster Hewitt handling game play. Toronto defeats Boston 3–2. Neither game is aired in its entirety, as NHL owners believe broadcasts will hurt arena attendance.

A promotion for *Hockey Night in Canada* telecasts.

▶ 1952–53 Jacques Plante's Stanley Cup debut. Mid-playoffs, goalie Gerry McNeil suffers acute anxiety and is replaced by rookie Jacques Plante, who only worked three regular-season games before his playoff baptism by fire: a must-win Game 6 against Chicago with the Canadiens facing elimination, down 3–2 in games. Plante earns a 3–0 shutout and backstops Montreal 4–1 in Game 7 to reach the Cup Final. Against Boston, Plante gets a win and a loss before McNeil returns with three straight wins. Elmer Lach pots the Cup clincher at 1:22 of overtime in Game 5. No Hockey Hall of Famer has played fewer regular-season games to win the Cup than Plante.

Maurice Richard and Butch Bouchard hoist Stanley Cup–winning scorer Elmer Lach.

▸ 1953–54 "If I had shaken hands, I wouldn't have meant it. I refuse to be a hypocrite."

—Incensed coach Dick Irvin, on leading his Canadiens off the ice before the ceremonial handshakes, following Detroit's Game 7 victory in the 1954 Stanley Cup Final

Gerry McNeil with captain Butch Bouchard, 1952.

Al Rollins, 1954–55.

▴ 1953–54 Al Rollins wins the Hart Trophy. Rollins remains the only NHL goalie on a last-place team to receive MVP honors. He records 47 losses of 66 matches played to keep the Black Hawks close in 15 one-goal games.

Jean Béliveau, with Frank Selke Sr. (left) and Dick Irvin, Sr. (right), 1953.

◂ 1953–54 Jean Béliveau signs with the Montreal Canadiens. Before salary disclosure, it was unheard of to know any player's wage, except for Béliveau's, whose unprecedented contract with Montreal was so rich, it couldn't be kept from the media. Inking a five-year guaranteed deal worth a then-astronomical $105,000 before bonuses, Béliveau, a 22-year-old rookie of only five NHL games, immediately became the league's highest-paid performer, earning more than bankable stars Gordie Howe and Maurice Richard.

▴ 1953–54 Detroit defeats Montreal in Stanley Cup overtime. The mutual hatred between the Red Wings and the Canadiens of the 1950s becomes very real during 1954's Cup Final when the two clubs, tied 1-1, head into Game 7 overtime. At 4:29, Tony Leswick's shot glances off the glove of Montreal defenseman Doug Harvey and over Gerry McNeil's right arm into the Canadiens net. It is a bitter pill. After rallying back from a 3-1 deficit in games to knot the series, Montreal loses the championship on a greasy goal to its sworn enemy. An incensed Canadiens coach Dick Irvin leads his team off the ice before the routine handshakes. "If I had shaken hands," said Irvin, "I wouldn't have meant it. I refuse to be a hypocrite."

McNeil knew the weight of playoff overtime better than most. In only six years of postseason play, he soldiered through three overtime Stanley Cup-deciding games. Backstopping Montreal, McNeil lost the 1951 Cup in Game 5 overtime, won the 1953 Cup in Game 5 overtime and, perhaps most harsh, reached Game 7 overtime and lost Stanley on that fluke goal.

▸ 1953 The Bee Hive Golden Corn Syrup player portraits. Available with proof of purchase, Bee Hive's famous 4¼-inch by 6¾-inch (10.8 cm × 17.2 cm) portraits of an estimated 1,025 different hockey players not only entertained young Canadians from 1934 to 1968 but inspired players like Gordie Howe and Bobby Hull to play the game. Production of the corn syrup quadrupled, and at its peak a reported 2,500 photographs were mailed daily to hockey fans from the St. Lawrence Starch Company's offices in Port Credit, Ontario. The hockey picture promotion is considered among the most successful marketing giveaways in Canadian history.

Fred Sasakamoose.

▲ 1953–54 Fred Sasakamoose, a Cree athlete from Saskatchewan's Sandy Lake Reserve, becomes the NHL's first "treaty" Indigenous player. His major-league career is brief, only 11 games with Chicago, registering no points and six penalty minutes. Sasakamoose later plays with the OSAHL Kamloops Chiefs, where he is named Chief Thunderstick by the Shuswap First Nation of British Columbia. He adopts the honorary title as the elected chief of the Sandy Lake Indian Band (Ahtahkakoop Cree Nation).

Richard Apologizes to Campbell; Posts $1,000 "Good Faith" Cheque

▲ 1954 "Mr. [Frank] Selke has brought this to my attention, and as the game of hockey has been very good to me, I humbly and most sincerely apologize to President Campbell and the Governors of the League."

—Maurice Richard apologizes for writing a newspaper column criticizing NHL boss Clarence Campbell

◂ 1954 Marguerite Norris, 25-year-old daughter of deceased Detroit owner James Norris and co-owner of the Red Wings, breaks the glass ceiling, as the NHL's first female executive and the first woman to have her name officially engraved on the Stanley Cup.

Detroit president Marguerite Norris (far right).

The 1954 World Champion Soviet Union team.

◂ 1954 **The World Championship.** Canada's conceit and sense of invincibility in hockey is shattered when the East York Lundhursts are routed 7-2 in the gold medal match against the Soviet Union. Built only eight years earlier in 1946 by Anatoli Tarasov, the Soviet hockey program, working with a few technical handbooks and the nation's best bandy players, devises a weave-and-pass game based on speed, skating, stick work and, perhaps most important, rock-hard athleticism. Canada is humiliated, but now has a true international rival.

Arrest 41 After Forum Hockey Riot
Crowd Loots Or Damages 50 Stores

TOP AND ABOVE Outside the Montreal Forum, March 17, 1955.

MAYHEM IN MONTREAL

The Richard Riot

For much of his stellar career, it seemed like it was Maurice Richard versus the world. As hockey's fiercest lightning rod, the acrimony toward him had been building for years. It wasn't just from NHL chief Clarence Campbell but from jealous managers of opposing teams and shadows like Ted Lindsay and Bill Ezinicki, game referees and linesmen, many in the media outside Quebec and, of course, entire fan bases of the other five NHL squads.

Finally, following a March 1955 fight against Boston's Hal Laycoe and the subsequent hostilities in which Richard punched linesman Cliff Thompson, Campbell suspends Richard for the final three games of the season and the entire playoffs. At the next match a tear-gas bomb explodes at the Montreal Forum. The game is forfeited to Detroit. A riot breaks out along 15 city blocks of Sainte-Catherine Street. Stores are looted, police cars damaged and dozens arrested. Only radio and television appeals by Richard quiet Montreal's impassioned fan base.

The suspension thwarts Richard's best career chance at the Art Ross Trophy, losing the 1954–55 scoring crown to teammate Bernie Geoffrion by one point. Geoffrion is vilified by Montreal's faithful. His kids are bullied at school. He receives telephone threats and hires a bodyguard. In the playoffs, without the suspended Richard, the Canadiens lose to the despised Red Wings in Game 7 of the Stanley Cup Final.

1954–55 The number of players in uniform is set at 18 (then reduced to 16), plus goaltenders. Teams agree to wear colored uniforms at home and white uniforms on the road.

The Boston Garden Zamboni, 1957.

▲ 1954 **The Zamboni.** Before rink resurfacers were invented, NHL ice sheets were cleaned and flooded between periods by maintenance men using shovels and barrels of water. The arrival of Frank Zamboni's motorized ice-cleaner changed everything during the mid-1950s. Its first appearance came on January 1, resurfacing Boston Garden prior to a Boston–New York game. The demonstration went well, and that fall the Bruins took delivery of Zamboni's Model E21. It quickly became standard equipment at NHL rinks.

Vsevolod Bobrov, IIHF VP Bunny Ahearne and George McAvoy.

▲ 1955 After being humbled by the Soviet Union in 1954, Canada returns to the world stage to reclaim its top ranking at the World Championship. The gold medal is determined in the final game. The Penticton Vees, led by the Warwick brothers, Grant, Bill and Dick, exact revenge, whipping the Soviets in a 5–0 blowout.

▲ 1955–56 **The Toe Blake coaching era begins.** Tough but honest, Blake fully grasped the task of running a Montreal Canadiens squad that included Maurice Richard, Jean Béliveau and Jacques Plante. "I was nervous," he admitted. "I felt I had to produce with a club like that. So much potential." Most importantly, Blake had to control Richard. No one wanted another riot. "Sometimes," recalled Blake, "I'd have to cool the Rocket on the bench. He'd glare at me, but he took it from me, too."

Despite his star-loaded bench — one good enough that even his checking line could fill the top lines on lesser teams — Blake was no "caretaker coach." He hated nothing more than losing, once getting so incensed after controversial officiating in 1961, he leaped onto the ice and threw a punch at referee Dalton McArthur, earning a record-high $2,000 fine. Under Blake, Montreal won eight Stanley Cups in 13 seasons.

The Soviet Union at the 1956 Olympics.

Soviet Superpower

The results were devastating for Canada. The Soviets had signaled a new era in international competition after winning their first Olympic gold medal at the 1956 Cortina d'Ampezzo Winter Games. The crushing 2-0 defeat of the Kitchener-Waterloo Dutchmen confirmed that the Soviets' 1954 World Championship victory against Canada two years earlier was no fluke.

After 36 years of Olympic dominance, Canada was in its final days of world supremacy. The USSR's hockey program created a new superpower to usher in the great Canada–Soviet Union rivalry.

The final games on February 4 would determine the gold medal. Canada played the Soviets outdoors before a capacity crowd of 12,700 at the Olimpico del Ghiaccio arena. Based on rankings, Canada would likely win silver or possibly gold if they beat the Soviets. A loss would mean the bronze medal. After a scoreless first period, the Soviets took a 1–0 lead on a screened shot by Yuri Krylov at 6:20 of the second frame. They scored again on a Valentin Kuzin goal 37 seconds into in the third. Canada fired 23 shots at Soviet goalie Nikolai Puchkov. Five struck iron.

The Soviets won gold in the 2–0 victory, leaving Canada with an embarrassing bronze after the Americans took the silver by crushing the Czechs 9–4 that same day. The Canadians' third-place finish was a first at the Worlds and the Olympics, trailing behind the two teams that had beat them, the Soviets and the Americans in an earlier 4–1 defeat.

Following the 1956 Olympics, the Soviets would soon monopolize international play. During their reign they were nearly invincible, capturing six Olympic and 18 World Championship gold medals until their demise with the political breakup of the USSR and ensuing fall of communism in 1991.

▲▼ 1956 *Sports Illustrated* waits two years from its magazine launch in 1954 to feature a hockey player on its January 23 cover. Gordie Howe and Maurice Richard seem like solid picks. *SI*, however, likes 24-year-old Jean Béliveau, who's exceeding all expectations, maturing into a scoring champion and racking up penalty totals while fighting for respect. His elegance and intuitive puck sense belie a sporting bravery seldom seen before. Béliveau wins the Art Ross Trophy as top scorer with 47 goals and 88 points, amassing a third-highest total of 143 penalty minutes. Béliveau adds the Hart Trophy, earning him the most box time ever by an MVP.

Béliveau's highlight-reel performance is his hat trick on November 5, 1955—the league's fastest on one power play, as Boston's 2-0 lead evaporates in 44 seconds when Béliveau erupts for three goals. Not by coincidence, the next season, 1956-57, the NHL changes its penalty rules. No longer will penalized teams serve the full duration of their minor infractions when scored upon. The rule stands today.

Most Penalty Minutes by an NHL MVP, One Season*

Player	Year	Team	GP	PIM
Jean Béliveau	1956	Montreal	70	143
Bobby Clarke	1976	Philadelphia	76	136
Bobby Orr	1970	Boston	76	125
Bobby Clarke	1975	Philadelphia	80	125
Nels Stewart	1926	Montreal Maroons	36	119

*Current to 2024-25

Leapin' Lou Fontinato, 1960.

▲ 1955-56 Lou Fontinato: the first NHLer penalized 200 minutes in one season. During his sophomore campaign to ascend the ranks as the league's chief pugilist, Leapin' Lou amasses an NHL-record 202 minutes with the New York Rangers, one of three times he led in box time during a nine-year career.

RULE CHANGE

1956-57 Players serving minor penalties are allowed to return to the ice when a goal is scored by the opposing team.

Late 1950s

The curved blade. While the evidence is mostly anecdotal, it's believed that Andy Bathgate was the first to use a bent stick blade on a consistent basis. He experimented with curving his blades before turning pro and then refined the technique in the big leagues. "I would heat up the blade with hot water and then I could bend them. I would put them in the toilet-stall door and leave them overnight. The next day they would have a hook in them," said Bathgate. The curved stick was popularized by Bobby Hull and Stan Mikita during the mid-1960s.

Stan Mikita planes his curved blade.

Ted Lindsay

THE NHLPA

The NHL's first players' association was intended to give members some power over their pension fund, its investments and television revenues. An inertia had long settled in over hockey. Player salaries were stagnant and benefits practically nonexistent. There was no collective bargaining, nor anything like profit-sharing, free agency or salary disclosure. Hockey had no player agents. League owners kept player contracts and pension ledgers locked away. They hid revenues and underrated assets. The game, they said, was monetarily fragile. League expansion was a dirty word. Stay small, stay profitable was the order of the day.

Ted Lindsay and others like Doug Harvey knew full-well the players' value—something Lindsay had learned growing up the son of pioneer goalie Bert Lindsay. Knowing management's reaction to a players' association, all 120 NHLers were signed up in secrecy. League owners were stunned at February 1957's announcement. Toronto's Conn Smythe was irate, seething at his players' "betrayal."

As expected, the league dialed up the drama into a full-blown crisis, making it their mission to bust the fledgling PA. Key figures were harassed and traded. On the ice players found themselves on mismatched lines and penalized with benchings. Lindsay was dealt to Chicago that summer, Detroit GM Jack Adams calling him "over the hill" even though the 33-year-old had just played his best offensive season, with 85 points in 70 games. Others were demoted to the minors. In the case of Marty Pavelich, he quit hockey altogether.

The players were pitted against one another, publicly admonished as troublemakers and accused of putting themselves above the game—a tactic meant to exploit their concerns for being branded a labor union, knowing their pride as professionals and their working-class backgrounds.

Lindsay's ill-fated association finally capitulated a year later, crushed by several factors including league pressure and intransigence and membership fatigue. The players did receive minor concessions from owners, which was a critical step to a sanctioned NHLPA in 1967, this time headed by lawyer Alan Eagleson.

Doug Harvey, Claude Provost, Gordie Howe and Ted Lindsay.

Maurice Richard against Harry Lumley, 1954–55.

▲ 1957–58 Maurice Richard scores number 500. The big moment comes on October 19 against Chicago's Glenn Hall after a Jean Béliveau pass to Richard, who fires it home to become the NHL's first 500-goal scorer. Reports note a "thunderous standing ovation" persisted for 37 seconds and "a buzz circulated among the crowd" for another minute afterward.

Richard developed a particular liking for the Black Hawks, scoring milestone goals number 100, 200 and 400. Chicago also succumbed to Richard's 325th, the historic marker that topped NHL career goal-leader Nels Stewart.

◂ 1957–58 **Willie O'Ree becomes the first Black player in NHL history, a decade after Jackie Robinson's Major League Baseball start. The 22-year-old winger from Fredericton, New Brunswick, debuts in the Boston–Montreal away-and-home contests on January 18 and 19, before returning to the minors. In a career marked by countless racial slurs, O'Ree plays 43 games for the Bruins in 1960–61, scoring four goals and 14 points. The first goal by a Black NHLer comes on January 1, 1961.**

▲ 1957–58 **Frank Mahovlich: Rookie of the Year.** Based on their exceptional major junior play, both Mahovlich (St. Michael's in Toronto) and Bobby Hull (the OHA St. Catharines Teepees) are bound to contend for the NHL's Calder Trophy. Hull outpoints Mahovlich but Mahovlich hits the 20-goal plateau, which likely sways Calder voters. Mahovlich receives 82 first-place votes and 38 second-place votes, while Hull has 39 and 77.

Butterfly-style originator Glenn Hall against Toronto, 1961–62.

▲ 1957–58 **The Glenn Hall trade.** Despite the accolades in his first two complete seasons with Detroit, including top rookie honors, and First and Second All-Star Team berths, Hall, the original butterfly-style goalie, is dealt to Chicago. He becomes their future in the crease, setting a games-streak record unbroken today, earning 11 All-Star Team appearances and backstopping the Black Hawks to the 1961 Stanley Cup against, who else, his original trade team, the Red Wings. Sweet payback. It's Chicago's first Cup title since 1938.

▲ 1957–58 **The Johnny Bucyk trade.** In a straight-up deal, Boston acquires Johnny Bucyk and cash from Detroit in exchange for goalie great Terry Sawchuk. It's Sawchuk's second tour with the Red Wings. Bucyk becomes a 21-year career Bruin and a main star in the Bobby Orr–Phil Esposito era. In 1970–71, Bucyk, in his 14th Bruin season, scores 51 goals at age 35. For Boston, it's the trade that keeps on giving.

Connie Broden.

The 1958 World Champion Whitby Dunlops.

▲ 1957–58 Connie Broden becomes the first and only Stanley Cup and world champion in one season. After retiring from the Montreal Canadiens' farm team, Broden, with permission from the Canadiens, jumps to the Whitby Dunlops, who win gold at the World Championship in Oslo, Norway. Broden plays a key role for Canada, scoring 19 points. Six weeks later, Broden is a spare for Montreal, seeing action in only one game during its six-game sprint against Boston in the Cup Final. No one except Broden has managed double championships, an impossibility today, given that the only NHLers participating at the Worlds come from teams eliminated from Cup contention.

1958–59

The beating on Leapin' Lou.

Hockey's premier tough guy, Lou Fontinato, mistakenly challenges Gordie Howe to fight on February 1. After Fontinato lands a few, Howe repeatedly drives his fist into the Rangers defenseman's face, rearranging his nose and cheekbone. Referee Frank Udvari said the pounding noise was "the sound of somebody chopping wood." Fontinato never plays the same again.

Referee Red Storey called the shots in more than 2,000 NHL games, 1950s.

◂ 1958–59 **"But [Red] Storey is one of my senior officials and he just froze."**

—NHL chief Clarence Campbell, on Red Storey, who "missed" calling two tripping penalties by Montreal players on Chicago's Eddie Litzenberger and Bobby Hull late in a 4–4 game during Game 6 of 1959's Stanley Cup semifinal at Chicago Stadium. Montreal scores the winning goal, which ends the series in six games and the Black Hawks' season. Black Hawk fans erupt, as three spectators attack Storey on the ice. Days later, Storey resigns over Campbell's comments.

Jacques Plante against Billy Harris, 1959–60.

◂ 1958–59 **"The other teams could have done the same thing as Jacques, but I guess nobody is as quick as Plante. He can get away with things that other goalies can't."**

—Coach Toe Blake, on Jacques Plante's nomadic wanderings to stop pucks outside the crease, then freezing them to force a stoppage in play. His actions enacted the 1959 rule whereby goalies can only fall on or cover the puck inside the crease.

Johnny Bower against the New York Rangers.

▴ 1958–59 Hockey's great warhorse Johnny Bower becomes a Maple Leaf. Bower labors 12 years in the minors and plays with New York before Toronto claims him in the NHL's inter-league draft. By then, Bower is already 33 years old. Even after all that pain and punishment in the maskless era, Bower backstops Toronto another 12 seasons, winning four Stanley Cups. Nicknamed the China Wall, he truly was that ageless wonder. He later becomes the league's oldest netminder in the playoffs at 44 years old.

▸ 1958–59 **The shot heard around the hockey world.** On November 1, Jacques Plante's nose is shredded by an Andy Bathgate backhand at Madison Square Garden. After stitch work for the umpteenth time in his career, Plante now seizes on the opportunity to wear his mask. With only house goalies available, a reluctant coach Toe Blake agrees.

Plante steps onto Garden ice armed with his practice mask—a primitive fiberglass protector with holes for the eyes and mouth. The Canadiens beat New York that night and roll 10-0-1 through November. Still, any falter by Plante, and Blake blames the mask.

He eventually comes around, backpedaling after the Canadiens' fifth-consecutive Stanley Cup that season, calling Plante magnificent. "I don't care what kind of mask he wears in the future," utters Blake.

Interestingly, who should be honored together at the Hockey Hall of Fame induction ceremonies 20 years later in 1978 but Plante and his unintended antagonist, Rangers forward Andy Bathgate.

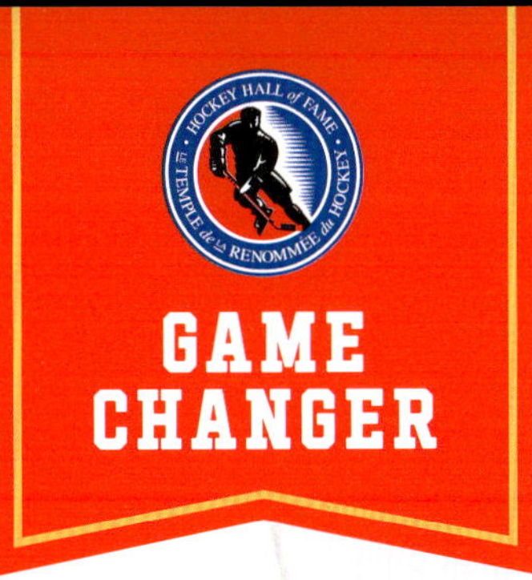

GAME CHANGER

Jacques Plante

His sheer talent and net brilliance aside, no player revolutionized more technical aspects of his position than Jacques Plante. His innovations advanced the game immeasurably in an era lacking safe equipment and any proper training. While the same is said of contemporary Glenn Hall's break with the classic "stand-up" pose to create the butterfly style of modern netminding, Plante's influence set numerous standards in today's play. As others observed, he didn't leave the game the way he found it.

Because of Plante, all goalies wear masks, leave the crease to play the puck and communicate with skaters by barking out orders and by raising their arms on icing calls. Puckstoppers now have their own goalie coaches, physiotherapists and training manuals thanks to Plante, who was hockey's first netminding coach and its first author on goalie instruction. Plante, an analytic puck-control freak, had the temerity to command a game as a goalie. "He studied goaltending with the methodical approach of a scientist," wrote author Todd Denault.

A man of invention and wild eccentricities, his mask was perhaps his greatest breakthrough. In his time, blocking shots barefaced came with the territory. The mask challenged authority and jeopardized job security. Few favored his decision, including his own fraternity and the press. "They figured a goalie had to be scared to play well," Plante once said. "When shots are coming at you 100 miles per hour, you're scared whether you have a mask or not."

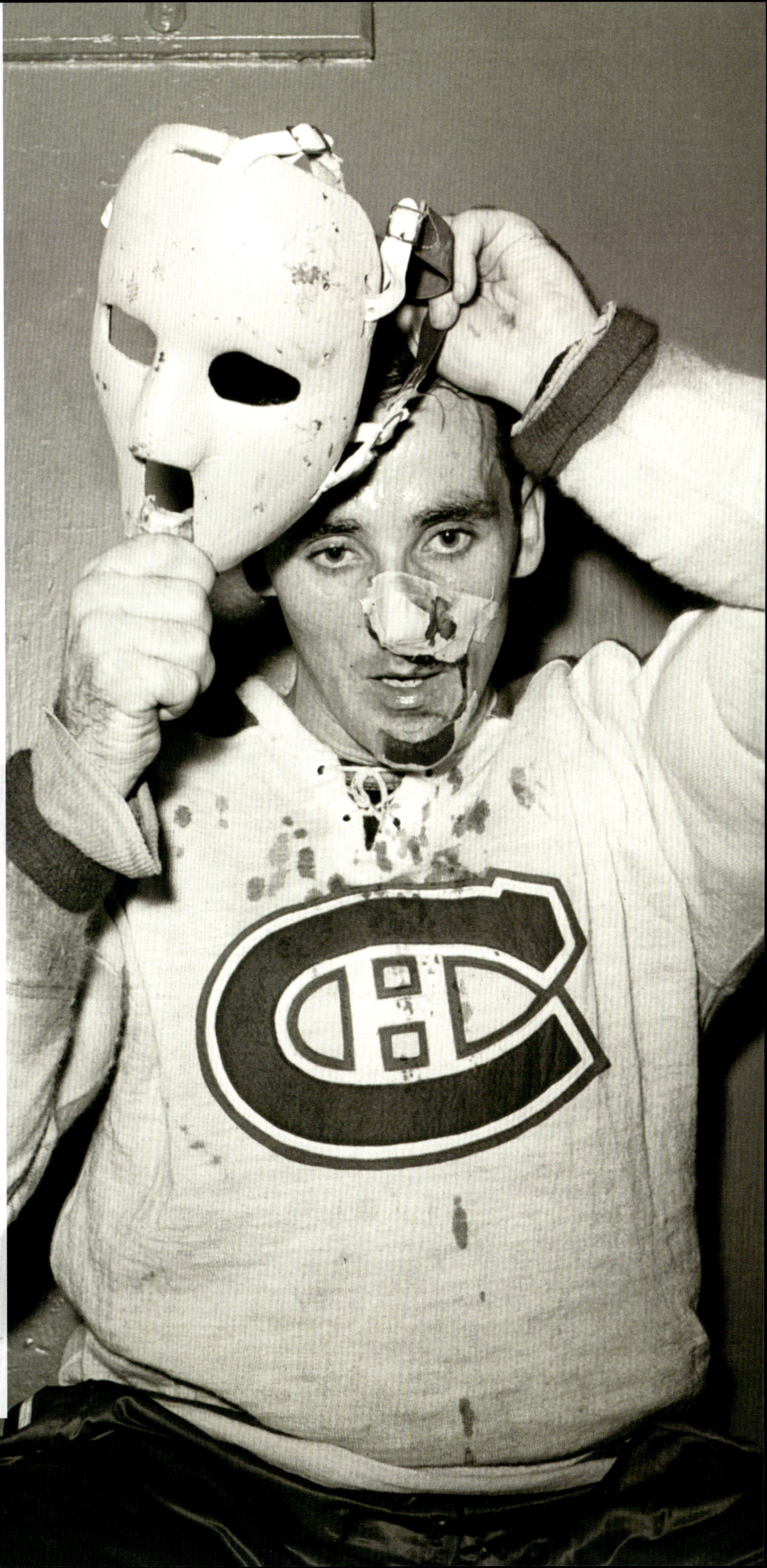

The five-year dynasty Montreal Canadiens, 1960.

▲ 1959–60 Montreal's dominance in league play is undisputed, sweeping both Chicago and Toronto in its record-setting fifth-successive Stanley Cup. A masked Jacques Plante limits the two clubs to 11 goals in eight games. The powerhouse that GM Frank Selke assembled and coach Toe Blake inherited—fielding a core of Maurice Richard, Doug Harvey, Jean Béliveau, Dickie Moore, Bernie Geoffrion and Plante—played 49 games of a maximum 70 during five Cup-winning playoff seasons from 1956 to 1960. Playing 10 series (two best-of-seven rounds each year), the Canadiens won three rounds in four straight and went to five games twice. Montreal never trailed in a playoff round and never played a Game 7. The 1959-60 Canadiens were the last team to go unbeaten in one playoff year. "It's the best of all the great Canadiens' teams," assessed Selke.

RULE CHANGE

1959–60 Players are not permitted to leave their bench to enter into any altercation.

Little-known Bronco Horvath comes within one point of equaling Bobby Hull in the NHL scoring race.

▲ 1959–60 Bobby Hull vs. Bronco Horvath. All season Hull and Horvath duel for the NHL scoring lead—until the season's last game in a head-to-head matchup between Chicago and Boston. Hull scores two points to overtake Horvath, who goes scoreless in the match. The 21-year-old Hull wins the Art Ross Trophy by one assist. Hull had 39-42-81 in 70 games, Horvath 39-41-80 in 68 games.

Andy Tabbed Cry-Baby By NHL Players, Brass

▲ 1959 Andy Bathgate writes *Atrocities on Ice*. Bathgate's first-person tell-all in *True* magazine exposes hockey's stickwork nastiness, creating a publicity firestorm for the NHL. The Rangers' star names six "spearing specialists," a controversial first for the league's closely guarded clubhouse. "I'm warning the National Hockey League," Bathgate wrote, "unchecked brutality is going to kill somebody." The backlash is near universal. Players, coaches, even officials chime in. Toronto's Punch Imlach calls Bathgate "the league's biggest cry-baby." NHL boss Clarence Campbell fines Bathgate $500—the amount he reportedly receives for writing the article.

Red Kelly chats with George Armstrong, alongside Frank Mahovlich.

▲ 1959–60 **The Red Kelly trade.** After some negative press, spiteful Detroit boss Jack Adams trades Kelly, his 12-year playmaking defenseman, to last-place New York. Kelly refuses and five days later, on February 10, in hockey's most lopsided trade Toronto acquires Kelly for low-impact rearguard Marc Reaume. Under Punch Imlach, Kelly moves from defense to forward, centering wingers Frank Mahovlich and Bob Nevin on Toronto's top scoring line. In the next seven seasons Kelly helps guide the Maple Leafs to four Stanley Cups. He's the most successful player to switch positions mid-career.

▲ 1960 **Team USA wins Olympic gold.** No one has the Americans in 1960. Affectionately called Riley's Irregulars after coach Jack Riley of West Point Military Academy, his bench is just a "pick-up team" of players of uncertain talent and varied vocations. Still, in the medal round, Riley's never-say-die squad overcomes the world's best four teams (and Germany) in seven days of competition, including edging Canada and the Soviet Union in 2–1 and 3–2 nailbiters. In the final game against Czechoslovakia, USA comes from behind in a 9–4 character win, showing absolute determination with five unanswered goals in the third period.

▲ 1960–61
Boston forward Jerry Toppazzini becomes the last skater to tend goal in an NHL game, replacing an injured Don Simmons with just 30 seconds remaining and Chicago up 5–2 on October 16. Toppazzini subs without goalie pads.

▸ 1960
Gordie Howe becomes the first 1,000-point NHLer on a Howie Glover goal in a 2–0 win against Toronto on November 27. It was Howe's 938th game.

Gordie Howe against Tim Horton and Terry Sawchuk.

SMOKIES CHAMPS

The Trail Smoke Eaters Jackie McLeod and Dave Rusnell against the Soviets, 1961.

◂ **1961** The Trail Smoke Eaters are the winningest world amateur champions in Canadian hockey history. In 1939 they defeat USA 4–0, outscoring opponents 42 goals to one, in eight-straight matches. In this second championship, the Smokies are locked in a three-way gold-medal race against the Soviet Union and Czechoslovakia. The Czechs look the favorites. They beat the Soviets 6–4 and tie Trail 1–1. Canada now must defeat the Soviets in the finale. With two minutes left Norm Lenardon strips defenseman Nikolai Sologubov of the puck. Off-balance, he fires high into the net, locking up the 5–1 win and the championship, which is based on goal differential. Lenardon is mobbed and carried from the ice by jubilant teammates at game's end. Canada doesn't win at the Worlds for another 33 years, until 1994.

Seth Martin, who backstops Canada in multiple events during the 1960s, becomes the most popular Canadian player in Europe. He serves as a role model to the Soviets' Vladislav Tretiak and Czech legend Jiri Holecek, who themselves would influence next-generation netminders like Vladimir Dzurilla, Pelle Lindbergh and Dominik Hasek.

Bill Hay, Eric Nesterenko and Bobby Hull.

▴ **1960–61** **Chicago halts Montreal's hockey dynasty.** Playing nothing like the thoroughbreds that had humbled opponents through five-straight Stanley Cups from 1956 to 1960, the Canadiens fall to Chicago, ending their reign in a six-game Cup semifinal. The hard-fought series turns on a Murray Balfour goal scored in triple overtime in Game 3. Montreal wins the next match 5–2, but Glenn Hall buries the Canadiens with double 3–0 shutouts. In the Cup Final, the Black Hawks down Detroit in six, as Bobby Hull and Stan Mikita make their inaugural Cup appearances. As one reporter said of Chicago's rise, the Hawks went "from drinking beer in the cellar to drinking champagne in the penthouse."

Bobby Baun, Allan Stanley and Carl Brewer of the champion Toronto Maple Leafs.

▴ **1961–62** Coach Punch Imlach's work ethic and keep-it-simple game play propels Toronto from last place in 1958 to Stanley Cup champion, as the Maple Leafs beat New York and Chicago, each in six games. Toronto hadn't won the Cup since 1951, the year Cup-winning scorer Bill Barilko disappeared and died in a plane crash. His body was only found in June 1962, furthering the myth that the Leafs couldn't win another Cup until he was laid to rest.

Don Simmons becomes the second goalie after Jacques Plante to wear a mask regularly in NHL play, subbing for Toronto's Johnny Bower in the Cup Final, when Bower pulls a leg muscle on a Bobby Hull shot in Game 4. Simmons backstops Toronto the rest of the series to win the Cup.

▲ 1961 **The Doug Harvey trade.** After six Stanley Cups, multiple individual awards and All-Star Team berths on Montreal's blueline, GM Frank Selke trades Harvey for New York's resident brute, Lou Fontinato. On the Rangers, Harvey serves as playing-coach. How good is he at 37 years old? Without batting an eye he claims his seventh Norris Trophy as top defender in eight seasons and leads New York to its first playoff spot in four years. Harvey remains the oldest Norris Trophy winner and the only NHLer to win a player trophy in the same season he coached.

Billy McGimsie.

▲ 1962, 1963 and 1965 The Hockey Hall of Fame makes up for lost time by venerating several overlooked trailblazers. Some old-timers, like six-time Stanley Cup champion Jack Marshall, are enshrined posthumously. Others, like Billy McGimsie, who won the Cup with the 1907 Kenora Thistles, waited 55 years for Hall acknowledgment. McGimsie was 82 years old when his induction was announced in 1962.

Jack Adams (center) with Harry Lumley and Mud Bruneteau, 1945.

THE NATURAL

Jack Adams

Jack Adams is the most accomplished individual etched on the Stanley Cup. He won as a player, coach and general manager, and, quite remarkably, Adams did it in each of the first five decades of NHL play. The Cup came twice as a player, with Toronto in 1918 and the Ottawa Senators in 1927. During one NHL Final, the Canadiens "cut Jack Adam's head to ribbons," reported the *Toronto Mail*. Despite the battering, he refused to quit, "dashing up and down the boards with blood streaming from cuts over his eyes and ears." Author Trent Frayne noted that during the game "he was water-sloshed and plaster-stuck from his hairline to his Adam's apple."

Little changed managing the Red Wings, the ever-combative Adams orchestrating seven championships between 1936 and 1962.

His success and endurance made him the paragon of sporting achievement. In real life he was a tough, mostly humorless chief—despite his nickname Jolly Jawn. A voluble autocrat schooled by a crude and cruel pro career, as Frayne noted, Adams operated no differently behind Detroit's bench nor as its front-office man, being not just of another time but of another hockey culture. In one famous instance, he was indefinitely suspended by the league after inciting his players and Detroit Olympia spectators to riot and physically attack game officials following a pivotal loss to Toronto during the 1942 Cup Final.

After that dustup, the Red Wings, ahead 3-1 in the series, lost confidence and luck and never got their spine back. One Toronto scribe called Adams unbridled and a scallywag who "falls victim to spasmodic attacks of ungovernable fury." In defeat, that just compounded the damage to the team.

Today, we might say Adams couldn't stay on message. His messages vacillated with his tantrums. However, Detroit's farm system bested any American-based team at the time and, despite a few hair-brained deals, Adams was the shrewdest of traders, a quality that ensured the Red Wings a long run of triumphs.

John Ferguson, in typical fashion, making the play in 1967 and leaving his man beaten. Here, Terry Sawchuk lies in Fergy's wake.

▲ 1963–64 John Ferguson debuts as peacemaker-enforcer with Montreal to provide protection for its slick forwards. Regarded as hockey's first policeman, Ferguson establishes his credentials 12 seconds into his first match, scrapping with Bruin tough guy Ted Green on Boston home ice on October 8. Ferguson also figures in three goals, scoring twice and assisting on a Bernie Geoffrion marker.

BRUINS TIE HAWKS; DEJORDY IN NETS

► 1962–63 Glenn Hall's ironman streak is halted at 502 games. Hall had bad nerves, tossed his cookies before every game and once said, "Playing goal is a winter of torture for me." Ironically, he becomes the NHL's game-endurance record-maker to somehow string together 502 complete consecutive games and 49 more in the playoffs. All without the safety of a mask. His streak ends at 10:21 of the first period against Boston on November 7. Hall, 31, suffering from an aggravated pinched nerve in his back, is relieved by AHL Buffalo Bisons goalie Denis DeJordy. It's the first game Hall doesn't finish in seven seasons.

Glenn Hall, OHA-Junior Windsor Spitfires, 1949–50.

◄ 1962 Father David Bauer, a Catholic who chose the priesthood over a professional hockey career, lobbies the Canadian Amateur Hockey Association to create a national team program of top amateurs that would compete internationally, and would replace the then-current practice of using club representation, which was typically Canada's best senior team—the Allan Cup winners. Upon the CAHA's approval, Father Bauer's national team is established. But facing increasingly stronger competitors from Europe, Canada fails to win gold, taking home bronze medals at the 1966 and 1967 Worlds and an Olympic bronze at Grenoble in 1968. Within a decade, his national program of amateur-only teams is discontinued at international events.

1963 The first NHL universal amateur draft. **On June 5, clubs select 21 players not currently playing with league-sponsored amateur clubs. Montreal and Detroit draft Garry Monahan and Peter Mahovlich, first and second overall. Both are 16 years old.**

The 1964 Stanley Cup champions (left to right) Billy Harris, Frank Mahovlich, Jim Pappin, George Armstrong, Bob Pulford, Bobby Baun and Red Kelly.

▲ 1963–64 The overtime heroics of Toronto's Bobby Baun. Tied 3–3 in Game 6 and facing elimination against Detroit in the 1964 Stanley Cup Final, the worst is expected when Baun is stretchered off after blocking a Gordie Howe slapper. At 1:43 of overtime, Baun, with his lower leg taped tightly and shot full of novocaine, lobs a shot that bounces past a confused Terry Sawchuk. Baun's sudden-death goal propels Toronto to Game 7 and a 4–0 Cup victory against Detroit. The rugged defenseman never misses a shift. Baun attends the Leafs' victory party, before allowing doctors to X-ray him and put his leg in a cast. The X-rays reveal a fracture of a small bone in his leg.

Howe Now Greatest Scorer of 'Em All

Gordie Howe scores his record-setting 545th career goal.

▲ 1963–64 Detroit's double record-setter game. On November 10, Gordie Howe tops Maurice Richard's 544-career-goal record with his 545th goal, while Terry Sawchuk equals George Hainsworth's 94 shutouts record in a 3–0 win — both against Richard and Hainsworth's former team, the Montreal Canadiens. Howe's record-breaker comes short-handed on a wrist shot from inside the face-off circle versus Charlie Hodge. The ovation by "the sardine-packed sellout of 15,027 fans" at Detroit's Olympia lasts seven minutes. Sawchuck breaks Hainsworth's shutout mark on January 18 with his 95th career zero, making 36 saves in a 2–0 win versus, again, Montreal.

The "shared" penalty box.

RULE CHANGE

▲ 1963–64 The separate penalty box. An October 30 on-ice fight between Montreal's Terry Harper and Toronto's Bob Pulford that resumed in the penalty box and led to a lengthy delay in play is credited with initiating the installation of separate boxes and doors in both the Forum and the Gardens. Each player blamed the other, with Pulford contending that Harper "said something that would make any man fight."

1963 The NHL's first player agent. Toronto's Carl Brewer hires lawyer Alan Eagleson to help negotiate his new Maple Leafs contract.

◄ 1963 The Jacques Plante–Gump Worsley trade. In a four-for-three swap dealing away two of hockey's most controversial netminders, Montreal acquires the "pudgy, acrobatic" Worsley, a highly-underrated and opinionated goalie who, except for a Calder Trophy in 1953, comes to the Canadiens with no major awards (on the defense-deprived Rangers, where he handled almost twice as many shots as any other NHL goalie). In Plante, New York acquires Montreal's 10-year starter, a six-time Vezina Trophy winner, six-time Stanley Cup champion and the 1962 MVP honoree of the Hart Trophy. During Plante's time the Canadiens allow the fewest goals scored against. But according to GM Frank Selke, Plante "had become complacent ... cocksure." Both goalies were 34 years old. Plante never won another Cup. Worsley became the Canadiens' starter, a Cup winner in 1965, 1966, 1968 and 1969.

"Bobby could shoot the puck through a car wash and not get it wet ... Dennis would do the same, if only he could hit the car wash."

—Anonymous, on the difference between the Hull brothers, with Dennis shooting equally hard but with less accuracy than Bobby

Terry Sawchuk and Johnny Bower.

▲ 1964-65 The Vezina Trophy becomes a joint award when Terry Sawchuk insists that Toronto teammate Johnny Bower share the trophy. While Bower had a league-best goals-against average (2.38), Sawchuk officially won the Vezina with a 2.56 average, but only because he had played 36 games compared to Bower's 34. At the time the Vezina went to the goalie who had played the most games on the team that gave up the fewest goals.

▸ 1964-65 **The first European-trained NHLer.** Among the best all-time Swedes, Ulf Sterner plays his first big-league game, sans helmet and mouthguard, with New York against Boston on January 27. For all of his international success, including scoring twice in Sweden's historic 5-3 gold medal win against Canada in 1962, Sterner, 23, goes pointless and only stays four games, unable to adjust to the physical demands of pro competition. He returns home to play another decade in world tournaments.

Ulf Sterner.

George Armstrong, Tim Horton and Frank Mahovlich.

▲ 1964 A small donut and coffee shop opens on Ottawa Street in Hamilton, Ontario, called Tim Horton Donuts. The store's first franchisee is Ron Joyce, who becomes the hockey legend's full partner in 1967. Today, that single location has grown into a quick-service restaurant chain of about 5,700 establishments worldwide.

Bobby Hull hands the Art Ross Trophy to Stan Mikita, 1964.

◂ 1964-65 Stan Mikita records the two highest penalty totals ever by an NHL scoring leader, 146 minutes and 154 minutes in 1963-64 and 1964-65. By 1966-67 and 1967-68 Mikita was winning his Art Ross Trophies with 12 and 14 minutes in box time.

1964-65 Ever the competitor, Ted Lindsay, 39 years old, ends a four-year retirement and scores a decent 14 goals and 28 points in his comeback season. But it's his 173 penalty minutes, only four shy of Carl Brewer's league-high total, that spotlight "Terrible" Ted's reputation as one of hockey's all-time punishing players. No NHL scoring champion (1949-50) recorded more box time than Lindsay's 1,808 career minutes.

Jean Béliveau.

Pierre Pilote against Henri Richard.

▲ **1964–65** **The first Stanley Cup MVP.** The Conn Smythe Trophy was originally presented in 1965 to Jean Béliveau, who scored eight goals and 16 points in 13 playoff games. The Montreal captain had four game winners, including Game 7's climactic clincher, which came after only 14 seconds of play. Chicago never got on the board after that in the Canadiens' 4-0 Cup victory.

▲ **1964–65**
Pierre Pilote surpasses Babe Pratt's 21-year scoring record of 58 points by a defenseman by notching 59 points with Chicago. The wily Pilote snags his third-consecutive James Norris Trophy as top blueliner.

RULE CHANGE

1964–65
Teams are required to dress two goalies. The maximum stick length is increased to 55 inches.

Roger Crozier, Ron Ellis and Bob McCord, 1966.

◂ **1965–66**
Roger Crozier wins the Conn Smythe Trophy. Detroit finishes 16 points behind league-leading Montreal, but Crozier pushes the Stanley Cup Final to six games, stealing Games 1 and 2 from the Canadiens. Playing on a twisted ankle (from a goal-crease crash), Crozier loses Games 3, 4 and 5 before managing a 2-2 tie going into a Game 6 overtime. In OT, Henri Richard slides toward the net, and redirects the puck past Crozier for the controversial Cup winner. Crozier is named MVP with a 2.34 goals-against average in 12 playoff games.

BOBBY'S 50-FOOT SLAP SHOT IN THIRD PERIOD SETS MARK

▲ 1965–66 Bobby Hull finishes the season with 54 goals, becoming the first NHLer to score more than 50 goals in a season. Hull's 51st is a 50-foot slap shot through the skates of Rangers goalie Cesare Maniago in Chicago's 4–2 win on March 12. Chicago Stadium erupts as 18,000-plus fans celebrate in a seven-minute uproar that reports describe as "one of the most hysterical demonstrations in Stadium history." The game is further delayed so workmen can clear the rink of "happy debris."

NHL EXPANSION

1966 The NHL sheds its eastern-league image and grants six U.S. cities franchise operating rights, doubling league size to 12 teams by adding a Western Division lineup of clubs in Minneapolis-St. Paul, Philadelphia, Oakland, Los Angeles, St. Louis and Pittsburgh. Franchise fees are $2 million each. The first NHL expansion in 40 years, Vancouver and Buffalo are snubbed. One Vancouver bid executive labels the all-American expansion "a cooked-up deal," as accusations of cronyism surface after reports that St. Louis didn't officially apply and St. Louis Arena is owned by Chicago owners Jim Norris and Arthur Wirtz.

1966–67 Chicago center Stan Mikita performs an historic NHL first in his hardware haul, winning the Art Ross, Hart and Lady Byng Trophies as top point-earner, MVP and most gentlemanly player in the same season.

▸ 1966–67 **The Maple Leafs' Stanley Cup.** Toronto upsets first-place Chicago in six games of the semifinal to face the defending Cup-champion Montreal Canadiens in a classic all-Canadian final. Montreal nails down a convincing 6–2 win in Game 1 against a Leafs team with three geriatrics in their forties and another eight past-primers in their thirties. The combined age of 20 Leaf players is 620 years. Of the NHL's Top 20 twenty-goal scorers that season, just two are Leafs: Ron Ellis with 22 and Jim Pappin with 21. One seasoned observer labels the club "a collection of the diligent, the wise and the near-infirm." But veterans like Johnny Bower, Allan Stanley and Red Kelly find new life in Imlach's crypt of grizzled graybeards. "On the other hand," said Montreal GM Sam Pollock, "in a short series, when you're playing well, you can beat anybody." Pollock is right. Toronto wins four of the next five games. A brilliant two-way performance earns Dave Keon the Conn Smythe Trophy as playoff MVP on the fabled over-the-hill gang, the oldest team, with an average age of 31.4 years, to win Lord Stanley's Cup.

Stanley Cup champions George Armstrong and Ron Ellis.

1966 ▸ **“Kid, I don’t know what they’re paying you, but it’s not enough.”**

—Boston veteran Ted Green, after being deked on several plays by rookie Bobby Orr at his first Bruins practice. In fact, Orr’s landmark contract made him the NHL’s highest-paid rookie—which still wasn’t enough.

▲ 1966–67 **The Bobby Orr signing.** Before the days of player agents, when teams dictated salaries, players, especially rookies, had no negotiating power. They accepted whatever offer was tabled. That changed in 1966, when Toronto lawyer Alan Eagleson, who was repping Orr, hints that his client instead might join Canada’s Olympic team. Bluff or not, the Bruins blink and Orr, by his own account, receives $25,000 for two years, plus bonuses. The two-year entry deal tops the incomes of many NHL veterans.

▲ 1967 **The Phil Esposito blockbuster trade.** Boston GM Milt Schmidt already had Bobby Orr, but his core of frontline players only took shape on May 15 after acquiring Esposito, Ken Hodge and Fred Stanfield from Chicago for Pit Martin, Gilles Marotte and goalie Jack Norris. The Black Hawks got swindled, at least on goal totals. Esposito, Hodge and Stanfield scored 980 goals between regular season and playoffs, while Martin and Marotte collected 264 for Chicago. Within three years the cellar-dwelling Bruins morphed into Stanley Cup champions.

An Ed Giacomin pokecheck on Henri Richard, with Jean Ratelle checking him.

▲ 1966–67 A Six Team Era feat, Ed Giacomin notches a league-best nine shutouts, blanking all league opponents at least once to become the last NHL goalie to do so. The New York netminder zeroed Toronto three times, Chicago and Detroit twice and Montreal and Boston once.

NORTHLAN

A New Hockey Order

This time of great political and cultural change in society brought the beginnings of a new hockey order. Unprecedented NHL expansion and the rival WHA saw elite play reach numerous untapped markets. Bobby Orr, who would revolutionize the game more than any single player, symbolized the rebellion of that player generation and their want of better working conditions. As veteran Bobby Baun said, "We were tired of the way the establishment treated us, and we were ready to do something about it."

Wayne Gretzky, 1985.

OPPOSITE
Bobby Orr.

There was the brash Alan Eagleson, the man who repped Orr and finally grabbed hockey's old-boy's network by the throat to create the NHL Players' Association. The league's Amateur (Entry) Draft gave every team a winning chance, with the ultimate goal of parity. Canadian television finally broadcast entire games, not just portions of matches. The 1972 Canada-Soviet Summit Series stirred a national calling against a very real world enemy. A countrywide unifier, the series began the protracted process of narrowing the performance gap among hockey nations. The caliber of play would forever change the "amateur" IIHF World Championship and the Olympics.

This era had Guy Lafleur. Phil Esposito. Valeri Kharlamov. Scotty Bowman. Vladislav Tretiak. Wayne Gretzky. Mario Lemieux. The Canada Cups. Meanwhile, European talent like Borje Salming and Peter Stastny slowly trickled into NHL ranks, dramatically altering the character of North American play—as did goon hockey, courtesy of Dave Schultz and Philadelphia's Broad Street Bullies.

Tiger Williams and Bob Probert elevated the tough guy role. Their ferocity could give you shivers. They hit to hurt, but they could score. Los Angeles had the Triple Crown Line, the first scoring unit with three 100-point players. In 1980–81, Marcel Dionne collected 135 points, Dave Taylor 122 and Charlie Simmer 105.

Despite the societal changes of the 1960s, hockey remained mostly a white man's game. For all that the women's movement had accomplished, there was little progress in their play, outside of local and university varsity teams, until 1990, when hockey held the first IIHF-sanctioned Women's World Championship.

This was an era of change and challenges to break through.

Alan Eagleson.

▲ 1967

The NHL Players' Association. Ten years after Ted Lindsay's crusade to form a players' association failed in 1957, NHLers like Bobby Baun and Bob Pulford took up the cause again. The inequalities of Lindsay's generation would not be their life in hockey—a politicized view that was treasonous in any previous era.

NHL economics, built by design, favored owners. League executives didn't want players controlling their own affairs or forming a players' association. It would likely lead to shared profits, meaning a stake in league ownership, as exists today through collective bargaining. Baun and Pulford found their change agent in Alan Eagleson, a lawyer and NHL outsider who gained quick acceptance among players after dealing in player representation matters, including Bobby Orr's contract in 1966. The next year, Eagleson created the NHLPA as a recognized bargaining group. It ultimately retooled league dynamics to shape the game's future.

Red Berenson became one of the biggest stars in the NHL's new West Division. Berenson led the Blues to three-straight Stanley Cup Finals.

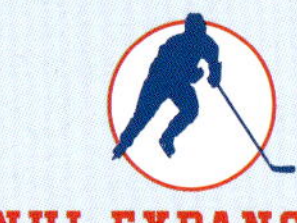

NHL EXPANSION

▲ 1967–68 Expansion doubles the NHL to 12 teams in the largest single-season growth spurt in league history. The East Division fields existing Six Team Era clubs and the West Division new franchises in St. Louis, Oakland, Philadelphia, Minneapolis–St. Paul, Pittsburgh and Los Angeles. The regular season is now 74 games with clubs playing 50 matches against division rivals and 24 against rivals outside their division.

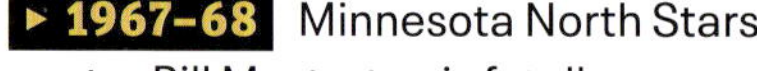

► 1967–68 Minnesota North Stars center Bill Masterton is fatally injured after suffering a skull fracture in an on-ice collision on January 13. Masterton's death encourages other players to begin wearing helmets. In his honor, the NHL creates the Bill Masterton Memorial Trophy, an annual award given to the player who best exemplifies the qualities of perseverance, sportsmanship and dedication to hockey.

Gerry Cheevers.

◄ 1967–68 Boston's Gerry Cheevers paints his mask with black stitch marks in jest after a shot from Fred Stanfield at practice scratches its white surface. Each time Cheevers took another shot to his head, "Frosty [trainer Frosty Forristall] would calculate where it would have been and how many stitches it would have taken," said Cheevers. The motif inspires goalies to decorate their own masks with team logos and more stylized imagery.

Pre-No.4 Bobby Orr and coach Harry Sinden.

▲ 1967–68 Bobby Orr wins his first of eight consecutive Norris Trophies as the NHL's top defenseman. Light years ahead of everyone in skill development, the Boston sophomore is just 20 years old, the youngest Norris winner to date. A knee injury limits him to 31 points in 46 games.

Phil Esposito against Bernie Parent.

▲ 1968–69 **The 100-point men.** Phil Esposito unleashes his lethal combination of inspired gamesmanship and garbage-goal getting to become the first 100-point NHLer on March 2. Esposito amasses a 126-point season, followed by triple-digits from Bobby Hull (107) and Gordie Howe (103).

Gump Worsley against Garry Monahan.

▲ 1968–69 **The last maskless Stanley Cup-winning goalies.** Neither Gump Worsley nor Rogie Vachon wore masks when they backstopped Montreal to the 1969 Stanley Cup. Vachon, 24, was in his third season with the Canadiens. Worsley, who once famously quipped "My face is my mask," went barefaced through four Stanley Cups with Montreal, his last in 1969, his 16th NHL season. He played another five years, almost exclusively without face protection, backstopping Minnesota. Vachon donned a mask the next season, 1969–70.

Jacques Plante and Glenn Hall, 1961.

▲ 1968–69 Once longtime rivals, St. Louis tandem Jacques Plante and Glenn Hall win the Vezina Trophy. Plante goes 18-12-6 with five shutouts. Hall has a near identical 19-12-8 and eight SOs to hand the Blues top spot in the West Division. At age 37 and six months years old, Hall's eight zeroes make him the league's oldest shutout leader ever.

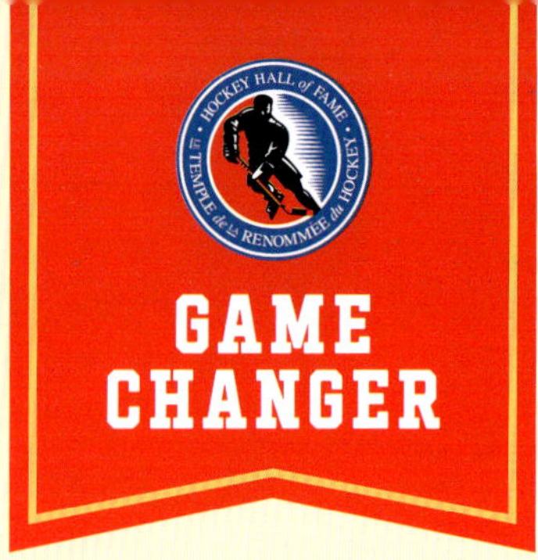

Television

"The game will suffer."

—NHL boss Clarence Campbell, on televised hockey games

Clarence Campbell's old-world assessment of television's reach was correct, even prescient. The NHL he presided over, the game as he knew it—one without union representation, profit sharing, free agency or any real television revenues—would "suffer" and go through a course correction, wholly impacting hockey everywhere.

A deer-in-the-headlights posture prevailed among league bosses, who, faced with any change, seemed paralyzed by progress. For example, until the late 1960s, only portions of matches were televised in Canada. Still, team owners understood enough to prejudge the influence of television on their sport. When the minor pro Western Hockey League spoke of expansion and television deals during the mid-1960s, the NHL countered with multiple expansions of its own and, in 1968–69, full game broadcasts starting at 8 p.m.

Television dollars brought unprecedented growth through the years, initially sparking unionization that launched the NHLPA and, in turn, triggered labor disputes that brought NHL lockouts and strikes, salary disclosure, salary caps and, eventually, league parity. Television's revenue streams lengthened season schedules and restructured team and league managements, both at the NHL level and its many feeder circuits.

Unlike any medium before it, television magnified the star power of players and broadened the game's fan base and commercial product, further ratcheting up franchise prices and ticket costs. It introduced a host of broadcasters and commentators, many becoming household names across the sports world, while treating its fan base to multi-platform sports programming. All of it gave hockey an elite league status in the sporting marketplace.

***Hockey Night in Canada*'s Danny Gallivan and *La soirée du hockey*'s René Lecavalier.**

Czechoslovakia defeats the Soviet Union 4–3, 1969.

▲ 1969 "We said to ourselves, even if we have to die on the ice, we have to beat them."

—Czechoslovak captain Jozef Golonka, on meeting the Soviets at the 1969 World Championship. Several months earlier, Soviet forces had invaded Czechoslovakia when Warsaw Pact tanks rumbled through Prague to stop national reforms made by the liberal Czechoslovak government. While the Czechs settle for the bronze medal, they stun the gold medalist Soviet team with 2-0 and 4-3 mid-series victories, which have been described as the most emotionally charged games in world hockey history.

1968–69

St. Louis center Red Berenson scores six goals against Philadelphia on November 7 to establish a modern record for most goals in a game. "Tonight, everything was going in," said Berenson. Darryl Sittler equals that goal output with six against Boston in February 1976.

▼ 1968–69

Bobby Hull, owner of the most lethal slap shot in hockey and among the game's most popular players, wins his final Art Ross Trophy. Hull led all NHL goal-scorers in seven of 10 seasons.

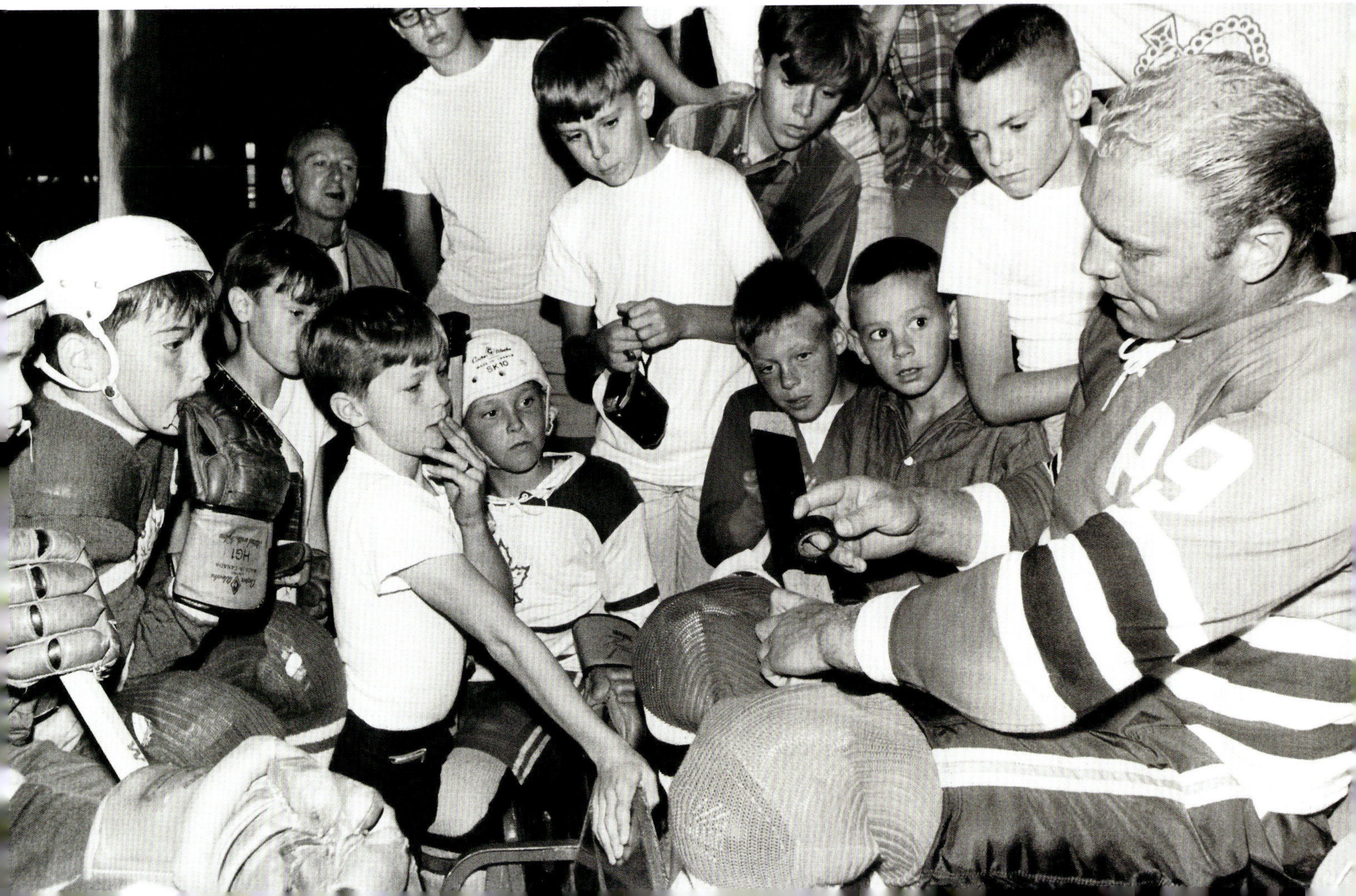

George Armstrong checks Serge Savard.

▲ 1968–69 Serge Savard wins the Conn Smythe Trophy. Charting one of the lowest point totals ever by a playoff MVP (10 points in 14 games), Savard captures the Conn Smythe for his on-ice leadership and his compete game, providing crucial scoring and D-zone coverage during Montreal's Stanley Cup semifinal against Boston and Cup-winning Final versus St. Louis. Only Dave Keon has fewer points among Conn Smythe skaters, with eight in 12 games in Toronto's 1967 championship.

1968–69 The *Hockey Night in Canada* theme song makes its debut on national television. Composed by classically trained composer Dolores Claman, the promotional song with the "Dan-da-da-da-dan-da" fanfare remains as popular as ever today.

▲ 1969–70 Bobby Orr claims four major individual awards. An NHL first, Orr's foursome includes the Art Ross Trophy as scoring leader, the Hart Trophy as league MVP, the Norris Trophy as outstanding defenseman and the Conn Smythe Trophy as playoff MVP. Orr, 22, becomes the only defenseman to win the NHL scoring title, racking up 120 points on 33 goals and 87 assists, the second-most by any NHLer to that time. Orr's historic season is capped by leading the Bruins to their first Stanley Cup in 29 years.

Orr's box time illuminates his fierce competitive edge. Better described, Orr had a mean streak. On a Big Bad Bruins squad stocked with bangers Don Awrey and Dallas Smith, Orr led everyone with 125 minutes. Ted Green tactfully said of Boston, "Certainly on our club, I don't think there are too many guys who wear lace panties out there."

◂ 1969–70 Tony Esposito posts 15 shutouts. Esposito's modern record of 15 zeroes equals the four-decade-old total of Alec Connell and Hal Winkler, who played during the dead-puck era before forward passing was permitted. George Hainsworth recorded the impassable mark of 22 blanks in 1928–29. In 63 games, Tony O logged a shutout almost every fourth start.

Ted Green.

▲ 1969–70 Wayne Maki fractures Ted Green's skull. Maki's vicious two-hander across Green's right temple during a September exhibition match sets a new low in ugly hockey. The stick blow left Green convulsing on the ice. He pulled through following major operations that included a steel plate implant. St. Louis Blues broadcaster Dan Kelly called the stick-swinging incident "one of the most horrifying, most violent exchanges I've ever seen in hockey." Green missed the entire season. Both men were given match penalties and later acquitted of assault charges.

▲ 1969–70 Bobby Clarke enters the NHL. During the Philadelphia Flyers' heyday of the 1970s, Clarke was the heart, soul and captain of the team of punishers nicknamed the Broad Street Bullies. Clarke won two Stanley Cups with the brawling Flyers, in 1974 and 1975, and three Hart Trophies as league MVP. He was among the first few to make plays behind an opponent's net, which Wayne Gretzky famously adopted as his "office" to great success during the 1980s.

1970 Canada won't return to world play "until the rules permit us to enter a team that is truly representative of Canadian hockey, so that we can play our best players as all other countries do."

—CAHA president Earl Dawson on Canada withdrawing from the World Championship and the Olympics, which it did until 1977, after modern eligibility rules eliminated any categorization of players, amateur or pro.

Terry Sawchuk chases the puck behind his net, with Claude Provost in pursuit, followed by Allan Stanley, 1967.

▲ 1970 Terry Sawchuk is the first goalie to survive 20 NHL seasons, but an innocent off-ice altercation with teammate Ron Stewart on the lawn of their rented house leads to a critical injury that ends his life. Following multiple surgeries, Sawchuk, 40, dies of cardiac arrest. It's a wasteful, needless passing, apropos of life's fragility, especially given his everyday courage manning the pipes.

1969
The NHL amateur draft expands to become the NHL Universal Amateur Draft. It includes all available amateur players of qualifying age who are not already signed under the old sponsorship system of junior farm teams.

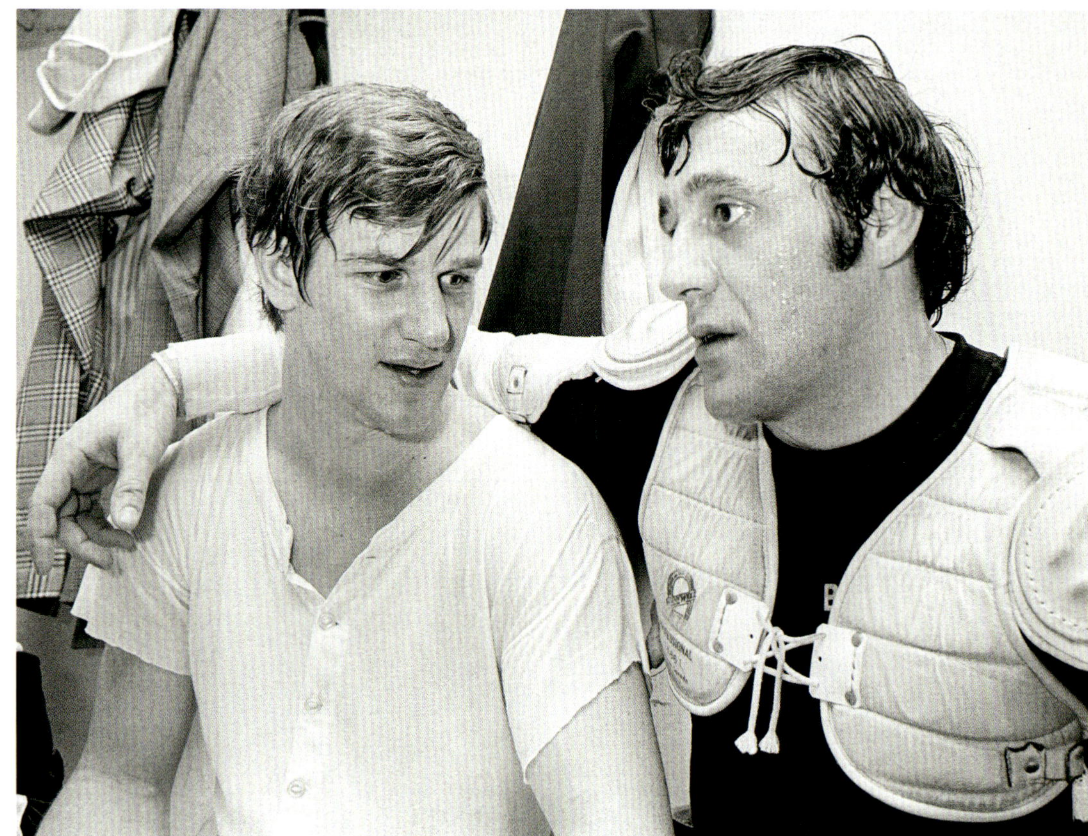

Bobby Orr and Phil Esposito.

▲ 1970–71 The Boston Bruins' record-breaking season left few NHL scoring standards untouched, as 37 team and individual records are set. The Bruins establish marks with 57 wins, 121 points and a blistering 399 goals, or 108 more goals than runner-up Montreal. Phil Esposito amasses records of 76 goals and 152 points, and the all-time NHL shot count of 550. Bobby Orr reaches triple digits with 102 assists and a league all-time high of plus-124. Boston's puck blitz propels Esposito, Orr, Johnny Bucyk and Ken Hodge to the top four spots in NHL scoring. Seven of the top-10 league scorers are Bruins.

Gilbert Perreault.

NHL EXPANSION

▲ 1970
Vancouver and Buffalo become the 13th and 14th NHL franchises. The Sabres win the wheel spin, selecting Gilbert Perreault first overall. The Canucks take Dale Tallon second. The NHL now has an 11:3 ratio of American-to-Canadian-based franchises.

► 1970–71 **The Ken Dryden show.** Montreal stages one of the greatest heists in playoff annals, gambling on Dryden, a rookie of six NHL starts, whose nimble acrobatic maneuvers ambush heavily favored Boston in their Stanley Cup quarterfinal, subdues Minnesota in their semifinal and outclasses Chicago's Tony Esposito in the Cup Final. Dryden faces down 709 shots, about 35 per game. Under siege, he allows 61 goals, the most by a Cup-winning netminder. Still, the rangy, lunging puckstopper keeps Montreal alive, after falling behind in two series. Dryden arrived unheralded, untested and, as Phil Esposito described, "a thieving giraffe."

Bobby Orr, 1970.

Bobby Orr

In a league of his own, "Bobby was a star from the moment they played the national anthem in his first NHL game," said Boston coach Harry Sinden. At 14, Orr signed the standard NHL "C" form, which gave the Bruins lifetime rights in exchange for $2,800, a used car and the unfulfilled promise of a new wardrobe. After signing for what was then a king's ransom of $25,000 over two years, Orr proceeded to show the hockey world his electrifying raw talents as rookie of the year, even though the Bruins finished last in 1966-67.

Orr didn't practice the stay-at-home trade of hard hits and standard defensive positioning. Like contemporaries Doug Harvey and Tim Horton, Orr was a game-breaker—even on ravaged knees. He could control game flow and tempo, orchestrate headlong rushes almost effortlessly through heavy forechecking and serve up pinpoint passes. Only faster than anyone before.

Rarely was there an errant pass or a missed backcheck on the blue line. His hockey IQ, superior instincts and creativity revolutionized the position and dominated individual point scoring for six NHL seasons. In 1969-70, Orr won the Art Ross Trophy as top scorer, another NHL first for a defenseman.

It was the sign of things to come. That year he scored the prettiest Stanley Cup-winner ever. Orr and teammate Phil Esposito made the Art Ross their own personal race between 1969-70 and 1974-75, alternating first and second positions every year, except 1972-73. Orr had an ornery side. As many points as he put up, they never topped his box time. He collected 915 points and 953 penalty minutes during a 12-year career. When Wayne Maki stick-chopped Ted Green across the head in 1969, Orr was the first off the bench to get at Maki. He was the consummate team player, harm's way be damned.

Orr's career ended in Chicago, where he signed a $3-million, five-year contract with the Black Hawks. It seemed wishful thinking. He played only parts of two seasons.

Orr was unlike any defenseman before him. His impact on hockey influenced the next generation in Denis Potvin, Paul Coffey, Ray Bourque and Nicklas Lidstrom.

Guy Lafleur.

▲ 1970 & 1971 **The Guy Lafleur draft pick trade.** California (Oakland) deals François Lacombe, its first-round pick of 1971, and cash for Montreal's first-round pick of 1970 (Chris Oddleifson) and Ernie Hicke. All goes according to plan for Montreal GM and master wheeler-dealer Sam Pollock. The Golden Seals finish in last place in 1970–71, delivering the Canadiens their first overall pick of 1971, Guy Lafleur. Lafleur becomes the keystone sniper of Montreal's dynasty teams of the 1970s. California's woeful finish falls on goalie Gary Smith, who sets the all-time NHL record with 48 defeats.

Gordie Howe's gloves.

▲ 1970–71 **Gordie Howe retires—the first time.** Still not finished with hockey at age 43, Howe, to this point in time, has won four Stanley Cups and collected six Hart Trophies as league MVP and six Art Ross Trophies as scoring leader after 25 years with the Detroit Red Wings. The NHL waives its customary three-year waiting period and elects Howe to the Hockey Hall of Fame in 1972.

Hellbent, Eddie Shack always took the shortest route from A to B. Here, Shack rides Gerry Ehman.

▲ 1970–71 Worth a thousand words, this Eddie Shack picture says just about everything of hockey's most "energetic, entertaining, combustible, whacky" skater of the 1960s and early 1970s. Shack not only could play the game, he had that rare commodity, personality. During his 17-year, 1,047-game NHL career, Shack played on six teams, had 20-goal seasons with five of them and won four Stanley Cups, all with Toronto, where the Brian McFarlane song "Clear the Track, Here Comes Shack" defined his maniacal yet methodical gamesmanship.

RULE CHANGE

1971–72 The third man entering an altercation is assessed an automatic game misconduct penalty. The number of players in uniform is set at 17, plus two goaltenders.

▸ 1971–72 Montreal (Verdun)-born, Scotty Bowman steps behind the hometown Canadiens' bench stocked with a dynasty-in-waiting team that features Guy Lafleur, Bob Gainey, Yvan Cournoyer, Serge Savard, Ken Dryden, Jacques Lemaire, Guy Lapointe and Larry Robinson. Under Bowman, Montreal captures five Stanley Cups in eight seasons during the 1970s.

Scotty Bowman.

"We played them pretty even, but they had Bobby Orr and we didn't."

—New York's Vic Hadfield, on the 1972 Stanley Cup Final between Boston and the Rangers

Jean Béliveau, Bobby Orr and Gerry Cheevers.

1971-72 **The NHL's all-time longest undefeated streak.** Gerry Cheevers never led the league in goals-against average, but few netminders were better at winning, especially backstopping a Boston Bruins powerhouse. His 32-game streak had a 24-0-8 record. Pete Peeters, on a less-dominant Bruins team, almost equaled Cheevers a decade later, falling one game short with 31 straight matches (26-0-5).

Longest Undefeated Streak, One Season

Player	Team	Season	Streak	Start-End Date
Gerry Cheevers	Boston Bruins	1971-72	32	11/14/1971-03/25/1972
Pete Peeters	Boston Bruins	1982-83	31	11/13/1982-02/13/1983
Pete Peeters	Philadelphia Flyers	1979-80	27	10/14/1979-02/14/1980
Frank Brimsek	Boston Bruins	1940-41	23	12/22/1940-02/23/1941
Glenn Resch	NY Islanders	1978-79	23	10/17/1978-01/14/1979
Grant Fuhr	Edmonton Oilers	1981-82	23	10/21/1981-01/13/1982

1972 **Czechoslovakia wins the World Championship.** The Czech national team earns some political payback at the Worlds when it halts the Soviet Union's streak of nine-straight World Championships and three Olympic titles. In the penultimate contest to largely determine the gold medal, the Czechs defeat the Soviets 3-2—sweet revenge in the host city Prague, the site of the Prague-Spring rebellion, where four years earlier Warsaw Pact troops entered and occupied the country. Their triumph in Prague sent the entire Czech nation into pandemonium. Two days later, World gold is secured in an 8-2 thrashing against Finland.

A Czechoslovak postage stamp promoting Czechoslovakia's 1972 World Championship.

Harold Ballard.

1972
Harold Ballard becomes majority shareholder of the Toronto Maple Leafs and Maple Leaf Gardens. During his lengthy tenure as president and owner, Ballard stripped the once-proud club of its championship sheen. Incompetent, ignitable, ego-driven and in over his head, Ballard was hockey's greatest media antagonist/manipulator. He ran the team with almost no NHL experience, refusing to take a back seat in its hockey operations. As sports writer William Houston pithily put it, Ballard's firm grip equaled his tight fist.

▲ 1972 **"The Canadians battled with the ferocity and intensity of a cornered animal."**

—Anatoli Tarasov, Soviet Union coach and "the father of Russian hockey," on Team Canada's play during 1972's Summit Series

▲ 1972 **The Canada–Soviet Summit Series.** The eight-game tournament was supposed to determine supremacy between hockey superpowers. However, something else happened that neither side expected. The geopolitics of communism versus capitalism were competing in a merciless game of brinkmanship on the ice that would sway hockey history and lead to the globalizing of NHL play. As series hero Paul Henderson said, "It was Canada playing, not Team Canada. It was us against them and every Canadian somehow seemed to have a sense of ownership of that team." Canada won, but only on Henderson's Summit Series winner with 34 seconds remaining in Game 8's cliffhanger at Moscow's Luzhniki Palace.

► 1972–73 **The World Hockey Association.** The NHL never fully grasped what impact the upstart WHA would have on its monopoly of major league hockey and its talent pools—not until Chicago superstar Bobby Hull signed a $1-million deal with the new circuit. No longer was this motley league of misfits and B-players a simple annoyance. It had lured away a sports idol. The threat was real and persisted, with other defectors Derek Sanderson, Bernie Parent and John McKenzie. Soon after, Gordie Howe and Dave Keon signed on, as did teenage prospects Wayne Gretzky and Mark Messier. New hockey markets popped up in franchise cities of Houston, Birmingham and San Diego. In the bidding wars, player salaries skyrocketed three-fold. The war of attrition ended in 1979, with WHA teams in Winnipeg, Edmonton, Hartford and Quebec joining the NHL.

The blind leading the blind. Aislin, 1977.

Marty, Gordie and Mark Howe

▲ **1973–74** Retiree Gordie Howe signs as a free agent with the WHA Houston Aeros in order to play alongside sons Mark and Marty. Howe spends four years in Houston, and then two more with the New England Whalers before his final NHL season as a Hartford Whaler when the WHA folds in 1979.

► **1973–74** **The coming of Borje Salming.** The NHL's experiment with European players really began with Salming, a superb rushing defenseman with speed and stickhandling and shot-blocking skills. No "chicken Swede," he survived the taunts, intimidation and physical abuse of the 80-game grind to play 1,148 matches with Toronto and Detroit. The six-time All-Star blueliner received Hockey Hall of Fame honors in 1996. His greater achievement, however, was breaking the stereotype of the skilled European who lacked brawn. Salming became that point man for the European invasion, pioneering the way for future arrivals to North American shores.

The 1974 Stanley Cup champion Philadelphia Flyers.

▲ **1973–74** The two-time Stanley Cup-winning Philadelphia Flyers were always more than their goon-squad tactics. Brawlers like Dave Schultz, Bob Kelly and Andre Dupont did bulk-up the bench and had opponents so unnerved that many contracted the alleged "Philly flu" game day to avoid playing them, mainly at the dreaded Spectrum. While the Flyers' thug-game strategy created space on the ice for their skaters, they still had to score and stop goals to win. Fifty-goal scorer Rick MacLeish and the LCB line of Reggie Leach, captain Bobby Clarke and Bill Barber provided the offensive force. Bernie Parent's crease work chalked up an NHL-record 47 wins and a league-leading 44 the following season, 1974–75. Both were Cup-winning seasons, with Parent picking up the Conn Smythe Trophy twice as playoff MVP. The Flyers were the first expansion team crowned Stanley Cup champions.

Denis Potvin and Rollie Melanson against Wayne Gretzky and Glenn Anderson.

▲ 1973–74 Denis Potvin wins the Calder Trophy. The New York Islanders drafted Potvin first overall in 1973 and the offensively gifted rookie defenseman played like a veteran, not only scoring 17 goals and 54 points to win top freshman honors, but compiling a Calder Trophy-high 175 penalty minutes—broken by Barrett Jackman's 190 minutes in 2002-03. No Bobby Orr, when Potvin won the Norris Trophy in 1976, he was still the first rearguard not named Orr to do it since 1967.

Tim Horton, Pittsburgh Hornets, early 1950s.

▲ 1974 Tim Horton is killed in a car accident. The 44-year old defenseman loses control and crashes near St. Catharines, Ontario, after a game on February 21. Horton was driving a Ford De Tomaso Pantera sports car, the signing bonus from the Buffalo Sabres that lured him out of retirement.

NHL EXPANSION

1974–75 NHL expansion welcomes Washington and Kansas City, which brings an 18-team, four-division realignment, named after NHL builders Lester Patrick, James Norris, Charles F. Adams and Conn Smythe.

"I should have skated over her wires."

—Islander goalie Billy Smith, griping about anthem singer Kate Smith singing "God Bless America" from center ice at Philadelphia Spectrum, 1975 playoffs

Phil Esposito, Johnny Bucyk and Bobby Orr.

▲ 1974–75 Bobby Orr and Phil Esposito's last hurrah. Orr and Esposito record their fifth 1-2 finish as teammates in NHL scoring. Orr wins his second NHL scoring title with 135 points, netting an NHL record 46 goals by a defenseman and his eighth-consecutive Norris Trophy. Esposito scores 61 times to lead the league for the sixth-straight season. Neither player records such totals again. Orr doesn't play another full season and Esposito is traded the following year.

1975 ▸ **"I can't remember a goaltender who could stare down the guys the way he did that night."**

—Referee Wally Harris, on Vladislav Tretiak, who backstops the Soviet Union in an epic 3-3 tie, despite being outshot 38-13 by the Montreal Canadiens on New Year's Eve, 1975. Some consider it the finest hockey game ever played.

Vladislav Tretiak.

Lars-Erik Sjoberg.

▲ 1974–75 The WHA Winnipeg Jets become the first European-stocked North American team, icing as many as 10 European expats during some seasons. The first wave included Bobby Hull's Swedish linemates Anders Hedberg and Ulf Nilsson and Swede veteran defenseman Lars-Erik Sjoberg, who captained Winnipeg to three Avco World Trophy championships. When the Jets joined the NHL in 1979, Sjoberg became the league's first European-trained team captain.

▲ 1975 **Marcel Dionne signs with Los Angeles.** Seeking a bigger payday and playoff experience, Dionne, third in 1974–75's scoring race behind Bobby Orr and Phil Esposito, departs Detroit, in effect, as a free agent. Without precedent (probably an NHL first), he signs with the Kings. The league intervenes to orchestrate a trade involving Dan Maloney, Terry Harper and a second-round draft pick as compensation. Dionne teams up with Charlie Simmer and Dave Taylor to form the Triple Crown Line. Six 50-goal seasons and nine playoff appearances later, Dionne is fated as the highest scoring NHLer (731-1,040-1,771) never to win the Stanley Cup.

◂ 1975–76 Darryl Sittler's record 10-point night. Boston's Dave Reece was having a so-far-so-good rookie season. He owned a healthy 7-4-2 record, with two shutouts. But then Sittler lit him up for six goals and four assists on national television in an 11-4 scorefest on February 7 that made the Toronto forward the league's first 10-point player. Reece never played NHL hockey again.

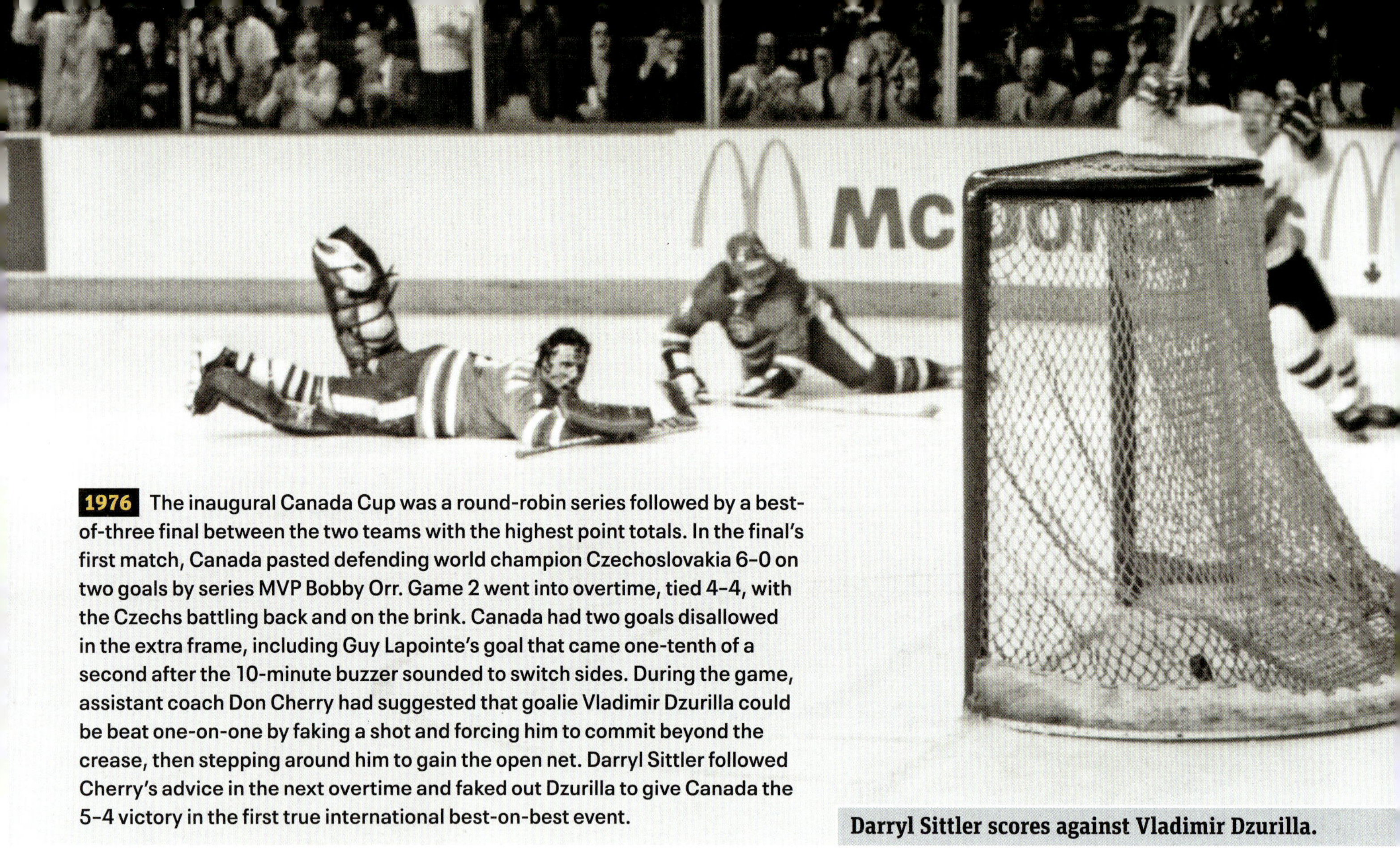

1976 The inaugural Canada Cup was a round-robin series followed by a best-of-three final between the two teams with the highest point totals. In the final's first match, Canada pasted defending world champion Czechoslovakia 6-0 on two goals by series MVP Bobby Orr. Game 2 went into overtime, tied 4-4, with the Czechs battling back and on the brink. Canada had two goals disallowed in the extra frame, including Guy Lapointe's goal that came one-tenth of a second after the 10-minute buzzer sounded to switch sides. During the game, assistant coach Don Cherry had suggested that goalie Vladimir Dzurilla could be beat one-on-one by faking a shot and forcing him to commit beyond the crease, then stepping around him to gain the open net. Darryl Sittler followed Cherry's advice in the next overtime and faked out Dzurilla to give Canada the 5-4 victory in the first true international best-on-best event.

Darryl Sittler scores against Vladimir Dzurilla.

1975-76 **"We had a feeling amongst ourselves that the whole league wanted us to win, just because of what they stood for ... you know, the Broad Street Bullies and all that. They tried to intimidate the whole league."**

—Montreal's Larry Robinson, recognizing much more than just a Stanley Cup was at stake after his Canadiens dispatched the Philadelphia Flyers four straight at the 1976 Cup Finals

▲ 1976 Bobby Orr signs with Chicago. In what may be the first free agent signing without compensation, Boston gets nothing for the game's greatest player. Hobbled by knee injuries, Orr plays only 26 games over two years before retiring.

A 16-year-old Wayne Gretzky battles Aleksandr Kozhevnikov.

◄ 1977 **The World Junior Championship.** Initially started as an invitational tournament in 1974 to fill the void for international hockey after Canada withdrew its national teams from world play in 1970, the World Juniors receives full IIHF recognition. The event endures its own growing pains to become a proving ground used by pro scouts to judge next-generation player performance.

Team Ugly made it easy for the Soviets

▲ 1977 Canada resumes World Championship play. After seven years of isolation from playing against the world's best teams, Canada returns to Europe with a stellar NHL lineup in Phil and Tony Esposito, Ron Ellis, Pierre Larouche and Rod Gilbert. They play well against some teams, but get thumped 11-1 and 8-1 versus the Soviets. Frustration sets in, which leads to game violence and public scorn in Europe and, worse, ridicule back home. Canada finishes out of medal contention in fourth place.

1977 *Slap Shot* debuts in movie theaters. Based on the Johnstown Jets of the Eastern Hockey League, the cult classic stars Paul Newman as Reggie Dunlop, playing-coach of the fictional Charlestown Chiefs. With the Pennsylvania factory town in decline, the Chiefs resort to violence to increase game attendance. The Hanson brothers are hired. Playing the trio of goons are former WHA bangers Dave Hanson and Jeff and Steve Carlson.

1977 "It's almost embarrassing to say you took away one of Orr's records. He was so much better than the rest of us, it was ridiculous."

—Tom Bladon, after breaking Bobby Orr's single-game seven-point record by a defenseman by scoring four goals and four assists in Philadelphia's 11-1 thrashing against Cleveland on December 11. The Flyer rearguard is the first NHLer to record a plus-10 in one game.

◂ 1976-77 The 60-8-12 Montreal Canadiens. Montreal reels off hockey's most dominant season as the first NHL team to win 60 games, registering a home-stand blitz without a loss over a five-month stretch to salt a 33-1-6 record and, perhaps the best test of absolute supremacy, a regular-season differential of 216 goals, with Guy Lafleur, Yvan Cournoyer and company scoring 387 times and Montreal's Big Three of Serge Savard, Larry Robinson and Guy Lapointe, backstopped by Ken Dryden, giving up just 171 goals.

Serge Savard and Larry Robinson, 1978.

▸ 1977-78 Mike Bossy: hockey's first 50-goal rookie. A 15th overall pick, Bossy was considered too fragile for NHL play. A huge miscalculation, given how Bossy proved himself every bit the sniper-warrior of four junior seasons of 118, 149, 136 and 126 points with the Laval National. In 73 freshman NHL games, Bossy netted 53 goals to break Rick Martin's 44-goal rookie mark of 1971-72. Overshadowed by Guy Lafleur and Wayne Gretzky, Bossy has nine-straight 50-goal seasons in a 10-year NHL career that brought the Islanders four Stanley Cups.

1977-78 "[If] you can't wear one 9, wear two."

—Junior B coach Muzz MacPherson to a 16-year-old Wayne Gretzky, on not being able to wear sweater No. 9 with the Sault Ste. Marie Greyhounds

1977 Detroit Red Wings Vice President John Ziegler replaces Clarence Campbell as NHL president. Campbell served as league chief for 31 years. Ziegler is the first American to hold the top office in hockey.

Patrick Roy and Bob Gainey, 1986. Through 16 NHL seasons Gainey led by example, shutting down the opposition's top scoring threats while providing leadership in five Stanley Cup campaigns.

▲ 1977-78 Inspired by the defensive, gritty team leadership of forward Bob Gainey, the NHL creates the Frank Selke Award and honors Montreal's frontline checker with the first four Selkes, a total only surpassed by Patrice Bergeron's six awards.

▸ 1977-78
Captain Video. Toronto coach Roger Neilson pioneers the use of game footage, using videotape as a teaching tool. Neilson experimented with video while coaching junior hockey with the OHA Peterborough Petes.

Roger Neilson.

Guy Lafleur.

▲ 1977-78 Guy Lafleur notches his second-straight Hart Trophy as league MVP and his third-consecutive Art Ross Trophy as NHL scoring leader, amassing 125-, 136- and 132-point seasons from 1975-76 to 1977-78. Lafleur records plus-ratings of +67, +89 and +73, just under Wayne Gretzky's highest plus-minus of +100 in 1984-85.

Serge Savard and Yvon Lambert.

▲ 1978-79 **The bench minor that likely cost Boston a Stanley Cup.** Leading the Canadiens 4-3 with 2:34 remaining in Game 7 of the Cup semifinal, the Bruins take a too-many-men-on-the-ice penalty. On the power play, Jacques Lemaire streaks across Boston's blue line and drops the puck to Guy Lafleur, who ties the game with a 30-foot bomb past a startled Gilles Gilbert. In overtime, Yvon Lambert scores, eliminating Boston. The humiliating defeat costs coach Don Cherry his Bruins job. Montreal beats the New York Rangers handily in the Cup Final to win their fourth-straight Stanley Cup.

◂ 1978–79 **Bryan Trottier wins the Art Ross Trophy.** A beast on the ice, Trottier was the tenacious passer-playmaker who centered gritty corner man Clark Gillies and pure scorer Mike Bossy on the dynasty New York Islanders. Trottier led the league with 134 points. But the point total obscures a finer scoring detail. His 46 goals on a measly 187 shots earn him a shot conversion rate of one goal every four shots on net.

▴ November 8, 1978 **Bobby Orr says goodbye to the game.** At age 30 the only thing stopping him from playing is his wonky knees. The following year, Orr, 31, becomes the youngest Hockey Hall of Fame inductee.

Frank Mahovlich, WHA Toronto Toros.

NHL EXPANSION

◂ 1979–80 A seven-year battle for the hearts of hockey fans ends with the WHA folding into the NHL, as Edmonton, Hartford, Quebec and Winnipeg create a 21-team league. Along the way, the WHA did its share of heavy lifting, opening up new markets to pro hockey, ridding the game of its reserve clause, pumping up salaries to unprecedented levels for a fraternity of players from underage 17-year-old prospects like Wayne Gretzky to marquee superstars in Bobby Hull and Frank Mahovlich.

RULE CHANGE

1979–80

Helmets are mandatory for players entering the NHL.

▴ 1979–80 **Gordie Howe plays in his fifth decade of pro hockey.** On October 13, Howe, with the Hartford Whalers, beats Pittsburgh's Greg Millen to become the first player to score an NHL goal after being elected to the Hockey Hall of Fame. Howe is 51 years old.

◂ 1978–79

The signing of Wayne Gretzky. After only eight games as an Indianapolis Racer, Gretzky's original $850,000 personal services contract is sold by Racers owner Nelson Skalbania to Edmonton Oilers owner Peter Pocklington. Shortly after, on January 26, Gretzky celebrates his 18th birthday by inking a new deal at a pregame, center ice ceremony at Northlands Coliseum in front of 12,321 fans. The "steal of a deal" was a nine-year agreement worth $2,325,000, including bonuses.

Team USA's 1980 Olympic Gold

A Miracle on Ice. Unthinkable. Unimaginable. The highly favored Soviet Union hadn't lost a gold medal since the 1960 Olympics. Team USA was a spirited squad of American collegiates with future NHLers Neal Broten, Ken Morrow and Craig Ramsey, but also unknowns like Mike Eruzione and Jim Craig. That changed in dramatic fashion on February 22 at Lake Placid, when the Americans scraped out a 4–3 victory on Eruzione's third-period wrist shot from outside the slot to beat Vladimir Myshkin for the go-ahead goal. With 10 minutes remaining, USA hung on, as Craig served up a training seminar in clutch netminding, facing 18-12-9 shots per period, and being outshot 39 to 16.

Team USA went on to play Finland for the gold. Coach Herb Brooks reportedly said, "If you lose this game, you'll take it to your grave ... your (bleeping) grave." Brooks spent 18 months building his roster and another four months preparing for this very moment, playing exhibition games in Europe and North America. His fanatical preparation and training emphasized speed, conditioning and discipline. It's widely known, he made himself an enemy of his players, challenging them physically and psychologically.

Against Finland, down 2–1, the Americans pulled off a three-goal third-period comeback to claim Olympic gold. *Sports Illustrated* called their triumph "the single most indelible moment in all of U.S. sports history" and rate their gold medal as the greatest sports moment of the 20th century. America's victory not only came to define Olympic competition, where even a *miracle* is possible, it inspired the next generation of American kids to dream of hockey glory.

1980 "Do you believe in miracles? Yes!"

—Al Michaels, ABC Sports, 1980 Winter Olympics, calling America's most memorable hockey quote

▲ 1979-80 **The Butch Goring trade.** Goring, an 11-year veteran center of nine 20-plus goal seasons with Los Angeles, is the puzzle piece the New York Islanders want for one reason: the Stanley Cup. It works better than anyone expected. Goring scores 19 points in 21 games in the Isles' 1980 Cup victory and plays a major role in the club's four-straight championships, including as playoff MVP in 1981.

► 1979-80 Wayne Gretzky hits NHL ice. Gretzky, 19, exceeds all expectations, tying Marcel Dionne for the scoring lead with 137 points in his first NHL season. He nets the first 50-goal season and the first 100-point season by a teenager. His WHA pro status, however, prevents his eligibility for the Calder Trophy as top rookie and, because Dionne scores more goals, Dionne gets the Art Ross Trophy.

Wayne Gretzky, as a WHA Oiler, March 1979, months before Edmonton joins the NHL.

Coach Pat Quinn, Stanley Cup Final, 1980.

▲▼ 1979-80 **The NHL's longest unbeaten streak.** Pat Quinn's first full season coaching Philadelphia was impressive. The Flyers wouldn't quit on Quinn, staging a 12-week undefeated streak of 35 games, racking up 25 wins and 10 ties. Rookie goalie Pete Peeters went 14-0-4 and Phil Myre 11-0-6 between October 14 and January 6.

Longest Undefeated Team Streak, One Season

Team	Season	Streak	Start-End Date
Philadelphia Flyers	1979-80	35	10/14/1979-01/06/1980
Montreal Canadiens	1977-78	28	12/18/1977-02/23/1978
Boston Bruins	1940-41	23	12/22/1940-02/23/1941
Philadelphia Flyers	1975-76	23	01/29/1976-03/18/1976

Mike Bossy.

▲ 1980-81 Mike Bossy matches Maurice Richard's magical 50-in-50 milestone of 1944-45, scoring his 50th goal in his 50th game against Quebec's Ron Grahame with just 1:29 remaining in the New York Islanders' 7-3 win on January 24. Bossy had been stuck at 48 goals, feeling the pressure after going goal-less throughout Games 48 and 49 and much of Game 50, until he got his 49th with 4:10 left in the third period and his 50th with few seconds to spare. "I had never been so frustrated in all my hockey career," said Bossy.

◂ 1980 Peter and Anton Stastny defect from Czechoslovakia to play in Quebec. In covert meetings during the European Cup in Innsbruck, Austria, Nordiques' GM Marcel Aubut meets and signs the Stastny brothers. Their escape, after the final game on August 24, stuns the hockey world and brings instant respectability to the struggling Nordiques, who reach the playoffs in their sophomore NHL season. The brothers finish first and third in team scoring, as Peter sets a rookie-record with 109 points and wins the Calder Trophy. The Stastnys' defection attracts other Czechoslovak players to North American play the next season.

Marian, Peter and Anton Stastny, 1982.

1980 **The Flames move north.** Atlanta becomes the first U.S.-based NHL franchise to move to Canada when majority owner Tom Cousins sells the franchise to Vancouver businessman Nelson Skalbania for $16 million, a record price at the time.

1980–81 Wayne Gretzky's shredding of the NHL record books begins in earnest with his dismantling of two major NHL scoring records: Phil Esposito's 152 points and Bobby Orr's 102 assists. Gretzky finishes the season with 109 assists and 164 points and sets a modern-era record with a 2.05 points-per-game average.

Wayne Gretzky versus the New York Islanders.

▴ 1980–81 **The Edmonton Oilers puck blitz—first edition.** Led by Wayne Gretzky's record-demolishing 92-goal and 212-point season, Edmonton tops the 400-goal plateau, pumping in 417 goals, the first 400-goal team in league annals. The Oilers' young guns set a mesmerizing pace. In an eight-day span in November, Edmonton wastes Vancouver 8–3, Detroit 8–4, Los Angeles 11–4, Chicago 8–1 and Winnipeg 10–2. Gretzky becomes the fastest 50-goal scorer ever. The Great One then scores once against Vancouver, four times against Los Angeles and notches his 50th with a five-goal night against Philadelphia in Game 39.

Ron MacLean and Don Cherry.

◂ 1980–81 Don Cherry joins CBC's *Hockey Night in Canada*. Following his days coaching Boston and Colorado, Cherry and sportscaster Dave Hodge (later Ron MacLean) co-host *Coach's Corner*, where Cherry becomes a hockey icon and household name for his bombastic tirades during their popular intermission segment.

"He had nice soft hands but he could also knock over a moose."

—NY Islanders GM Bill Torrey, on scoring stud and inspirational leader Bryan Trottier, who sets the all-time NHL playoff record for the longest point streak in one season (18 games in 1981) and in multiple seasons, with 43 points in 27 games

Longest Point Streak, Multiple Playoff Years

Player	Team	Start-End Date	Point Streak	G	A	P
Bryan Trottier	NY Islanders	05/10/1980-04/08/1982	27	17	26	43
Gordie Howe	Detroit	03/29/1960-04/11/1963	22	10	22	32
Al MacInnis	Calgary	04/13/1989-04/06/1990	19	9	20	29

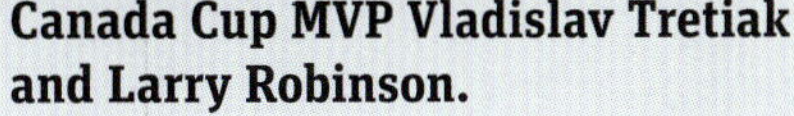

Canada Cup MVP Vladislav Tretiak and Larry Robinson.

Soviet players celebrate their 8–1 Canada Cup victory. A shocked Team Canada bench and Montreal Forum fans look on in disbelief.

▲ 1981 **The Canada Cup blowout.** The Soviets lose two earlier games against Canada, then in the one-game showdown final, they hammer the Canadians 8–1, suggesting to some that the Soviets misled Canada, under-playing their true game. Coach Viktor Tikhonov even hyped Canada's dominance, slyly saying mid-tournament, "The Canadians were superior to us when it came to guts and courage. My players reminded me of a boxer who comes into a ring with the notion in his mind that he's going to get beat up."

▲ 1981 **"That's a game I'm going to have to live with for the rest of my life."**

—Goalie Mike Liut, after giving up five goals in the third period of Canada's disastrous 8–1 loss to the Soviets at the 1981 Canada Cup

Wayne Gretzky and Billy Smith.

▼ 1983–84 The rookie NHL season of Tom Barrasso. A graduate of Acton-Boxboro high school in Massachusetts, Barrasso, 18, jumps directly to the Buffalo Sabres and plays with the poise of a seasoned pro, netting a 26-12-3 record, winning First All-Star Team honors, the Calder Trophy as top rookie and the Vezina Trophy as best netminder, with a 2.84 goals-against average.

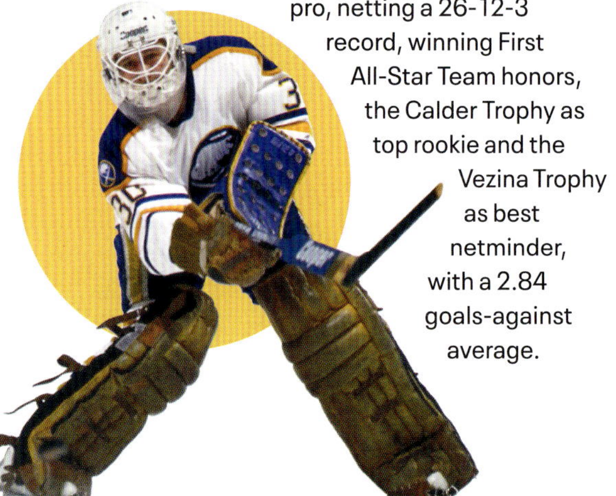

▲ 1982–83 New York's Billy Smith wins the Conn Smythe as playoff MVP as the Islanders crush high-flying Edmonton in a Stanley Cup Final sweep to claim their fourth-consecutive championship. Smith establishes series momentum in Game 1, blanking the Oilers 2–0, to become the first goalie in 199 games to shut out Edmonton. Smith allows just six goals and zeroes Gretzky and company in seven of 12 periods. Clearly, the Islanders were motivated. "The Oilers are so damn cocky," said Islander Bob Bourne. "The thing that really bugs me is they don't give us any respect ... Edmonton doesn't respect anyone."

RULE CHANGE

1983–84

A five-minute sudden-death overtime is adopted in regular-season games that are tied at the end of regulation time.

1983–84 **"I have four guys who don't understand a word I'm saying, 10 guys who do understand but don't do a thing I tell them to do, and another four who aren't good enough to do what I tell them to do."**

—Coach Tom McVie, on New Jersey's franchise-record 56 losses

1983–84 **The Good Friday Massacre.** No game better epitomized the rivalry between Montreal and Quebec than the 35-minute bench-clearing brawls on April 20. It was what one report called "a vendetta ... that became frightening in its bitterness and duration." Every dressed player was involved, either in the second or third period skirmishes. Bodies and equipment littered the Montreal Forum ice. In all, 10 players were ejected and a record 252 penalty minutes called, only 46 minutes off the all-time playoff record later set by Detroit and St. Louis in 1991.

Rod Langway.

▲ 1983–84

Paul Coffey loses the Norris Trophy. Neither extraordinary offensive totals nor a top-six finish in plus-minus persuade Norris voters, as Coffey's red-hot 40-86-126 and plus-52 finishes second to Rod Langway's 9-24-33 record and a plus-14. Coffey's 126 points is second only to Gretzky's 205 in the scoring race.

Dave Lumley, Wayne Gretzky and Lee Fogolin Jr.

▲ 1983–84 Edmonton settles scores with the New York Islanders, defeating the four-time Stanley Cup champions in a five-game Final. Mark Messier scores 26 points in 19 games and wins the Conn Smythe as playoff MVP.

1983–84 The Edmonton Oilers' puck blitz— second edition. Edmonton elevates firewagon hockey to another dimension, pumping in an all-time NHL-high 446 goals with three 50-goal scorers: Wayne Gretzky (87 goals), Glenn Anderson (54) and Jari Kurri (52). Gretzky wins the scoring title with 205 points and a 79-point margin over his closest rival, Oiler teammate Paul Coffey's 126 points. Gretzky becomes the first NHLer to hit the 100-goal mark, scoring 87 in the regular season and 13 in the playoffs. Even goalie Grant Fuhr sets scoring marks. Despite only playing 45 games, Fuhr nets 14 points, outscoring 30 NHL skaters with as many or more games that season.

Brad Park.

◄ 1984–85 Brad Park retires as among the most dominant rear-guards of his time, but without any major silver-ware, except, fittingly, a Bill Masterton Trophy for his dedication to hockey. Competing against hardware hogs Bobby Orr and Denis Potvin, Park never receives the most important prize of his position, a Norris Trophy, nor the ultimate team achievement in a Stanley Cup. During his 17-year career, he finishes second in Norris voting a record six times. In playoff futility, Park's teams qualified every postseason, losing with the Rangers (7 seasons), Boston (8) and Detroit (2). Park played 1,113 games and earned a high-scoring 213-683-896.

Mario Lemieux.

▲ 1984–85 No. 66: the savior of Pittsburgh. Refusing to go to the podium at the 1984 NHL draft without a "good contract" from Pittsburgh GM Eddie Johnston, first overall pick Mario Lemieux later signs a reported multi-year $1-million deal with the Penguins. To prove his worth, Lemieux scores his first goal on his first shot on his first shift in his first game, against Boston on October 11. Lemieux nets a 100-point season and the Calder Trophy as top rookie.

Dave "Tiger" Williams.

▲ 1984–85 Tiger Williams becomes the first NHLer penalized 3,000 minutes. A heavyweight with offensive skills, Williams played wrecking ball around the net, his best season coming in 1980–81 with Vancouver. As a Canuck he accrued a league-leading 343 penalty minutes and scored 35 goals and 62 points, the highest scoring totals ever by an NHL penalty leader.

◀ 1984–85 **Pelle Lindbergh wins the Vezina Trophy.** In his fourth NHL season, Lindbergh out-ballots Tom Barrasso for the top goalie award with a 40-17-7 record, propelling Philadelphia to first in regular-season standings with 113 points to Edmonton's 109, only to lose to the Oilers in the Stanley Cup Final. Lindbergh is the first non-North American netminder to win the Vezina. Months later, the 26-year-old Swede marvel dies in a high-speed, alcohol-related car crash in New Jersey.

Team Canada's John Tonelli (left) and Paul Coffey react to their overtime win against the Soviets.

▲ 1984 **The Canada Cup.** After being humiliated by the Americans at the 1980 Olympics, a retooled Soviet national team went on a championship streak, winning the Canada Cup in 1981, three-consecutive world titles in 1981, 1982 and 1983, gold at the 1984 Olympics and five-straight victories at this year's Canada Cup. Canada, meanwhile, was playing hot and cold through the tournament but secured a 2–2 tie after three periods in their one-and-done semifinal against the Soviets. Twelve minutes into overtime, Vladimir Kovin and Mikhail Varnakov got a two-on-one break, with only Paul Coffey between them and Canada's Pete Peeters in net and a potential second Soviet Canada Cup victory. Coffey read Kovin's saucer pass to Varnakov perfectly and intercepted the puck. He counterattacked into the Soviet zone. Some dogged work by John Tonelli got the puck back to Coffey, whose shot deflected off Mike Bossy to give Canada a 3–2 win. In the best-of-three final Canada beat Sweden two straight to reclaim world hockey dominance.

Grace Sutter, her sons and Stanley.

◀ 1984–85 The only NHL family to ice six brothers in one season, the Sutters combine to score 138 goals, the most by siblings in one season. Brent scores 42 goals, Brian 37, Darryl 20, Duane 17, Ron 16 and Rich 6. The six sons of Grace and Louis Sutter of Viking, Alberta, amass 316 points, a league record. The brothers followed the same path to the NHL, playing junior with the WHL Lethbridge Broncos. At least one Sutter played in the NHL for 24 seasons, from 1976 to 2001.

1985 “I feel very upset, not only for myself ... but for all the other little girls who won’t be able to play in higher levels of hockey.”

—Justine Blainey, the 12-year-old girl who tried to overturn the OHA ban on girls playing on boys’ teams, after making the roster of the Toronto Olympics, a boys’ team in the Metro Toronto Hockey League. Blainey’s case went to the Supreme Court of Ontario, whose September 1985 landmark decision upheld the ban, ruling that girls can’t play on boys’ sports teams.

Paul Coffey against Brian Hayward.

◄▼ **1985–86** **Paul Coffey breaks Bobby Orr’s goal record.** Coffey’s epic season sets several offensive numbers for defensemen. He beats Orr’s “unbreakable” 46 goals in 1974–75 with 48 goals, nets an all-time NHL record 28-game point streak (of 55 points) and ties Tom Bladon’s 1977–78 mark for eight points in a game. Coffey falls one point shy of Orr’s all-time mark of 139 points (1970–71), held pointless in Edmonton’s final game with 138 points.

The NHL’s Longest Point Streaks by Defensemen

Player	Team	Season	Start-End Dates	GP	G	A	P
Paul Coffey	Edmonton	1985-86	11/27/1985-01/25/1986	28	16	39	55
Ray Bourque	Boston	1987-88	01/16/1988-03/05/1988	19	6	21	27
Bobby Orr	Boston	1970-71	12/13/1970-01/24/1971	18	9	26	35
Brian Leetch	NY Rangers	1991-92	11/23/1991-12/31/1991	17	5	24	29
Ray Bourque	Boston	1984-85	10/27/1984-12/03/1984	17	4	24	28

1986 “I was talking to my goalposts.”

—Patrick Roy, on being asked by New York reporters (after winning a May 5 playoff game) why he stared at his net after the national anthem. Much later, when his English improved, Roy said he simply creates a vision of the nets getting smaller.

1985–86 Wayne Gretzky continues to break his own assists and points marks with 52-163-215 totals. He is the NHL’s only 200-point scorer, this being his fourth time in five seasons.

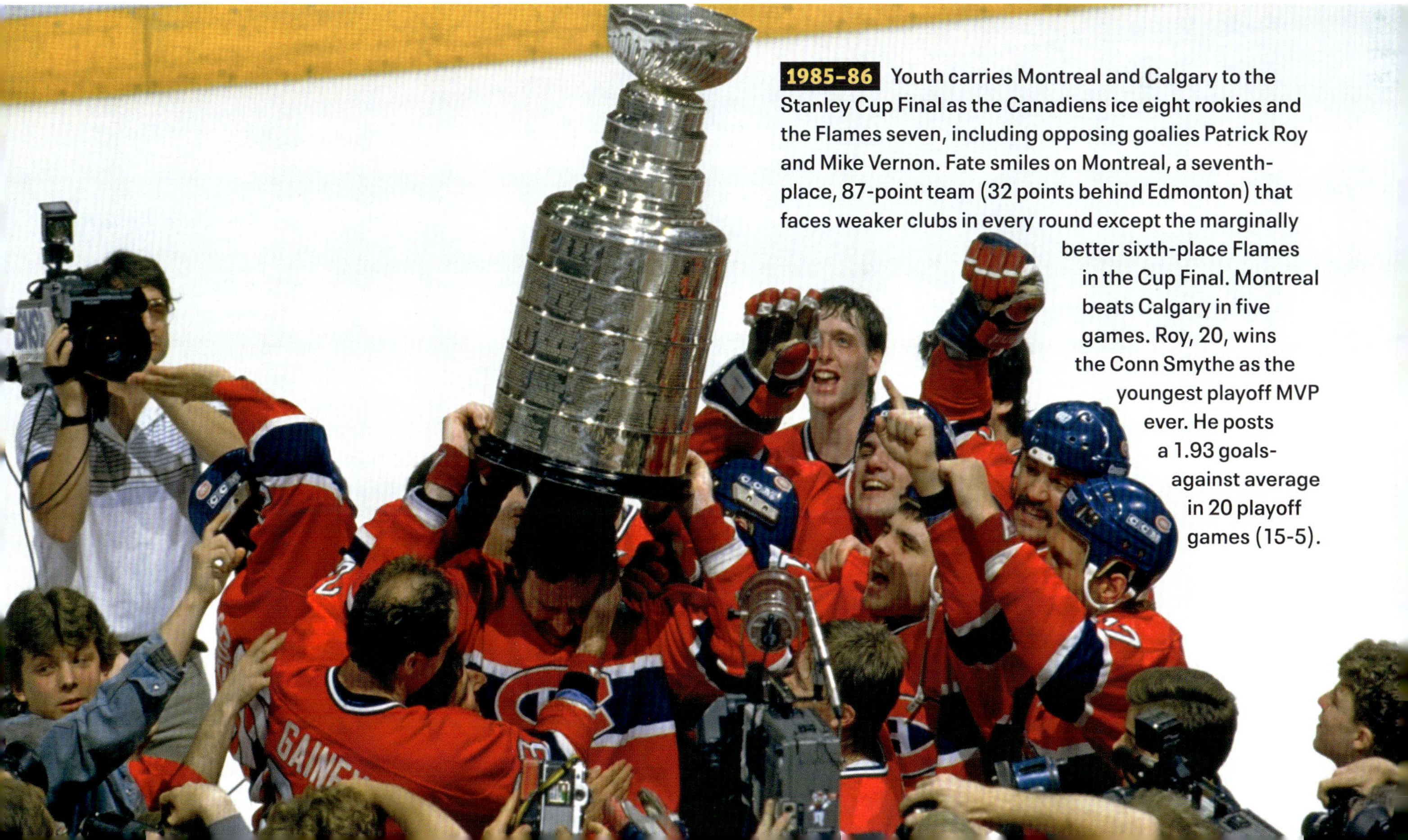

1985–86 Youth carries Montreal and Calgary to the Stanley Cup Final as the Canadiens ice eight rookies and the Flames seven, including opposing goalies Patrick Roy and Mike Vernon. Fate smiles on Montreal, a seventh-place, 87-point team (32 points behind Edmonton) that faces weaker clubs in every round except the marginally better sixth-place Flames in the Cup Final. Montreal beats Calgary in five games. Roy, 20, wins the Conn Smythe as the youngest playoff MVP ever. He posts a 1.93 goals-against average in 20 playoff games (15-5).

1986 "I don't know if I will ever live this down, but I will have to keep on living."

—Edmonton rookie Steve Smith scores an own goal, banking a cross-ice pass off the leg of goalie Grant Fuhr and into his own net, handing Calgary a 3-2 lead in Game 7 of their 1986 Stanley Cup Divisional Final. The Flames hold the lead and spoil the Oilers' chances of a third-straight Stanley Cup. Following Edmonton's Cup victory in 1987, who does Wayne Gretzky choose for the first ceremonial skate with the Stanley Cup? Gretzky hands the silverware to Smith.

1986-87 Doug Jarvis breaks Garry Unger's NHL ironman streak of 914 games on December 26. Jarvis played 12-plus seasons without missing a game.

4 hockey players die in crash of team bus

1986 Tragedy strikes hockey when a bus carrying the Swift Current Broncos loses control on black ice and flips over while traveling to Regina. Scott Kruger, Trent Kresse, Chris Mantyka and Brent Ruff die in the accident. Survivors include Joe Sakic and Sheldon Kennedy. The Broncos somehow finish the season and later win the Memorial Cup in 1989.

Ron Hextall against Esa Tikkanen.

▲ 1986-87 The rookie season of Ron Hextall. Among the first grandsons of an NHLer to play in the league, Hextall establishes his own reputation as a fearless battler, accruing a 37-21-6 record backstopping the overachieving Flyers, winning the Vezina Trophy and earning a goalie record of 104 penalty minutes. Coached by Mike Keenan, Philadelphia plays 26 of a maximum 28 playoff games, gutting it out to a Stanley Cup Game 7 before losing 3-1 to Wayne Gretzky's Oilers. Of little consolation, Hextall takes home the Conn Smythe Trophy as playoff MVP.

◄ 1986-87 The last NHL bench-clearing brawls. Only months apart, clashes on February 26 and May 14 change hockey history and eliminate bench-clearing brawls once and for all, due to stiffer suspensions and heavier fines. In February's free-for-all, the contagion spreads on the ice after Quebec's Randy Moller squares off against Boston's Nevin Markwart. The Bruins' Bob Sweeney leads the attack off the bench, bringing both teams into the skirmish. Officials whistle 10 game misconducts, 11 fighting majors and six minor penalties.

The pregame playoff fight between Montreal and Philadelphia in May deals the death blow to full-scale brawling. It erupts following the warm-up skate when two Montreal players, still on the ice, shoot the puck into the Flyers' empty net. Within seconds, players, always superstitious of such rituals, pour out of their dressing rooms, some half-dressed and with bare feet. The brawl lasts 11 minutes. League fines total $24,000. That summer Rule 70.1 is introduced, penalizing players who leave the bench to fight. "I played two more years after that game," Flyer Ed Hospodar said. "It just wasn't done any more."

1987 Montreal's Chris Chelios battles Philadelphia's Mike Stothers during a playoff brawl.

▲ 1987 **The Piestany punch-up.** Considered the gravest melee in international hockey, Canada and the Soviet Union square off on the final day of the World Junior Championship in Piestany, Czechoslovakia. The Soviets aren't going to medal. Canada needs a five-goal differential to win the title. Any fewer goals would mean a silver to Finland's gold. With Canada ahead 4–2 in the second period, a fierce 20-minute, bench-clearing brawl erupts, sparked, some believe, by Soviet forward Pavel Kostichkin's slash on Canada's Theoren Fleury. Unable to control the bedlam, the officials leave the ice and order the arena lights darkened. Both teams are disqualified. Finland gets its first gold medal at the tournament.

▸ 1987–88 **The first shoot-and-score NHL goalie.** In his sophomore season, Ron Hextall cements his status as Philadelphia's big mobile netminder with pinpoint passing skills. Among the first goalies to use a curved stick, he shoots as hard as some forwards. On December 8, with Boston down 4–2 and an empty net late in the contest, Hextall fires the puck rink-length and scores the league's first shoot-and-score goal.

Ron Hextall.

▸ 1986–87 **The Cam Neely trade.** On paper, it looked a toss-up. Neely was underachieving in Vancouver with one 20-plus goal year and dreadful plus-minus numbers. Veteran center Barry Pederson's production had slowed following seasons of 40-plus goals and 100-plus points in Boston. The Canucks thought so much of Pederson they threw in a first-round pick (Glen Wesley). The club culture switch was huge for Neely. He notched three 50-goal seasons and never had another minus rating again. Pederson looked ordinary and played just three-plus seasons with Vancouver. Neely entered the Hockey Hall of Fame in 2005 and became Bruins president in 2010.

Cam Neely.

The Gretzky-to-Lemieux Canada Cup goal.

▲ 1987 **The Canada Cup.** The fourth Canada Cup showcases Canada and the Soviet Union's strongest rosters in a three-game final. The two teams couldn't have been more evenly matched or the games more tightly contested, as all three contests had identical 6–5 scores, with the teams splitting two overtime decisions. Late in Game 3's epic finale, with the score at 5–5, Canada launches an electrifying three-on-one break with only Soviet defender Igor Kravchuk back. Using Larry Murphy as a decoy on right wing, Wayne Gretzky feeds the puck back to a trailing Mario Lemieux, who sails into the zone and buries a wrister in the top corner behind Sergei Mylnikov with 1:26 remaining, sending fans into pandemonium at Hamilton's Copps Coliseum. Lemieux, 21 years old, leads all scorers with 11 goals, this tournament marking a turning point in his hall-of-fame career.

▲ 1987–88 **The Brett Hull trade.** Despite Hull's 26-24-50 numbers in 52 games, Calgary trades Hull and Steve Bozek on March 7 for St. Louis' Rob Ramage and Rick Wamsley. Defensive liabilities and poor conditioning dog Hull, but with the Blues he quickly morphs into a sniping weapon, especially following Adam Oates' arrival in 1989–90. Paired with Oates for two-plus seasons, Hull knocks off league-leading 72-, 86- and 70-goal years, a 228-goal count that only rivals Wayne Gretzky's three best years of 250 goals. Calgary does win the 1989 Stanley Cup, but Wamsley plays backup to Mike Vernon, and Ramage is traded following those playoffs. Meanwhile, Hull has 10 seasons in St. Louis, collecting five 50-plus goal years and multiple individual awards. He wins Stanley Cups in his first seasons with Dallas (1999) and Detroit (2002).

◂ 1988–89 In his coming-of-age season, Mario Lemieux handily wins his second NHL scoring race, with a formidable 199 points, outpointing Wayne Gretzky by 31 points. Lemieux's most inspired effort comes on December 31, when he scores goals in five different ways—at even-strength, on the power play, short-handed, on a penalty shot and into an empty net in Pittsburgh's 8–6 win against New Jersey. Of the Penguins' 347 goals, Lemieux has a hand in 57 percent of them, on his 85 goals and 199 points.

Mario Lemieux against David Volek.

1988–89
In a crease crash with St. Louis rookie Steve Tuttle, Clint Malarchuk's throat is sliced open by Tuttle's skate blade. Malarchuk is rushed to hospital, where he receives some 300 stitches to close the six-inch laceration. He was back in the Sabres' net 11 days later.

▸ **1989** **"This is the most peaceful feeling in hockey. I wish I could describe it to people outside. I think you appreciate it a lot more after you've been trying to win it for 16 years, like I have."**
—Lanny McDonald, on finally winning the Stanley Cup

▴▾ **1988–89** **Al MacInnis wins the Conn Smythe Trophy.** Among a select few defensemen to ever outscore every other playoff scorer in one season, MacInnis collects a postseason-high 31 points on seven goals and 24 assists. Twenty-six points come from MacInnis's 17-game consecutive point-scoring streak, the second-longest in postseason play and the longest ever by a defenseman.

Longest Point Streaks, One Playoff Season

Player	Team	Year	Start-End Date	Point Streak	G	A	P
Bryan Trottier	NY Islanders	1980-81	04/08/1981-05/21/1981	18	11	18	29
Al MacInnis	Calgary	1988-89	04/13/1989-05/25/1989	17	7	19	26
Wayne Gretzky	Edmonton	1987-88	04/09/1988-05/26/1988	16	12	27	39
Pavel Bure	Vancouver	1993-94	04/22/1994-05/31/1994	16	13	10	23

▴ **1988** **The Wayne Gretzky trade.** Not just a player move, Gretzky's signing with Bruce McNall's Los Angeles Kings altered North American play. Saying goodbye to Canada was hard for Gretzky, but harder on Canada. If a Gretzky trade was possible, so too seemed anything else. Within a decade, NHL franchises opened in San Jose, Tampa Bay, Miami, Anaheim, Dallas, Phoenix, Carolina, Nashville and Atlanta. NHL commissioner Gary Bettman orchestrated that shift to southern markets, but it was Gretzky's arrival in California that foretold of a new NHL order, one dominated by powerhouse clubs across America. The August 9 deal was Gretzky, Marty McSorley and Mike Krushelnyski for Jimmy Carson, Martin Gelinas, three first-round draft picks and $15 million.

Vladislav Tretiak.

▲ 1989 The greatest goalie never to play in the NHL. Despite serving his country faithfully while backstopping his national team to a record 10 World Championship gold medals, plus three Olympic golds and one silver and one Canada Cup victory, Soviet Union authorities block Vladislav Tretiak's 1984 request to play in the NHL. The most successful netminder in international hockey, Tretiak, only 32, retires the next year. Five years later, Trekiak becomes the first non-NHL European star elected to the Hockey Hall of Fame, ironically coinciding with the initial breakup of the Soviet Union, which would ease restrictions on fellow Soviets to play NHL hockey.

Mats Sundin, Canada Cup, 1991.

▲ 1989 The first European first overall NHL draft pick. The lowly Quebec Nordiques select Swede sniper Mats Sundin, an 18-year-old junior with Nacka HK, as its top draft choice. Several European notables that year include Bobby Holik (10th), Olaf Kolzig (19th), Nicklas Lidstrom (53rd), Sergei Fedorov (74th) and Pavel Bure (113th).

◂ 1989–90 **Wayne Gretzky passes Gordie Howe.** Howe's once unassailable 1,850 career points are broken by Gretzky on October 15, fittingly in Edmonton, where the Great One rose to fame and celebrity. A Los Angeles King, Gretzky made a night of it for the Edmonton crowd, first to tie Howe's mark with a first-period assist for his 1,850th point, then, with 53 seconds left, sets the record with his 1,851st point by beating Bill Ranford with a backhand shot that sends the 4–4 game into overtime. An ovation of five minutes follows. The game is halted as Howe takes part in ceremonies honoring the NHL's new point king. Not done, Gretzky caps the festivities by scoring the 5–4 OT winner.

Wayne Gretzky is congratulated by Gordie Howe, Wayne's wife Janet and father Walter.

The Europeans

The European invasion of North American pro ranks began with the WHA Winnipeg Jets signing top-ranked Swedes and Finns in the 1970s and gained momentum after early player defections from Soviet-satellite countries like Czechoslovakia during the 1980s.

Nothing, however, signaled the imminent rush of elite talent into NHL play like the open defiance of Soviet star Igor Larionov. One third of the famed KLM Line, Larionov, in an October 1988 letter of protest in the magazine *Ogonyok*, condemned the authoritarian rule of coach Viktor Tikhonov and his regimented world of interminable practices and conditioning workouts of 11 months each year, all while confined to training-camp quarters with little time off, even for married players.

As a result, Larionov was cut from the team. Captain Viacheslav Fetisov joined him in protest, a major sports story that reflected the changing state of affairs in current Russian society on the eve of *glasnost*, the new Soviet political policy of openness.

If Larionov cracked open the door to freedom, it was blown off its hinges by the May 1989 defection of 20-year-old Alexander Mogilny, the future of Soviet hockey and the youngest Soviet player ever to medal Olympic gold (1988).

"I couldn't see myself growing as a person and as a hockey player in Russia at that time. I didn't see any different way to do it," said Mogilny, who was found guilty of desertion as a conscripted army officer on the Central Red Army team and branded a traitor.

Sergei Fedorov.

With the Big Red Machine in chaos, the Soviet Ice Hockey Federation consented to permit veterans to play in North America. Larionov, 28, and Vladimir Krutov, 29, inked deals with Vancouver. Viacheslav Fetisov, 31, and Sergei Starikov, 30, signed with New Jersey. Sergei Makarov, 31, jumped to Calgary.

In July 1990, the poster boy of a new NHL generation, Sergei Fedorov, 20, signed with Detroit, adding to the great influx of young talent from Eastern Europe that would globalize the game, while stocking new NHL markets and their feeder leagues with international competitors at every position.

Peter Stastny.

▲ 1980s **The Peter Stastny decade.** Following his arrival in 1980, the Czech-born Stastny notches six consecutive 100-point seasons for the Quebec Nordiques to become the first European-trained player to score 1,000 NHL points. He finishes second only to Wayne Gretzky with the highest point total during the 1980s.

Susana Yuen is shouldered by teammates after Canada defeats USA.

▲ 1990 **The first Women's World Championship.** Despite a hockey history dating to the 1890s, the first real effort at women's world play only comes in 1987 in Toronto. University hockey and national competitions aside, this event inspires other major tournaments in Europe and Asia, including the first IIHF-sanctioned championship in Ottawa in 1990. Eight teams participate in the round-robin and medal rounds. In some games, Canada wears pink uniforms. The Canadians beat USA 5–2 for the first-ever gold medal awarded by the IIHF in women's hockey.

1990 NHL salary disclosure ends pay secrecy and becomes a mechanism for wage escalation, while shaping contract negotiations and player compensation. The first player salary survey is released in February. Studies find that underpaid players begin scoring more goals, since goal and point totals are more highly valued and compensated, but in some cases become less defense-oriented, allowing their teams to be scored upon more often than their additional goal totals.

RULE CHANGE

1990–91 All ice markings, including the goal lines, blue lines and defensive zone face-off circles, are moved 1 foot (30 cm) out from the end boards, creating 11 feet (3.3 m) of room behind the nets and shrinking the neutral zone from 60 to 58 feet (18.3 to 17.7 m).

Mario Lemieux against Jon Casey, 1991.

▲ 1990–91 The Stanley Cup comes to Pittsburgh. Putting up Gretzky-like numbers, Mario Lemieux fires a playoff-high 93 shots, scores 16 goals and assists on 28 others for a 44-point postseason, just three shy of the Great One's all-time record of 47 points. His most important goal happens in Game 2 of the Cup Final against Minnesota. Leading 2–1, Lemieux wheels through center ice, niftily splits Minnesota defensemen Neil Wilkinson and Shawn Chambers, then dekes goalie Jon Casey and flicks a backhander into the twine as he falls to the ice. A healthy Lemieux is unstoppable. It's the play that defines the series.

1991 The Mats Sundin goal that ends Soviet-era hockey. The youngest player on the ice, Sundin, 20, begins his celebrated end-to-end rush near his own net in the last 11 minutes of play, the tension pinning with the score tied 1–1 and the gold medal at stake at the World Championship final between the Soviet Union and Sweden. Sundin maneuvers through center ice and crosses the blue line, puts a deke on arguably international hockey's best defenseman, Viacheslav Fetisov, and fires a low shot beyond goalie Andrei Trefilov. Sweden wins gold. Sundin becomes a national hero. With the fall of the Soviet Union, it's the last game ever played by the Soviet national club. It claims an uncharacteristic bronze medal. The next year the team is known as Russia.

Ron Francis against Bob Sweeney.

▲ 1990–91 **The Ron Francis trade.** Mario Lemieux's Penguins were already Stanley Cup contenders with Jaromir Jagr, Paul Coffey and Tom Barrasso, but heisting Hartford captain Ron Francis, Ulf Samuelsson and Grant Jennings from the Whalers in exchange for John Cullen, Jeff Parker and Zarley Zalapski on March 4 clinched back-to-back Cup championships, 1991 and 1992. Francis was the key trade member, bringing his nothing-fancy clutch playmaking and dogged puck pursuit to Pittsburgh for another seven seasons.

Scott Stevens.

▲ 1990–91 **High stakes free agency.** St. Louis GM Ron Caron signs Washington restricted free-agent Scott Stevens to five years and $5.1 million. The NHL's new CBA forces the Blues to yield five first-round draft picks to the Capitals as compensation. Stevens plays only one season in St. Louis before he's awarded as compensation to New Jersey after the Blues sign another free agent, Brendan Shanahan.

◂ 1990–91 Ed Belfour wins the Calder Trophy. Undrafted and ever adept at defying his critics, Belfour produces one of the greatest rookie seasons of all-time, racking up a 43-19-7 record in Chicago and dominating in just about every category — games, wins, minutes played, goals-against average, saves and save percentage — to claim the Calder and Vezina Trophies as top rookie and top goalie, the Jennings Trophy for best GAA and a First Team All-Star berth.

Ed Belfour.

▲ **1991–92** **The return of Scotty Bowman.** Following four years of retirement as hockey's winningest coach, Bowman replaces the late Bob Johnson as Pittsburgh's new bench boss. In a season dedicated to Johnson, Pittsburgh repeats as Stanley Cup champions under Bowman, his first of another four Cups. Bowman finally retires in 2002, a five-team NHL coach with a record haul of nine NHL championships.

RULE CHANGE

1991–92
The NHL introduces video replay to help officials rule in goal / no goal situations. The size of the goal crease is increased and changed to a semi-circular configuration. Major and game misconduct penalties for checking from behind into boards are introduced.

San Jose's Pat Falloon.

1991–92
NHLPA executive director Alan Eagleson loses the support of the players and steps down on December 31, to be replaced by Bob Goodenow.

NHL EXPANSION

◂ **1991–92**
The San Jose Sharks begin play, following a 1990–91 agreement whereby the Gund Brothers sell the Minnesota North Stars in exchange for a new franchise in San Jose. The North Stars protect 14 players and two goalies; the Sharks select four North Stars, one goalie and minor-leaguers.

▸ **1991**
The passing of Bob Johnson. Instrumental at the college and NHL levels in American hockey, Johnson is diagnosed with a brain tumor days before the Canada Cup. He is immediately admitted to hospital for surgery and, despite his state of health, remains its coach in absentia, forwarding messages of encouragement and game strategies to U.S. assistant coach Tim Taylor. "We want to win this thing for Bob, for ourselves and for all of America," said Joe Mullen mid-tournament. With one of its finest two-way lineups, Canada beats USA 4–1 and 4–2 in the final cup round, but not without each American player fully recognizing what "Badger Bob" meant to their individual development both as an inspirational light and, now, as fallen hero.

Eric Lindros.

▲ 1991–92 Eric Lindros stands his ground after declaring he won't join Quebec if the organization drafts him with its first overall pick of 1991. The Nordiques draft Lindros anyway and wind up trading him a year later to two teams, Philadelphia and the Rangers. On June 30, the NHL rules that Lindros is a Flyer. Quebec acquires six players, two first-round picks and $15 million.

Teemu Selanne.

▲ 1992–93 Teemu Selanne's rookie year of 76 goals and 132 points obliterates the rookie marks of Mike Bossy (53 goals) and Peter Stastny (109 points). His other rookie record, 387 shots on net, has since been topped by Alexander Ovechkin's 425 shots in 2005–06. However, Ovechkin didn't come close in scoring totals. To give perspective to Selanne's 76-56-132 count, in Ovechkin's amazing first season, he numbers 52 goals and 106 points.

1991–92 **The NHL's players walkout.** Despite several sticking points in negotiations, players mostly get what they want from the 10-day strike. With the Stanley Cup playoffs imminent, the league makes concessions on free agency and card-licensing earnings. It agrees to a $100,000 minimum salary (a 300 percent increase) and no salary cap. A settlement is reached on a two-year contract on April 10 to save the postseason. The walkout is the first of three more protracted labor disputes, each locking out the players during the next two decades.

Mario Lemieux fans, 1991.

▲▼ 1992–93 **The Mario Lemieux comeback.** Only hours after undergoing radiation treatment for Hodgkin's disease, Lemieux returns to action, scoring a goal and an assist on March 2 against Philadelphia. During his 23-game absence, the defending Stanley Cup–champion Penguins struggle through a 11-10-2 run. Lemieux himself lags Buffalo's Pat LaFontaine by 12 points in the scoring race with 20 games left in the schedule. In that time Lemieux sets a torrid pace, racking up 56 points, while trashing LaFontaine's lead to win the title with 160 points, 12 more than the Sabres center. The Penguins are equally impressive, winning an all-time record 17 straight games to finish first overall with 56 wins and 119 points. Half of Pittsburgh's losses occur in the 24 games that Super Mario misses.

Longest Winning Streak, One Season

Team	Season	Games	Start-End Date
Pittsburgh	1992-93	17	03/09/1993-04/10/1993
Columbus	2016-17	16	11/29/2016-01/03/2017
Edmonton	2023-24	16	12/21/2023-01/27/2024
NY Islanders	1981-82	15	01/21/1982-02/20/1982
Pittsburgh	2012-13	15	03/02/2013-03/30/2013

1993 "Nobody remembers who was picked second."

—Alexandre Daigle, after being chosen first overall in 1993 ahead of Chris Pronger (second), Chris Gratton (third) and Paul Kariya (fourth)

RULE CHANGE

1992–93 No substitutions are allowed in the event of coincidental minor penalties called when both teams are at full strength. A minor penalty is given for attempting to draw a penalty ("diving"). Major and game misconduct penalties are instituted for checking a player from behind into the goal frame.

▲ 1992–93 The Patrick Roy spectacle. Eleven of the 20 games Montreal plays during 1993's Stanley Cup playoffs are decided in overtime. The Canadiens win an astonishing 10 in large part due to playoff MVP Roy, who executes some of the best clutch hockey ever. Montreal records 12 one-goal wins, Roy earning a 16-4 record and 2.13 goals-against average. Three OT victories come when needed most, during the five-game Cup Final against Wayne Gretzky's Los Angeles Kings.

Manon Rhéaume.

▲ 1992 The NHL's first woman goalie. After Manon Rhéaume won gold tending Canada's nets at the 1992 IIHF Women's World Championship, she famously signs with GM Phil Esposito's Tampa Bay Lightning to publicize his new franchise in Florida. Rhéaume sees action for one period in a preseason game against St. Louis on September 23. Her short stint between the pipes creates plenty of media attention, both for the Lightning and Rhéaume, who appears on talk shows like *Late Night with David Letterman*. Given the era, *Playboy* offers her $75,000 to pose *au naturel*. She declines, stating, "If *Playboy* offered me a million dollars, I would still refuse."

Gary Bettman.

◄ 1992–93 Gary Bettman, former vice president of the NBA, is named the NHL's first commissioner on December 11. He takes office on February 1, replacing president Gil Stein, who was running the league since John Ziegler resigned in June 1992. Bettman declares, "I believe the opportunities that face this league are virtually limitless."

Cooper
96
SUNDIN
13
FINLAND
Škoda
БРУНЬКИ
PECA
HASEK
39

A World Game

This era in hockey is bookended by the NHL player lockouts of 1994-95 and 2004-05, which would reshape not only the sport's business, but also its game culture and its competitive play. The 10-year period introduced the hockey world to the league's first commissioner, Gary Bettman, who was instrumental in effecting those changes, which still govern hockey today.

For the first time North American play witnessed the mass arrival of European-trained scoring leaders and defenders, including Russians, who continued to be accessible following the easing of emigration restrictions under *glasnost*, the Soviet reform policy of greater freedoms.

Jaromir Jagr. Pavel Bure. Peter Forsberg. Dominik Hasek. Teemu Selanne. Sergei Fedorov. Markus Naslund. Igor Larionov. Mats Sundin. Nicklas Lidstrom. Alexander Mogilny. Ilya Kovalchuk. Each became a household name among fans on our shores.

We said goodbye to iconic figures we both lionized and despised. The likes of everyone from Wayne Gretzky to disgraced NHLPA boss Alan Eagleson. Mario Lemieux retired for three years before his return in 2000-01 as the first player ever to own his NHL team.

After Tampa Bay and Ottawa came into the league in 1992-93, expansion and team transfers opened up several southern markets under Bettman, in Miami, Anaheim, Dallas, Phoenix, Carolina, Nashville and Atlanta, followed by new northern clubs in Columbus and Minnesota in 2000-01. The NHL's Sun Belt strategy became very real when Tampa Bay hoisted the Stanley Cup in 2004, once an almost inconceivable notion — an NHL championship in Florida.

During this wave, Canada bore a net loss, adding an Ottawa franchise but losing Quebec and Winnipeg in their moves to Colorado and Phoenix. In an NHL first for Canadian fans, not a single local team won the Stanley Cup during this era. The country was not just losing franchises and Cup championships, it was losing its national pastime, the bedrock of the Canadian cold-weather experience.

Expansion, shored up by the welcomed flood of elite European talent, resulted in billion-dollar television contracts, subsequent streaming deals and, by extension, a wider footprint in America, and it increased USA Hockey's registration totals and Division 1 college programs, which would invite generations of new American players into the game.

Igor Larionov.

OPPOSITE
Clockwise, from top left: Pavel Bure, Mats Sundin, Nicklas Lidstrom, Dominik Hasek, Peter Forsberg and Teemu Selanne.

Erin Whitten, 1997.

▲ **1993–94** Erin Whitten becomes the first female goalie to record a victory in a professional game. On October 30, Whitten backstops the East Coast Hockey League's Toledo Storm to a 6–5 win over the Dayton Bombers. The native of Glens Falls, New York, played on boys' teams in high school before graduating to university hockey in New Hampshire and then onto the U.S. national women's team. She competed in four Women's World Championships.

Sergei Fedorov, Hart Trophy, 1994.

◂ **1993–94**

The first Russian NHL MVP. In his fourth season, Sergei Fedorov earns two Most Valuable Player awards, the Hart Trophy and the Lester B. Pearson Award, as voted by the players themselves. By now, Fedorov is the centerpiece of Detroit's 200-foot game, the best two-way player in hockey and its superstar of Stanley Cups in 1997, 1998 and 2002. As coach Scotty Bowman said, "Sergei could do it all."

RULE CHANGE

1993–94

High sticking is redefined to allow goals scored with a high stick below the height of the crossbar of the goal frame.

▸ **1993–94** The IHL Atlanta Knights hire John Paris Jr., the first Black coach in pro hockey. In a career that began modestly playing junior (he was scouted by Scotty Bowman) in Quebec during the 1960s, Paris would become a hockey trailblazer. Born in Windsor, Nova Scotia, Paris coached in the minor leagues during the 1970s. In 1987, he guided the Riverains du Richelieu to an Air Canada Cup national championship as the first Black coach in Midget AAA and was named coach of the year. Paris parlayed that success into becoming the first Black NHL scout for the St. Louis Blues and the first Black coach and GM in the Quebec Major Junior Hockey League, with Trois-Rivières and Granby. In 1993–94, Paris moved to Atlanta and led the Knights to the Turner Cup title. Throughout the years he faced racism on and off the ice. While playing alongside Guy Lafleur on the Junior A Quebec Aces during the 1960s, he earned the nickname, "Chocolate Rocket," which inspired Paris' book, *They Called Me Chocolate Rocket*.

John Paris Jr., Quebec Junior Aces, 1960s.

Mark Messier.

▲ **1993–94** The Rangers end a 54-year Stanley Cup drought at MSG by defeating Vancouver in an emotional seven-game Cup Final. Pavel Bure scores 16 times for the Canucks during postseason play. New York D-man Brian Leetch becomes the first U.S.-born Conn Smythe winner, with a playoff-high 34 points. The big moment, however, belongs to the "**Mess**iah," as one fan signboard read during the Conference Finals against New Jersey, after Mark Messier guarantees, "We're going to go in and win Game 6." That night Messier scores a natural hat trick in the third period to keep New York alive. In the Cup Final against Vancouver, he leads again in dramatic fashion, scoring the winner in Game 7. Messier is the first and only player to captain two different Cup champions, the Oilers in 1990 and the Rangers in 1994.

Los Angeles Kings fans in Vancouver.

Wayne Gretzky scores No. 802 into an open net.

▲ 1993–94 Wayne Gretzky overtakes Gordie Howe as the NHL's greatest goal scorer, potting his career 802nd against Vancouver's Kirk McLean on March 23. Gretzky, trailing on the play, takes a pass from Marty McSorley and scores on a poorly positioned McLean. The Great One had already surpassed Howe's all-time career marks as league leader in assists and points. His 130 points with Los Angeles earn him a 10th and last Art Ross Trophy—and a minus-25, the worst plus-minus by an NHL points leader ever. For the first time in his career Gretzky misses the playoffs.

The postage stamp depiction of Al Behrman's overhead shot of Peter Forsberg's 1994 Olympic winner against Corey Hirsch. The Canadian goalie refused to allow his likeness on a Swedish stamp, a decision he later regretted. The upshot? Sweden's national hero scores on an unidentified goalie who wears a blue sweater, not Canadian red, and No. 11, instead of Hirsch's No. 1.

▲ 1994 **Sweden's first Olympic triumph.** Following decades of early-round exits and bronze and silver medal finishes, Sweden's moment of Olympic glory comes down to a deadlocked 2–2 game against Canada. Sixty minutes have been played. Ten minutes of overtime settle nothing. Two shooters on each side score on the first four of six shots in the shootout. Next up are Peter Forsberg and Paul Kariya to claim gold. Forsberg, 20, sails in on Canadian goalie Corey Hirsch, shifts left, pulls Hirsch with him and slips the puck from his forehand to his backhand and with one glove on his stick pushes the puck under the outstretched arm of Hirsch and into the yawning net. Tommy Salo stops Kariya at the other end. Sweden wins its inaugural Olympic gold.

Mike Modano.

▲ 1993–94 The North Stars move from hockey-wild Minnesota to become the Dallas Stars. Scoring ace Mike Modano, not known for his defensive play, is soon transformed by coach Bob Gainey into a more complete player. In short order his scoring prowess warms Texans to the northern ice-game. Modano becomes the poster boy of hockey in the American Southwest, where, with few rinks and no high school programs, he helps establish the game and produces a Stanley Cup in 1999 for the Lone Star State.

Hakan Loob.

▲ 1993–94 The Triple Gold Club is established by founding members Tomas Jonsson, Mats Naslund and Hakan Loob in February 1994 when Sweden wins Olympic gold in Lillehammer, Norway. All three Swedes also claim a World Championship and a Stanley Cup to complete their trifecta of hockey titles.

Mats Sundin.

▲ 1994 **The Mats Sundin trade.** Maple Leaf fans are livid over Wendel Clark's exit from Toronto to Quebec for Swedish sensation Mats Sundin in an eight-player swap in June. The risks are high. Clark, their captain, is coming off his best season. Sundin has mesmerizing puck skills and huge potential as a game breaker. In Toronto, Sundin becomes the franchise face for the next 13 seasons. Clark stays one year in Quebec, then is traded before the Nordiques move to Colorado as the Stanley Cup-winning Avalanche in 1995–96.

◂ 1994–95
Jaromir Jagr claims the Art Ross Trophy. Jagr equals Eric Lindros' league-high 70 points in 1994–95's lockout-shortened 48-game season, but Jagr wins the NHL scoring title with 32 goals, compared to Lindros' 29. He's the first European-trained player, the first non-Canadian and the first champion to wear a face shield. No fluke, Jagr collects another four consecutive crowns in 82-game seasons beginning in 1997–98.

Luc Robitaille.

▸ 1994 **Canada strikes World Championship gold.** After 33 years in exile, Canada wins in Milan, Italy, with a bench of NHLers eliminated from Stanley Cup play that include Brendan Shanahan, Joe Sakic and Rob Blake. After subduing every opponent in the round-robin and defeating the Czechs and Swedes in the playoffs, Canada faces Finland for gold. They go into overtime. The shootout is tied 1–1. Each team scores twice before Luc Robitaille dekes out Finn goalie Jarmo Myllys (and Mika Nieminen misses against Bill Ranford), ending a 33-year drought that dates to the Trail Smoke Eaters' historic victory in 1961.

Gary Bettman

Gary Bettman.

At 32-plus years on the job, NHL Commissioner Gary Bettman has survived running the world's top hockey circuit longer than any former league boss. On occasion his tenure has been seriously questioned, especially during Bettman's season-long player lockout of 2004–05.

When he took office in 1993, the NHL game was a stagnant enterprise. As one observer noted, it was "already clinging to relevancy" with a clutch-and-grab, hook-and-hold on-ice product that neutralized game flow through ineffectual rules and inadequate officiating. Upstairs, owners couldn't control payrolls with players reportedly making three-quarters of every dollar grossed. Expansion team fees had to help balance their bottom lines.

Further, a compromised league president was in cahoots with a crooked labor boss. Neither could transform a weakened league economic structure that already lacked the moneymaker of a lucrative U.S. television contract.

The sport needed a change agent. Gary Bettman was that individual of the moment who would rescue North American hockey from itself. It meant a hefty restructure. Even Bettman, the ex-NBA executive of sterling repute, didn't know the absolute slog required to lead hockey's hidebound "old boys" establishment into a more corporate future.

It wasn't just about public perception, meaning the goons and toothless grins that negatively branded mainstream hockey, the player-crease violations or the tedious neutral zone trap that could win Stanley Cups (see the New Jersey Devils). Bettman had to contend with the $80-million payrolls of the high rollers versus the meager $20-million offerings of cash-strapped small-market franchises.

Hockey had the best in-person experience in sport, but the game left itself exposed to market vagaries as a gate-driven operation. It was freighted with the reportedly worst salaries-to-revenues ratios among the top-four major North American team sports.

Bettman inherited all this. He came aboard with a lot of nerve and sureness, which helped pave his vision of the future. Still, NHL owners took a chance on him. His acumen in sport business belied his hockey sense. Only later would he learn the finer points of the game and make franchises more valuable. Bettman ultimately proved the many skeptics and doomsayers wrong, at least concerning the game's financial stability.

While no Canadian team has won the Stanley Cup in 30-plus years, his protracted labor disputes would bring a crucial salary cap, greater team parity and tremendous revenue growth. He never wavered on the real risk. "I don't have any concerns that the fans will come back," he said.

That was everything.

Patrick Roy.

◂ 1995-96

The Patrick Roy trade. On December 2, Roy gets shelled for nine goals against Detroit, many of them due to the stubbornness of Canadiens coach Mario Tremblay, who reportedly decides to humiliate his all-star goalie in front of jeering fans just to tamp down Roy's ego. When Roy finally gets the hook mid-match he tells Canadiens president Ronald Corey that he's done in Montreal — this would be his last Canadiens game. Four days later Roy is traded to Colorado, where he guides the Avalanche to the Stanley Cup, his third of four championships. Montreal hasn't won the Cup since.

1995-96

In an October 2 meeting between the NHL, NHLPA and the IIHF, the Canada Cup is renamed the World Cup. An agreement is reached to allow NHL stars to play in the 1998 Olympics during a 17-day mid-season league break.

1995

The NHL introduces the draft lottery, a weighted system to determine the order of the first player picks in the annual league draft.

NHL EXPANSION

1990s

During this decade, the NHL expands from 21 to 30 teams, beginning with San Jose (1991-92), followed by Ottawa and Tampa Bay (1992-93), Anaheim and Florida (1993-94), Nashville (1998-99), Atlanta (1999-2000) and Columbus and Minnesota (2000-01). Teams relocate from Minnesota to Dallas (1993-94), Quebec to Colorado (1995-96), Winnipeg to Phoenix (1996-97) and Hartford to Carolina (1997-98).

The 1996 Stanley Cup champion Colorado Avalanche.

▴ 1995-96

Colorado becomes the first NHL team to win the Stanley Cup in its first year in a new city, as the Avalanche steamroll Florida in the Cup Final. Uwe Krupp scores Game 4's 1-0 Cup clincher at 4:31 of the third OT period. Stanley takes its first Atlantic crossing with Peter Forsberg, the first NHLer to bring the Cup to Europe. He parades the trophy to hometown folks in Ornskoldsvik, Sweden.

"My main trick was not to unite all five Russians every time. Often, I would wait until the second or even third period to get them out on the ice together. It always got other teams confused."

—Detroit coach Scotty Bowman, on the Soviet hockey system of creating a five-man combination in uniting Russian forwards Sergei Fedorov, Igor Larionov and Vyacheslav Kozlov with Viacheslav Fetisov and Vladimir Konstantinov on defense during the mid-1990s.

▲ **1996–97** **Craig MacTavish: The last helmet-less player.** Having signed with Boston before the mandatory cutoff date in 1979, MacTavish is grandfathered under the ruling and permitted to play bare-headed through to retirement. He plays his final NHL game, for St. Louis, during the 1997 playoffs.

RULE CHANGE

1996–97
All players must be clear of the attacking zone prior to the puck being shot into that zone. The opportunity to "tag-up" and return into the zone is removed.

▲ **1996** **Borje Salming perseveres through the bullying and verbal baiting as a "chicken Swede" to play 1,148 NHL games and become the first European-trained NHLer honored into the Hockey Hall of Fame.**

Detroit's Mike Vernon makes a save against Philadelphia. Nicklas Lidstrom and Vladimir Konstantinov defend during Stanley Cup Final play.

▲ **1996–97** Detroit wins its first Stanley Cup since 1955 by eliminating Philadelphia four straight in the 1997 Cup Final. Scoring comes from Brendan Shanahan and Steve Yzerman. When they score, the Red Wings go 15-1 in the postseason. When one of the Russian Five (Sergei Fedorov, Igor Larionov, Vyacheslav Kozlov, Viacheslav Fetisov and Vladimir Konstantinov) gets a point, Detroit goes 15-0. "We couldn't believe we were playing on the same ice as they were … and yet they were so different," noted Detroit center Kris Draper.

Goalie Mike Vernon racks up a 1.76 goals-against average, allowing only two goals or fewer in 17 of 20 postseason games. Six days after the Cup victory, three team members suffer injuries in a car accident. The crash ends the career of 30-year-old defenseman Vladimir Konstantinov but inspires the team to another Cup in 1998. During the summer, Larionov is among the first players to parade the Cup around Moscow's Red Square and pose for photos outside Lenin's tomb.

Team USA's Chris Chelios and a decidedly Canadian headline.

Brendan Shanahan celebrates Detroit's Stanley Cup win against Philadelphia.

▲ 1996 **The World Cup of Hockey.** Deploying a squad of rock-hard check-finishers in Keith Tkachuk and Bill Guerin and the offensive might of Pat LaFontaine, Brett Hull and Mike Modano, Team USA comes back from a 4–3 overtime loss in Game 1 to win the World Cup's best-of-three final with convincing, tightly contested double 5–2 victories. Goalie Mike Richter owns Team Canada. Selected tournament MVP, he stones the Canadians by making 17 saves on 18 shots in Game 2's third period and then, except for an Eric Lindros goal, kills off a 22-shot barrage in Game 3's explosive second frame. That period seemed to break Canada's back. Adam Foote gave the Canadians a 2–1 lead midway through the third, before USA struck four times in the last 3:18 of play to win the World Cup.

▲ 1996–97 **The Brendan Shanahan trade.** Detroit gave up some special talent in Paul Coffey, Keith Primeau and a first-round draft pick to acquire Shanahan (and Brian Glynn) from Hartford in October 1996, but he proved the difference maker in an already-stellar team on the verge of Stanley Cup stardom. Fronted by Steve Yzerman and coach Scotty Bowman's five-man Russian unit, the Red Wings capture three Stanley Cup championships during Shanahan's stay in the Motor City, with back-to-back Cups in his first two seasons.

1997 Los Angeles owner Bruce McNall, the man who brought Wayne Gretzky to California and the former chairman of the NHL Board of Governors, begins serving a five-year, 10-month prison sentence in March for swindling banks and investors out of $236 million.

"I don't want to be coach of the year. I only want to be coach for a year."

—Coach Pat Burns, of the Hull Olympiques in 1984 and the first three-time winner of the NHL's Jack Adams Trophy, with Montreal (1989), Toronto (1993) and Boston (1998)—which meant, based on the hired-to-be-fired perils of the profession, he was fired three times.

◄ 1997–98 **Dominik Hasek wins back-to-back Hart Trophies.** The Dominator's eccentric play continues to baffle shooters, coaches and critics alike, winning his second consecutive MVP award, an NHL first for goalies. During the season Hasek nets 13 shutouts against an NHL record 11 different teams. The following season he elevates the very average Buffalo Sabres to within two games of winning the Stanley Cup. It's an extraordinary rags-to-riches story from an unorthodox, sprawling flopper, who was drafted 199th overall 15 years earlier in 1983.

▸ 1997 **"Having my own child, I felt I had to come forward and deal with this issue."**

—Sheldon Kennedy, on going public about his years of sexual abuse from Swift Current Broncos coach Graham James. For his courage and inspiring others to tell their stories, Kennedy is voted Canada's top newsmaker of 1997.

Vladimir Konstantinov accepting the Stanley Cup from Steve Yzerman, 1998.

▴ 1997-98 Scotty Bowman claims his eighth Stanley Cup as coach in Detroit's sweep of Washington, the fastest series of the four rounds, the first three all going to six games. Captain Steve Yzerman is named playoff MVP. Upon accepting the Stanley Cup, Yzerman places the trophy in the lap of teammate Vladimir Konstantinov, who is wheelchair-bound after suffering brain injuries in a car accident the previous year.

1997-98 NHL scoring sinks to a 42-year low of 5.28 goals per game. Pittsburgh's Jaromir Jagr is the league's only 100-point player with 102 points, the lowest count in a full season since 1967-68. The culprit? The neutral zone trap, a defensive strategy whereby defenders clog mid-ice to stem offense attacks. Video goal judges reportedly disallow 110 goals of 304 reviews in player-crease violations.

1998 Former NHLPA boss and player agent Alan Eagleson pleads guilty to three counts of fraud in a Boston Court on January 6. The next day, Eagleson, 64, pleads guilty in Toronto to three more counts of swindling players, stealing disability-insurance money and embezzling Canada Cup proceeds. He's fined $1 million and sentenced to 18 months at the Mimico Correctional Centre, where the once most powerful man in hockey fetches coffee and works as a cleaner. Two months later, in March, after 18 Hockey Hall of Fame honorees threaten to quit the Hall, the disgraced PA boss resigns as a Hall member.

◂▸ 1997-98 For the first time a trio of Europeans lead the NHL scoring race, with players from five different countries finishing in the top five positions.

Pavel Bure.

The NHL's Top Five Scoring Leaders, 1997-98

Player	Team	GP	G	A	Pts	Country
Jaromir Jagr	Pittsburgh	77	35	67	102	Czech Rep.
Peter Forsberg	Colorado	72	25	66	91	Sweden
Pavel Bure	Vancouver	82	51	39	90	Russia
Wayne Gretzky	NY Rangers	82	23	67	90	Canada
John LeClair	Philadelphia	82	51	36	87	USA

RULE CHANGE

1998-99 The NHL institutes a two-referee system on a trial basis. The goal line is moved to 13 feet from the end boards and the goal crease is altered with squared sides and a rounded top.

1998-99 Goalie Vincent Riendeau becomes the first former NHLer to play as a member of a Russian team. After his NHL career ends in 1994-95, Riendeau bounces around leagues in North America, Germany, Switzerland, Britain and for Lada Togliatti of the Russian Superleague.

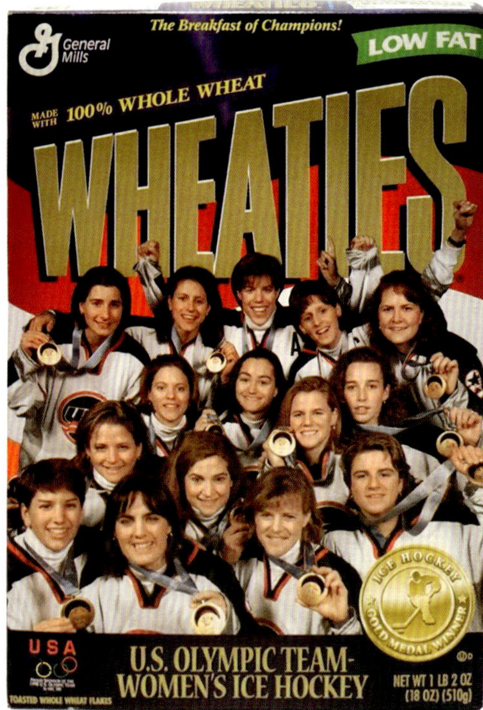

▲ 1998 **"It's every Olympic athlete's dream. First a gold medal and then your own Wheaties box."**

—USA captain Cammi Granato, on 1998's Olympic gold medal victory and appearing on an American sports fixture, "The Breakfast of Champions" cereal box

Dominik Hasek backstops the Czech Republic to its first Olympic gold medal.

▲ 1998 **The Olympic Games.** In two Olympic firsts, men's ice hockey has full NHL participation and women's hockey debuts with six nations competing. USA surprises tournament-favorite Canada, winning the first Olympic gold medal in women's play, with a 7–4 pasting in the round-robin and a 3–1 gold medal shocker on February 17. In men's action, Brendan Shanahan admits, "This is such a crushing feeling ... You feel like you let your team and your country down," as Canada falls to the Czech Republic in a dramatic semifinal shootout showcasing Dominik Hasek versus Patrick Roy. In the final, the Czechs win gold, blanking Russia 1–0. Hasek gives up just six goals on 160 shots throughout the event.

1998 **"This is the worst feeling in the world right now."**

—Wayne Gretzky, after Canada is defeated 2–1 in a semifinal shootout against the Czech Republic. Coach Marc Crawford is widely criticized for not picking Gretzky as one of the five shootout shooters.

Mario Lemieux, after winning approval to operate the Penguins.

▲ 1999 In September, Mario Lemieux becomes the first former NHLer to buy his team after his reorganization plan to purchase the Pittsburgh Penguins is approved by the U.S. bankruptcy court and the NHL Board of Governors. Lemieux becomes president, chairman and CEO of the Penguins.

RULE CHANGE

The IIHF elects to eliminate the red line for two-line passes (beginning in 1999), reducing the advantage of defense-oriented teams while opening up the ice to more creative offense. The NHL doesn't implement the rule for another seven years.

1999 The National Women's Hockey League is formed, superseding the old Central Ontario Women's Hockey League to become the first Canadian professional women's league. The NWHL fields stars like Cassie Campbell, Angela James and Geraldine Heaney on teams from several provinces. The circuit folds into the Canadian Women's Hockey League in 2007–08.

▼ 1999 "If it wasn't a real goal, wait till they see my ring."

—Brett Hull, on his disputed Stanley Cup-winning goal, which had his left skate inside Dominik Hasek's crease. Hull maintained possession before taking the shot. The NHL concluded he had control of the puck, which—contrary to their interpretation of the rule throughout the season—made it legal.

Brett Hull's controversial Stanley Cup winner, 1999.

▲ 1998–99 Dallas wins its first Stanley Cup on Brett Hull's controversial skate-in-the-crease goal at 54:51 of overtime against Dominik Hasek of Buffalo. Joe Nieuwendyk's 11 goals earn him MVP status, but it's Stars goalie Ed Belfour who outduels Colorado's Patrick Roy in the Conference Finals and then Hasek in the Cup Final.

1999 Maple Leaf Gardens hosts its final NHL game on February 13. Chicago spoils the celebrations with a 6–2 win against Toronto, which bookends the first game at the Gardens 67 years earlier when the Black Hawks won that contest 2–1 in 1931. Maple Leaf Gardens is the last of the Six Team Era arenas.

1998–99 **Wayne Gretzky says goodbye.** The Great One plays his final NHL game in New York on April 18. Gretzky collects his final point as a Ranger, an assist on a Brian Leetch second-period goal in a 2–1 overtime loss to Pittsburgh. Gretzky's NHL career spanned 20 seasons. He left the game with more milestones than anyone thought possible—a staggering 61 league records, including the centerpiece totals of 894 goals and 1,963 assists for 2,857 points. Commissioner Gary Bettman declares that No. 99 will be retired throughout the league.

"No way."

—New Jersey's Bobby Holik, after being asked if the club could have won the 2000 Stanley Cup with former coach Robbie Ftorek, who is replaced by Larry Robinson with just eight regular-season games remaining. Robinson's dressing room tirade, with the Devils down 3-1 in games to Philadelphia, is credited as the turning point. New Jersey wins the next three straight against the Flyers to face Dallas in the Cup Final.

RULE CHANGE

1999–2000 The crease rule is revised to implement a "no harm, no foul, no video review" standard. Teams to play with four skaters and a goaltender in regular-season overtime. If an OT goal is scored, the winner gets two points and the loser one point. If no OT goal is scored, both teams are awarded one point.

Mike Ricci.

▲ 1999–2000 **The 4-on-4 overtime.** The first team to record a point in a loss following the introduction of 4-on-4 overtime in a regulation tie is Edmonton, when San Jose's Mike Ricci scores on the power play in a 3-2 win on October 7. The first true 4-on-4 goal (with neither team penalized) is scored by Calgary's Valeri Bure a week later on October 13.

Heads-up hockey: Scott Stevens.

▲ 1999–2000 Dallas takes New Jersey to six games in the Stanley Cup Final. The Devils, however, prevail on Jason Arnott's Cup winner in double overtime, handing New Jersey its second championship. Nine players from that squad were on the 1995 Cup team, including captain Scott Stevens, who wins the Conn Smythe Trophy as playoff MVP, while scoring only 11 points, a true measure of his leadership in the postseason.

Czech Republic's Martin Stepanek holds Slovakia's Lubomir Sekeras.

▲ 2000 Seven years after the peaceful division of Czechoslovakia in 1993, the Czech Republic plays Slovakia in the gold medal game at the World Championship in St. Petersburg, Russia. The Czech Republic prevails 5-3, but the moment is significantly bigger than any medal victory, as the Czechs and Slovaks show the world their progress as independent hockey nations and the former might of the old Czechoslovak hockey program.

▸ 1999–2000 **The Marty McSorley suspension.** Frustrated following a fight with Vancouver's Donald Brashear, McSorley takes a vicious two-hander to the head of Brashear in a Bruins-Canucks game on February 23. Brashear is knocked unconscious when his head hits the ice. McSorley is suspended for a full year. Found guilty of assault with a weapon by a B.C. provincial court, McSorley receives 18 months probation. He never plays another NHL game. Brashear has another nine NHL seasons, retiring in 2009–10.

Vancouver's Donald Brashear during a team warm up at GM Place in October 2000. Eight months earlier Brashear had been clubbed with a baseball-style swing by Boston's Marty McSorley.

Rankin Inlet, Nunavut, the home of Jordin Tootoo, 2007.

▴ 2001 Jordin Tootoo becomes the first player of Inuit descent drafted into the NHL, selected 98th overall by Nashville. Growing up in the remote village of Rankin Inlet on the northern shore of Hudson Bay (near the Arctic Circle), Tootoo didn't play organized hockey until he was 14.

RULE CHANGE

2000–01 After using the two-referee system for 20 games beginning in 1998–99, the NHL institutes a two-referee and two-linesmen system to be played at all games.

2000 "Stitch me up quickly boys, we're on a power play."

—Columbus' Steve Heinze, on rushing the Blue Jacket trainers to get him back in a November 11 game after a slash by Phoenix Coyote Brad May. On the ensuing man-advantage, Heinze scores a power-play game winner. May receives a 20-game suspension.

▸ 2001 **Ilya Kovalchuk is drafted first overall.** Atlanta selects hockey's next biggest star and the first Russian-trained No. 1 pick. Kovalchuk was intractable, rebellious and selfish with the puck. In world competition he wore No. 71 and in North America he chose No. 17, in honor of Soviet star Valeri Kharlamov, whose virtuosity and pure wizardry in game play would be studied and adopted not just by Kovalchuk, but by superstars like Wayne Gretzky and Igor Larionov.

The NHL and the international play of Ilya Kovalchuk.

2000-01 **"We tried to open it up and it was like feeding a piranha."**

—Nashville coach Barry Trotz, on the risks of playing a high-tempo game against the speedy Vancouver Canucks in a December 4 match. The third-year Predators slow the pace, but still lose 6-3.

Ray Bourque, coach Bob Hartley, Patrick Roy and Avs captain Joe Sakic.

◂ 2000-01 The Colorado Avalanche win their second Stanley Cup, earning Ray Bourque a long-overdue championship after 22 seasons and 1,826 NHL games. Colorado needs wins in Games 6 and 7 against New Jersey. Patrick Roy delivers, stoning the Devils in 4-0 and 3-1 victories for the Avalanche. Roy is named playoff MVP, his third Conn Smythe Trophy in as many decades, in 1986 and 1993 with Montreal and in 2001 with Colorado.

▾ 2001-02 **"I can see them both there, and the pass goes practically to Mario's stick. He doesn't just not play it, he actually puts his stick there to play it, then moves his stick. It was a beautiful play, and a play you have to honor as a goalie. Obviously, I honored it a bit too much."**

—American goalie Mike Richter, on Chris Pronger appearing to feed a pass to a streaking Mario Lemieux. But Lemieux lets the puck go past him to Paul Kariya, who has the open net to tie Canada-USA's gold medal game 1-1 at the 2002 Olympics.

Paul Kariya scores against Mike Richter. Aaron Miller defends. Canada wins Olympic gold, 5-2, in 2002.

A double gold for Canada. Jayna Hefford scores on Sara DeCosta; Mike Richter stops Theoren Fleury.

▲ 2002 **The Olympic Games.** Exactly 50 years after the Edmonton Mercurys win Canada's last Olympic gold medal in 1952, Canadians celebrate the anniversary with two championship teams stepping up to the podium to hear "O Canada." Canada's women prevail in a 3–2 nail-biter versus USA, who had posted eight-straight wins against the Canadians in pre-Olympic play. Three days later, in gold medal competition against a formidable American squad on home ice in Salt Lake City, the Wayne Gretzky-managed Canadian team, with the No. 1 line of Mario Lemieux, Paul Kariya and Joe Sakic, captures gold in a 5–2 victory.

Jarome Iginla.

▲ 2001–02 Jarome Iginla becomes the first Black player—and the first player—to win both the Art Ross Trophy as NHL point-scoring champion and the Maurice "Rocket" Richard Trophy as goal-scoring champion in the same season since the latter trophy was inaugurated in 1999. Iginla records league-highs of 52 goals and 96 points. Alexander Ovechkin (2007–08) and Connor McDavid (2022–23) are also double scoring-award winners.

World champion Slovakia.

▲ 2002 **The World Championship in Sweden.** Slovakia makes history when its national team beats Russia 4–3 to capture that nation's first gold medal, a victory that not only validates its developing hockey program in the international arena but its stature as an independent nation from the Czech Republic. Peter Bondra breaks a 3–3 tie with only 100 seconds remaining in the championship match. Later, players kiss the Scandinavian ice in celebration, team manager Peter Stastny weeps at the bench and back home millions revel throughout the country. "This means more than a Stanley Cup to me," said Bondra. "The Cup is celebrated by one city. This belongs to an entire nation."

▸ 2001 "I told Trots that, if 20 years ago I'd seen 20 Bryan Trottiers skating around before the game, I would have just laid down at center ice."

—San Jose coach Darryl Sutter, on seeing the entire New York Islander team wearing Bryan Trottier's name and No. 19 during an October 20 pregame warm-up to honor the Islanders' retirement of Trottier's number, an NHL first that has become a tradition.

Kim Martin against Switzerland's Nicole Bullo.

▲ 2002 **The Olympic Games.** Fifteen-year-old Swedish goalie Kim Martin leads Sweden to its first-ever medal finish in elite competition in women's hockey, making 32 saves in a 2–1 upset over Finland for Olympic bronze.

RULE CHANGE

2002–03 "Hurry-up" face-off and line-change rules are implemented, due largely to the pace and style of play at the 2002 Olympics, which so impress NHL GMs that within weeks of the tournament, the league adopts the rules.

2002–03 Protective nets above the glass behind both goals become mandatory at NHL rinks following the death of 13-year-old fan Brittanie Cecil, who was struck by a deflected puck at Columbus' Nationwide Arena at a Blue Jackets–Calgary Flames game on March 16.

2001–02 In the pre-cap NHL era of have and have-not teams, the New York Rangers pay out a whopping $65 million in contracts. Meanwhile, in Atlanta, the Thrashers spend a league-low $15.2 million, as one of three clubs with payrolls under $20 million. In 2002-03, salaries on all 30 NHL teams topped the $20-million mark.

Nicklas Lidstrom.

▲ 2001–02 Detroit wins the Stanley Cup, icing several veterans who claim their first Cup, including Dominik Hasek, Luc Robitaille and Steve Duchesne. Hasek, 37, is the first European starting goalie to capture the Cup, setting an NHL playoff record of six shutouts. Igor Larionov becomes the NHL's oldest scorer of an overtime playoff goal, when the 41-year-old Russian ends a triple-overtime 3–2 game against Carolina. Swedish defenseman Nicklas Lidstrom earns the Conn Smythe Trophy, the first European-trained playoff MVP.

Mario Lemieux battles Bryan McCabe, 2002.

▲ 2002-03 **"I don't think it's the place of the NHL to try to embarrass players. If they would just call the obstruction, nobody would have to dive."**

—Mario Lemieux, on the NHL's new diving policy after the league outed Bryan McCabe, Darius Kasparaitis and Rick DiPietro during the league's first crackdown. Each was fined $1,000 and their names were listed in all dressing rooms throughout the league. "They don't call half the (crap) that goes on. I get speared in the (groin) the play before, then I get punched in the head and I go down and it's a dive?" fumed McCabe.

◂ 2003 **Grant Fuhr is inducted into the Hockey Hall of Fame** In his first year of eligibility, Fuhr becomes the first Black player honored in the Hall. The 19-year NHL veteran and a five-time Stanley Cup winner with Edmonton was the first Black goalie to crack the NHL in his Oilers debut in 1981-82 and the first Black player to win the Cup.

Hayley Wickenheiser.

▲ 2002-03 Hayley Wickenheiser—often credited with being the first female hockey player who isn't a goalie to play in a men's professional league—is reportedly bested by Maren Valenti, who played for Freibury of Germany's second division in 1998-99. Valenti didn't register a point in 24 games. Given that, Wickenheiser becomes the first woman to score a goal in men's pro hockey when she suits up for Kirkkonummen Salamat, a Division 2 league in Finland. Her celebrated goal comes in her sixth game, a 5-4 loss on February 1. Wickenheiser later wrote about chasing success. "I had something to prove."

Stanley Cup champions Martin Brodeur, Ken Daneyko and Patrik Elias, 2003.

▲ 2002-03 New Jersey wins its third Stanley Cup after clinching two Game 7s, in the Conference Finals against Ottawa and in the Cup Final versus Anaheim. Martin Brodeur shuts out the Ducks 3-0 in the Cup winner. Five Devils players, including Ken Daneyko, are members of all three championship teams.

José Théodore, 2003.

THE NATURAL
Outdoor Games

The idea of playing professional hockey outdoors is a natural. So thought Edmonton Oilers president Patrick LaForge, who originally pitched the concept to the NHL. As the story goes, LaForge was struck by market research in the 1990s on, who else, beer drinkers. Their hockey fantasy was seeing NHL players play pond hockey—the contest they played as kids, wearing toques and replica jerseys, calling for a pass, their skates slicing across a freshly plowed rink on a winter's day.

The notion stuck. The 2003 Heritage Classic became the league's first regular-season game played outside and featured the Oilers against the Canadiens at Edmonton's Commonwealth Stadium in temperatures of -1°F (-18°C). Mother Nature and technology created the ideal ice temperature of 22°F (-5°C) on a rink constructed over a football field. Except for being outdoors, it was anything but a throwback.

The 57,167 fans watched two games—the old-timer Megastars match and then the Canadiens-Oilers tilt—at a greater distance than the usual hockey experience. Nonetheless, fans were treated to Wayne Gretzky, Guy Lafleur and Mark Messier taking turns at the time-honored tradition of shoveling snow off the rink. More novelty than nostalgia, the game immediately connected with stadium fans and those watching at home. It scored the league a huge win that has since turned into the Stadium Series of outdoor matches and generated a revenue bonanza with record television ratings, sponsorship deals and attendances numbers of 100,000-plus fans at some stadiums, especially at the university and college levels with their own contests.

The league's showcase successor, the Winter Classic, became what author Jonathon Gatehouse called "the NHL's television salvation," as the most-watched regular-season match in America. Scheduled on New Year's Day, it was click-bait for hard and soft fans, making it hockey's "calendar" day, similar to the Fourth of July for baseball or Thanksgiving for football. Hockey's roots turned into its latest craze.

Martin St. Louis, Art Ross Trophy and Hart Trophy winner.

▸ 2003-04 Martin St. Louis wins the Art Ross Trophy with 38 goals and 94 points. For the first time since 1967-68 (besides 1994-95's lockout-shortened season) there is neither a 50-goal scorer nor a 100-point scorer. As well, it's the third time in five seasons there is no 100-point scorer, a strong indicator that the neutral zone trap continues to hamper NHL scoring. All-time records for total shutouts in a season are shattered. While the league does attempt to crack down on interference and obstruction, by mid-season the rules aren't being called.

RULE CHANGE

2003-04 Home teams wear colored uniforms and visiting teams wear white uniforms. The maximum length of a goaltender's pads is set at 38 inches (96.5 cm).

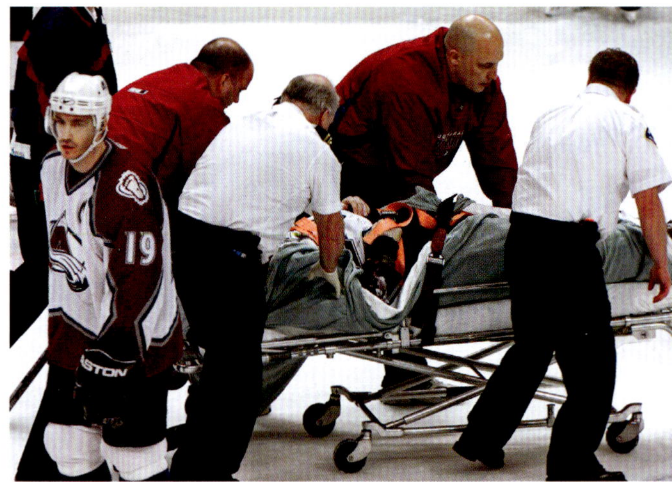

Joe Sakic skates away while Steve Moore is stretchered off the ice after after a retaliatory hit by Todd Bertuzzi.

▴ 2003-04 Todd Bertuzzi blindsides Colorado's Steve Moore on March 8, attacking him from behind in a revenge hit for Moore's cheap shot to the head of Vancouver captain Markus Naslund earlier in the game. Moore suffers a concussion, vertebral ligament damage, facial cuts and three fractured bones in his neck. Bertuzzi is suspended for the duration of the season and playoffs, forfeiting $501,926.39, the amount for the final 13 games of regular-season play. Moore never plays another NHL match.

Phoenix's Brian Boucher blocks a shot by Rangers forward Matthew Barnaby, 2002.

Brett Hull.

▲▼ 2003–04 **The longest modern-day shutout sequence.** Brian Boucher's career seemed near an end. Third on Phoenix's depth chart and on waivers, when no team claims him and a Coyotes spot opens up in November due to injuries, the 26-year-old takes full advantage, blanking opponents in a five-game stretch before a deflected shot by Atlanta's Randy Robitaille beats him on January 11. Boucher earns a 332:01 shutout streak—just 128 minutes and 48 seconds short of Alec Connell's all-time record set in the dead-puck days of 1927–28.

Longest Shutout Sequence, One Season

Players	Team	Season	Duration	Saves	Start-End Date
Alec Connell	Ottawa	1927-28	460:49	—	01/28/1928-02/22/1928
George Hainsworth	Montreal	1928-29	343:05	—	02/23/1929-03/10/1929
Brian Boucher	Phoenix	2003-04	332:01	145	12/22/2003-01/11/2004
Roy Worters	NY Americans	1930-31	324:40	—	11/11/1930-11/22/1930
Bill Durnan	Montreal	1948-49	309:21	—	02/24/1949-03/09/1949

▲ 2003 **"Bob Goodenow will kill me, but if we're going to be realistic about things, probably 75 percent of the league is overpaid."**

—Brett Hull, on skyrocketing player salaries in January 2003—a period in which NHL chief Gary Bettman and NHLPA boss Bob Goodenow wage war over a new CBA, set to expire in September 2004. The dispute led to the 2004–05 NHL lockout and cancellation of the entire season. Hull, at the time, earned $5 million a year.

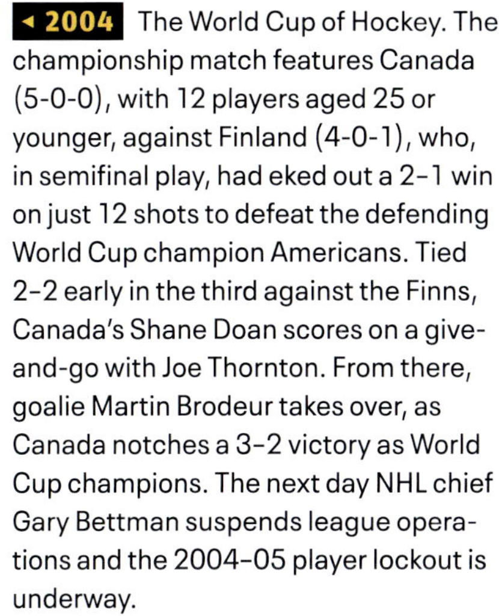

◀ 2004 The World Cup of Hockey. The championship match features Canada (5-0-0), with 12 players aged 25 or younger, against Finland (4-0-1), who, in semifinal play, had eked out a 2–1 win on just 12 shots to defeat the defending World Cup champion Americans. Tied 2–2 early in the third against the Finns, Canada's Shane Doan scores on a give-and-go with Joe Thornton. From there, goalie Martin Brodeur takes over, as Canada notches a 3–2 victory as World Cup champions. The next day NHL chief Gary Bettman suspends league operations and the 2004–05 player lockout is underway.

Shane Doan whips past an immobile Andreas Renz.

NHL fans at exhibition play between the World Stars and the Polish National Team during the league's lockout, December 2004.

"Get into a room, lock the door and don't come out until there's a deal done."

—Philadelphia's Jeremy Roenick, slamming both the NHL and the NHLPA for stalled talks during the league's players lockout, November 2004

▲ 2004–05 **The NHL lockout.** NHL chief Gary Bettman announces in September that the season start of league play has been postponed indefinitely. The main sticking point with the players association is what Bettman calls "cost certainty" in the form of a salary cap. NHLPA boss Bob Goodenow counters, "Until he gets off the salary-cap issue, there is no chance of getting an agreement."

Both sides restate their positions early on without any movement. There is talk of hiring replacement players. On November 3, Bettman cancels the All-Star Game scheduled for February in Atlanta. Flyer goalie Robert Esche calls Bettman a "madman" for his intransigence on the cap issue. Without any resolution, in January, Wayne Gretzky's dad, Walter, states, "I don't know how to solve it, but they're all greedy, the owners and the players."

To the dismay of fans, last-minute negotiations fail and on February 16 Bettman announces that "it is no longer practical to conduct even an abbreviated season" and cancels 2004–05. A new agreement is only reached July 21–22 after the players overwhelmingly accept the new collective bargaining agreement, 464 for and 68 against. The owners ratify the agreement that includes a salary cap, revenue sharing and a universal 24 percent cut to existing contracts.

Cammi Granato.

▲ 2004–05 **The Women's World Championship.** Once again, the title match pits Canada against USA, who have lost all eight previous World tournaments and an Olympic gold in 2002 to the Canadians. For their trouble, the U.S. women's team captured gold in the 1998 Olympics. Now in 2005, the scoreless finale is settled by shootout when USA scores three times to Canada's one goal. USA's Cammi Granato, on winning after losing eight previous World finals, confesses, "It's been a long time coming."

Team Canada.

▲ 2005 **The World Junior Championship.** After three successive silver finishes in 2002, 2003 and 2004 to Russia and USA, Canada sends its most experienced team to the Juniors. The 2005 edition features 17-year-old Sidney Crosby on the first line with Patrice Bergeron and London Knights star Corey Perry. The defense includes Dion Phaneuf and Shea Weber. A Canada–Russia final showcases the next generation of superstar rivals in Crosby versus Alexander Ovechkin. Canada's powerhouse routs the Russians 6–1, snagging the team a perfect 6-0-0 with a cumulative score 41–7. The Canadians never trail during the entire tournament.

Angela Ruggiero.

▲ **2004–05** Angela Ruggiero becomes the first woman who isn't a goalie to play a complete regular-season pro game in North America when she suits up for the Tulsa Oilers in a Central Hockey League game on January 28. In another first, her brother Bill backstops Tulsa, making them the first brother–sister tandem to play professionally together. In the 7–2 win against the Rio Grande Valley Killer Bees, Angela plays 13 shifts and records an assist, the first point by a woman in a North American pro game. "I'll remember that the rest of my life," she said.

◄ **2004–05** The NHL lockout prematurely ends the careers of several veteran stars after the league cancels the season. Among those who say goodbye are Ron Francis, Al MacInnis (at left) and Mark Messier, who played 1,756 games, just 11 shy of Gordie Howe's elusive 1,767 career-game mark.

Igor Larionov against Dan Quinn, 1989.

▲ **2004** Igor Larionov, 43, retires on April 24, following a 27-year career that included four World Championship titles, three Stanley Cups, two Olympic gold medals and a 1981 Canada Cup. In December, Larionov was feted with a farewell friendlies game at Moscow's Luzhniki Arena, featuring a who's who of Russian and North American teammates, from Sergei Fedorov to Steve Yzerman.

► **2004–05** With no quick resolution to the NHL lockout, players stay involved in hockey. Almost 400 NHLers compete in Europe. The World Stars Tour, a 10-game, 14-day European tour in December, features an NHL squad of elite talent against all-star and national teams from prominent hockey countries overseas. In Toronto, Brendan Shanahan organizes a two-day hockey summit on December 7–8, bringing together players, on-ice officials, executives and media members to brainstorm on improving game-play quality.

Daniel Brière, with SC Bern of the Swiss League.

LPHF
WASHINGTON
capitals
SUPREME
OILERS
PLAYALBERTA

The Next Big Thing

Sport is always about the next one—those alpha athletes with real potential for greatness. Rookies Sidney Crosby and Alexander Ovechkin held that promise and purpose, fortuitously arriving following the bitter NHL lockout of 2004–05.

This era of play also brought us Marie-Philip Poulin, Connor McDavid, Nathan MacKinnon, Brianna Decker, Auston Matthews, Carey Price, the shootout, 3-on-3 overtimes, the first women honorees into the Hockey Hall of Fame, Ovechkin's chase of Gretzky's 894, the golden goals of world play, an unprecedented American grip on the Stanley Cup and, finally, the long-anticipated PWHL.

The lockout had stolen a full season of the sport's best hockey. This fell on NHL commissioner Gary Bettman, who faced widespread resentment and condemnation from every corner of the game. As his corporate business model necessitated, Bettman got his salary cap, something that is meant to help all clubs, no matter their franchise base, by containing the gap between rich and poor. Despite sacrificing games and goodwill, it rebooted player-league dynamics, created more competitive play, swelled league revenues and, in time, player salaries and provided a geographic balance to a broader North American audience.

Brendan Shanahan's two-day summit on how to create more offense, curb player interference and bring about rules changes to inject more entertainment into hockey had much to do with that transformation.

Of immediate evidence, in Nashville's 2005–06 opener, Steve Sullivan took the puck in San Jose's corner, deked around Sharks winger Marco Sturm and turned defenseman Tom Preissing inside out before slipping a pass to winger Scott Walker at the far post for a tap-in. Sullivan later stated that in previous years after his second move he would have been sticked between the legs and driven and pinned against the glass—the type of clutch-and-grab hockey that Shanahan wanted eliminated for good.

The next big thing? The hockey establishment must reinvent the international model by better showcasing the elite talents of those like McDavid, Crosby, Ovechkin, Matthews, Nylander and Barkov in world competition, rather than, as one observer noted, "denying the global marketplace this version of itself."

Sidney Crosby. Illustration by Bruce MacKinnon, 2010.

OPPOSITE (FROM TOP)
Marie-Philip Poulin with Abigail Boreen, Alexander Ovechkin and Connor McDavid with Leon Draisaitl.

"Isn't that always the way it goes. The guy who pushes for the changes, who makes the world better, doesn't get to enjoy what he's worked for."

—Mike Modano, on Dallas teammate Brett Hull, who, after 18 NHL seasons of griping about bump-and-grind hockey, diluted skill levels and mediocre league marketing, doesn't get to experience the revamped game played under rules that curtail interference and increase game speed and goal scoring. Hull plays just five matches for Phoenix post-lockout.

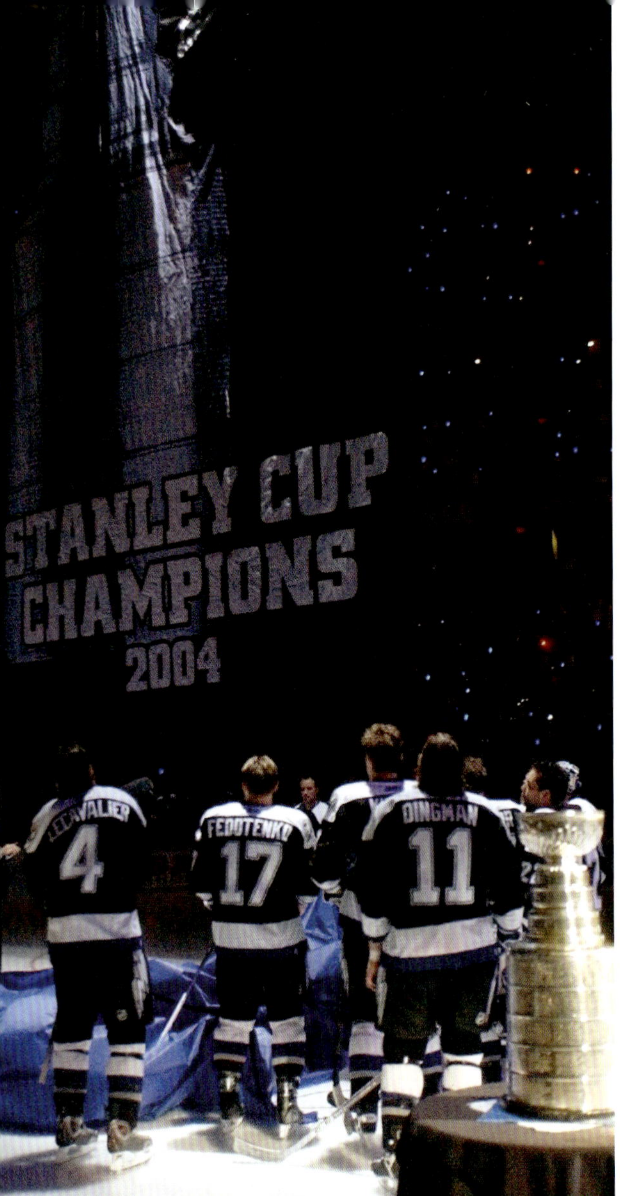

Tampa Bay raises its 2004 Stanley Cup banner.

▲ 2005–06 Emerging from the NHL lockout of 2004–05, a wellspring of stories grab headlines, including Tampa Bay finally raising the Lightning's 2004 Stanley Cup banner, Wayne Gretzky's coaching debut, rookies Sidney Crosby and Alexander Ovechkin, more stringent obstruction rules and the first ever shootout.

2005–06 **The shootout.** Criticized for being anti-team and unhockeylike, the shootout captivates fans and creates scoring heroes like Dallas winger Jussi Jokinen, who converts a perfect nine of nine shootouts until his 10th attempt on March 18. Jokinen finishes the season with a league-best 10 shootout goals on 13 tries, a glitzy 76.9 shot-percentage, the highest among NHLers with six or more attempts.

Joe Thornton with pals, the Art Ross and Hart Trophies.

▲ 2005 **The Joe Thornton trade.** A what-were-they-thinking hairbrained deal by underachieving Boston sends captain and franchise-face Joe Thornton to San Jose on November 30. In the four-player swap, the Bruins acquire Wayne Primeau, Brad Stuart and Marco Sturm, who play a combined 506 games and score 270 points in Boston compared to Jumbo Joe's 1,104 games and 1,055 points with San Jose. No coincidence, late in the season Boston GM Mike O'Connell is fired. Thornton wins the NHL scoring title and MVP award. While both teams improve their record after the trade, over the next five seasons, Boston makes the playoff three times, San Jose five. The Bruins win two series, the Sharks five.

RULE CHANGE

2005–06 The NHL adopts new rules to crack down on fouls and open up the game. Among other rules: The goal line moves to 11 feet (3.6 m) from the end boards, blue lines move to 75 feet (22.9 m) from the end boards, which reduces the neutral zone from 54 feet (16.4 m) to 50 feet (15.2 m). The center red line is eliminated for two-line passes. "Tag-up" offside rules are reinstituted. A team that ices the puck is not permitted to make any player substitutions prior to the ensuing face-off. The size of goaltender equipment is reduced. If a game is tied after five minutes of overtime, the winner is determined by shootout.

▸ 2005 **"I feel my dreams come true. I play in the NHL. First game, we win."**

—Alexander Ovechkin, 20, after scoring two goals, each less than 90 seconds after Columbus takes the lead in his first NHL game, handing Washington a 3-2 win.

Canada's Vicky Sunohara fist bumps Katie Weatherston and teammates after a goal against Finland, 2006.

▴ 2006 **The Olympic Games.** Canada's women cruise to gold glory, outscoring opponents 46-2 by trouncing Italy 16-0, Russia 12-0, Sweden 8-1 in the round-robin, then beating up Finland 6-0 in the semifinals and scoring a 4-1 gold medal victory against Sweden. Canada never plays archenemy USA, who lose to the surprising Swedes in a 3-2 semifinal shootout as 19-year-old goalie Kim Martin stops 37 of 39 shots and all four shootout attempts. It's the biggest upset in women's hockey and the first major championship not involving a Canada-USA finale.

Alexander Ovechkin against Petr Nedved.

▴ 2005-06 **The apprenticeship of Alexander Ovechkin.** Playing under obstruction-free rules on a scoring-addled Washington team, Ovechkin's once-in-a-generation skill set earns an NHL rookie record 425 shots, smashing Teemu Selanne's mark of 387 in 1992-93. Notably, Ovechkin remains the only freshman to top all NHLers in shots on goal in one season since the stat's first tabulation in 1959-60. Ovechkin's 52-54-106 total secures the Calder Trophy as top rookie, just the second time a rookie has potted 50 goals and 100 points in a season (after Selanne's 76-56-132). Calder runner-up Sidney Crosby nets a rookie 39-63-102.

◂ 2005-06 A consistent enforcement of hooking, holding and cross-checking rules creates league-wide offense, particularly in goals and power plays. The NHL's zero-tolerance decree boosts overall scoring 18 percent or a goal per game from a five-year low in 2003-04—the largest percentage hike since 1929-30. Man-advantage situations soar 38 percent and power play goals 48.2 percent.

Carolina's Eric Staal posts the biggest point-total jump (69) coming out of the lockout, from 31 as a rookie in 2003-04 to 100 points in 2005-06.

Sweden celebrates its 3–2 Olympic gold medal win against Finland.

▲ 2006 **Sweden's double world titles.** After claiming Olympic gold at Turin, Italy, in an unforgettable 3–2 win against Nordic-rival Finland in February 2006, Sweden's men test their national team's program again three months later at the Riga World Championship, this time gutted of its firepower in Mats Sundin, Peter Forsberg and Nicklas Lidstrom, who are back in NHL action. Also missing is goalie hero Henrik Lundqvist. In fact, only eight Olympians return to play in the Worlds.

The Swedes lose just once, a 5–2 defeat to Slovakia. Then, they batter USA 6–0 and hold on to a 5–4 win versus Canada before defeating the Czech Republic 4–0 for the gold medal. No national team since 1988, when the Soviet Union won Olympic and World golds in a combined tournament, managed to lock up both titles in the same year.

Carolina goalie Cam Ward.

▲ 2005–06 Carolina and Edmonton battle for the Stanley Cup, marking the first time two former WHA teams meet in the Cup Final since the league merged with the NHL in 1979–80. The Hurricanes defeat Montreal, New Jersey and Buffalo before their seven-game tilt with the Oilers, finally winning 3–1 in Game 7. Goalie Cam Ward is awarded the Conn Smythe as playoff MVP. Sophomore Eric Staal collects 28 points in 25 games to lead all playoff scorers.

2006–07 Toronto's Yanic Perreault records a league-high 62.77 winning percentage in the face-off dot, his seventh-straight NHL season with the best face-off count.

2006 **Team World vs. Team Russia at Red Square.** In celebration of three Russian milestones—the 60th anniversary of the birth of Russian hockey, the 50th anniversary of the former Soviet Union's first Olympic gold medal in hockey and the 25th anniversary of the famous KLM Line in the 1980s—Moscow organizes a December charity game of old-timers playing on outdoor ice in Red Square. The friendlies match features NHL stars, like Peter Stastny, Paul Coffey and Jari Kurri, squaring off against a squad of former Soviet greats, including Igor Larionov, Sergei Makarov and Viacheslav Fetisov. Team World and Russia tie 10–10.

Team Russia vs. Team World, Red Square, Russia.

2007 **The World Junior Championship.** Canada beats Russia 4-2 in gold medal play, but nothing surpasses the thrilling Canada-USA shootout in their semifinal matchup. Sixty minutes of regulation play and a 10-minute overtime settle nothing in the 1-1 deadlock, with Canada's Carey Price supplying the net heroics, stopping 12 shots compared to just two faced by USA goalie Jeff Frazee in 4-on-4 OT. The shootout goes on for six gripping rounds between Price and Frazee, with each team coach choosing any skater from their bench to go 1-on-1.

Canada's Jonathan Toews and USA's Peter Mueller each score twice, and in round seven they go again. Toews scores and Price denies Mueller. "I guess I was running out of ways to score so I gave him a little head fake ... I was able to beat him on the blocker side," said an 18-year-old Toews, who set the record for most shootout goals (3) by one player in one game at the World Juniors.

Months later, Toews wins the World Championship, making him the first Canadian to claim gold at the Worlds and World Juniors in the same year.

Canada's Jonathan Toews scores the semifinal shootout winner against USA's Jeff Frazee.

Sidney Crosby, winner of the Hart, Lester B. Pearson and Art Ross Trophies.

2006-07 **Sidney Crosby wins the Art Ross Trophy.** Crosby, 19 years and 244 days, becomes the youngest player to win the NHL scoring race, with a league-high 36-84-120 total. His Art Ross is accompanied by the Hart Trophy as league MVP and Lester B. Pearson Award for most outstanding player as voted by the players themselves.

2007 "I told him, I'm coming for him. But I didn't expect it to be this close."

—Jordan Staal, on scoring 29 goals in his rookie season with Pittsburgh, just one goal less than the 30 notched by big brother Eric. On February 10, Jordan becomes the youngest NHLer to score a hat trick at 18 years and 153 days.

2006-07 The Buffalo Sabres win 10 consecutive games to start the season, equaling Toronto's 10-game start in 1993-94. Sabre goalies Ryan Miller (8 wins) and Martin Biron (2) split net duties, with Miller claiming his first three victories all in shootouts—which turn ties into potential wins, an advantage over pre-shootout eras. What goes around comes around. In the possible NHL record-setting Game 11, Miller finally cracks. Buffalo is denied in his 5-4 loss to Atlanta, by, guess what, a shootout.

Longest Winning Streaks from Start of Season*

Team	Season	Streak	Start-End Date
Toronto	1993-94	10	10/07/1993-10/28/1993
Buffalo	2006-07	10	10/04/2006-10/26/2006
Montreal	2015-16	9	10/07/2015-10/24/2015
Carolina	2021-22	9	10/14/2021-11/03/2021

*Current to 2024-25

Most Wins, One Season

Player	Team	Season	GP	Games in Season	W	L	T	TOI
Braden Holtby	Washington	2015-16	66	82	48	9	—	3,841:11
Martin Brodeur	New Jersey	2006-07	78	82	48	23	—	4,696:33
C. Hellebuyck	Winnipeg	2024-25	63	82	47	12	—	3,741:22
Bernie Parent	Philadelphia	1973-74	73	78	47	13	12	4,307:25
Roberto Luongo	Vancouver	2006-07	76	82	47	22	—	4,490:16

2006-07 **Martin Brodeur wins the Vezina Trophy.** Brodeur and Roberto Luongo battle all season to break Bernie Parent's NHL record 47 wins until April 5, when Brodeur notches his 48th in a New Jersey 3-2 victory against Philadelphia. Luongo finishes with a career-high 47 wins for Vancouver, one shy of Brodeur, who claims the Vezina ahead of runner-up Luongo. Today, Brodeur shares top spot with Braden Holtby's 48 wins in 2015-16.

Jean-Sébastien Giguère and Rob and Scott Niedermayer.

▲ 2006–07 The Anaheim Ducks become the first California-based team to win the Stanley Cup, defeating Minnesota, Vancouver, Detroit and then Ottawa in a five-game Stanley Cup Final. Ottawa's Daniel Alfredsson, Jason Spezza and Dany Heatley lead all playoff scorers with 22 points each, but Anaheim's core of Ryan Getzlaf, Scott Niedermayer, Chris Pronger and goalie Jean-Sébastien Giguère establish a near-impenetrable 200-foot game, losing only five matches in postseason play. The Cup clincher in the Ducks' 6–2 win is an own goal by Ottawa's Chris Phillips, accredited to Travis Moen of Anaheim.

The Anaheim Ducks vs. the Los Angeles Kings, London, England.

▲ 2007–08 **The NHL's first regular-season game in Europe.** Ten years after the league played its first regular-season match outside North America — in Japan in October 1997 — the Anaheim Ducks and Los Angeles Kings play a two-game series in London, England, each team winning a match, 4–1.

2008
Alexander Ovechkin signs hockey's richest contract and second-longest term with Washington in January, a $124-millon deal for an average of $9.5 million per year over 13 years.

2008 The IIHF celebrates its 100th anniversary of its founding in May 1908 in Paris, France. Its Centennial All-Star team is named, honoring goalie Vladislav Tretiak (Russia); defensemen Viacheslav Fetisov (Russia) and Borje Salming (Sweden); wingers Valeri Kharlamov (Russia) and Sergei Makarov (Russia) and center Wayne Gretzky (Canada).

▼ 2008 **The NHL Winter Classic.** A league record crowd of 71,217 fans watch Pittsburgh beat Buffalo in a 2–1 shootout win at Ralph Wilson Stadium, near Buffalo. Sidney Crosby scores the winner. The league's showcase successor to 2003's Heritage Classic in Edmonton, the Winter Classic becomes the NHL's most-watched regular-season match.

Buffalo's Maxim Afinogenov skates past Pittsburgh's Adam Hall during the NHL Winter Classic at Ralph Wilson Stadium, Orchard Park, New York.

The Red Wings celebrate their franchise's 10th Stanley Cup.

▲ 2007-08 **Detroit wins the Stanley Cup.** The Red Wings defeat Pittsburgh in six games, breaking two playoff records for the oldest goalie and the games-played player on a Cup winner, as Dominik Hasek and Chris Chelios set new NHL standards. Hasek, age 43, ends the 41-year reign of Johnny Bower, age 42, from his 1967 Cup title with Toronto. Chelios tops Patrick Roy's NHL career record of 247 playoff games with his 248th on April 12 and extends his own mark to 266 games after playing in his 23rd career playoff season, 2008-09. Chelios, 46, remains the oldest U.S.-born player in NHL history.

The Montreal Stars, 2009 Clarkson Cup champions.

▲ 2008-09 The Clarkson Cup is awarded for the first time as a club championship trophy to the CWHL Montreal Stars, after defeating the WWHL Minnesota Whitecaps 3-1. The cup was commissioned by Canada's Governor General Adrienne Clarkson. It hasn't been presented since 2019, when the CWHL folded.

2008 **The World Championship.** For the first time in 100 years, since the Ligue Internationale de Hockey sur Glace organized itself in 1908, Canada hosts the 72nd World Championship, the IIHF's centennial year. The Cup finale heads into overtime with Canada and Russia dead-locked 4-4. Rick Nash takes a delay of game penalty. Ilya Kovalchuk whips a shot over Cam Ward's shoulder to deliver Russia its first gold medal in 15 years.

2008-09 The Kontinental Hockey League begins operations. An international pro league, the KHL has 24 member clubs in Russia, Latvia, Kazakhstan and Belarus. Later, it expands into Finland, Slovakia, Croatia and China.

Alexander Radulov fends off Steven Stamkos, with Derek Roy trailing, during the 2009 World Championship. Russia defeats Canada 2-1. Radulov scores the game winner and teammate Ilya Kovalchuk is named MVP.

2009 Canadian astronaut Robert Thirsk brings a classic piece of Canadian literature, Roch Carrier's *The Hockey Sweater*, on his Soyuz TMA-15 voyage to the International Space Station.

► 2008-09 Mike Green's power-play goal in Washington's 5-1 win against Tampa Bay sets an NHL rearguard record for goals in consecutive games on February 14. Green breaks Mike O'Connell's 25-year-old, seven-game stretch.

Longest Goal Streaks, Defenseman, One Season

Player	Team	Season	Start-End Dates	Goal Streak	G	A	P
Mike Green	Washington	2008-09	01/27/2009-02/14/2009	8	10	7	17
Mike O'Connell	Boston	1983-84	01/05/1984-01/17/1984	7	7	4	11

Several players with six games

Evgeni Malkin against Detroit's Brad Stuart and Niklas Kronwall.

▸ 2009 Former NHL goalie Kevin Weekes breaks the broadcasting barrier by becoming the first Black hockey analyst, working for the NHL network and as a color commentator on CBC's *Hockey Night in Canada*. In 2021 he makes his debut on *NHL on ESPN*. Among sporting icons admired by Weekes are Michael Jordan and goalie great Grant Fuhr. According to Weekes, Fuhr "was the one that proved to me that it was possible to play in the NHL and to look like me and to make the league and have a career."

▴ 2008–09 Evgeni Malkin captures the Art Ross Trophy. Malkin scores 113 points for Pittsburgh, three more than fellow countryman Washington sniper Alexander Ovechkin. Their 1-2 Russian finish reverses the previous year's NHL scoring race order when Ovechkin beat Malkin. In both years Ovechkin won the Hart Trophy as MVP and Malkin finished second.

Sidney Crosby.

▴ 2008–09 Pittsburgh wins the Stanley Cup. Maxime Talbot scores both goals in Game 7's climactic 2-1 championship victory against Detroit. Evgeni Malkin is named playoff MVP, scoring 36 points through postseason play. Despite the Penguins' series victory, during the Cup Final Detroit outscores Pittsburgh 17 to 14.

Martin Brodeur corrals a loose puck against Philadelphia.

▴▾ 2009–10 Martin Brodeur sets multiple NHL marks—still unbroken. Brodeur's 16th season in New Jersey shatters league records of two of hockey's best, Patrick Roy and Terry Sawchuk. On November 27, Brodeur breaks Roy's minutes-played record (60,214). Three weeks later, he relieves Roy of his games-played record (1,029) and, three days after that, on December 21, Sawchuk's indomitable 39-year, 103-shutout mark falls to Brodeur's 104th zero, a 4-0 win against Pittsburgh.

Most Minutes Played, Career

Player	Team(s)	GP	W	L	T	SO	TOI
Martin Brodeur	NJD, STL	1,266	691	397	105	125	74,438:25
Patrick Roy	MTL, COL	1,029	551	315	131	66	60,214:34

Most Shutouts, Career

Players	Team(s)	GP	W	L	T	OT L	SO
Martin Brodeur	NJD, STL	1,266	691	397	105	49	125
Terry Sawchuk	DET, BOS, TOR, LAK, NYR	971	445	336	171	—	103

▼ **2010** **“Talking makes the game so much easier ... Crosby talks great. That’s really the reason [the goal was scored]. If he didn’t say anything to me, I probably wouldn’t have passed it to him.”**

—Jarome Iginla, on Sidney Crosby yelling “Iggy” to get his attention for the split-second pass in tight quarters deep in USA’s zone that led to Crosby’s 2010 Olympic winner.

◀ **2010**

Team Canada wins Olympic gold. After falling 5-3 to USA in the preliminary round, Canada is forced into winning three-straight elimination games to reach the gold medal match, including a 7-3 quarterfinal smackdown against Russia, its first Olympic victory against its archnemesis in 50 years. The gold medal is within reach for Canada in a 2-1 game versus USA, until Zach Parise tucks the tying goal under Roberto Luongo with just 24.4 seconds on the clock. At 7:40 of overtime Sidney Crosby’s give-and-go with Jarome Iginla against USA is as good as gold. In jubilation, Crosby’s sends his stick and gloves flying, which, for many, defined those Winter Games. Crosby emerges a national hero of Canada’s eighth Olympic gold medal in ice hockey.

▶ **2010** **Canada’s women win Olympic gold against USA.** Eighteen-year-old Marie-Philip Poulin makes her Olympic debut and scores both goals in the 2-0 gold medal victory. Shannon Szabados, 23, nets the shutout, turning aside 28 shots in her first Olympic Games. Veterans Hayley Wickenheiser and Jennifer Botterill provide the leadership in Canada’s third-consecutive gold medal, but clearly a new generation of core players announce their arrival in 2010.

Shannon Szabados blocks a USA shot. Surrounding Szabados is Canada’s Catherine Ward, Caroline Ouellette, Meaghan Mikkelson and USA’s Jenny Potter.

Boston teammates lean over a concussed Marc Savard, 2010.

Angela James and Cammi Granato, along with 2015 Hall inductee Angela Ruggiero (center), 2015.

▲ 2010 Angela James and Cammi Granato make history as the first women enshrined into the Players category of the Hockey Hall of Fame.

James was among the first superstars of modern-day women's hockey, playing for Canada's national team in the first women's world tournament in 1987 and the inaugural IIHF Women's World Championship in 1990, when she led Canada to a gold medal, scoring a tournament-high 11 goals in five games. Three more golds came in 1992, 1994 and 1997. James, once Canada's greatest scoring threat, sadly never saw Olympic action.

Granato won Olympic gold and silver medals to go with one World Championship gold and eight silvers. In 2007, Granato was awarded the Lester Patrick Trophy for her contributions to U.S. hockey. The next year, Granato, James and Geraldine Heaney became the first three women inducted into the IIHF Hall of Fame. That same year, 2008, the U.S. Hockey Hall of Fame welcomed Granato as their first female inductee.

RULE CHANGE

▲ 2009-10 **An update to Rule 48: Illegal Check to the Head.** Pittsburgh's Matt Cooke delivers a legal blow to Marc Savard's head on March 7. The Boston center is sidelined for two months. In the interim the league announces Rule 48.1, a rare in-season rule revision (to take effect the following season) that penalizes the type of hit in which the head is the main point of contact in an avoidable situation. The previous version of this rule only made checks from the blindside illegal.

2010 **The World Championship.** The Czech Republic defeats Russia 2–1 in the Worlds final, ending Russia's 27-win streak dating to 2007. German goalie Dennis Endras is voted tournament MVP. Among the Czech stars are Jan Marek and Karel Rachunek, who tragically die the next year in the Lokomotiv Yaroslavl plane crash that kills 26 hockey players.

Chicago's Dustin Byfuglien and teammates.

2010-11 Sweden's Marcus Vinnerborg, 37, becomes the first European referee to officiate an NHL game, making his league debut when he calls the Anaheim-Dallas game on November 16.

◂ 2009-10 **The Stanley Cup.** Chicago wins its first Cup Final in 49 years, defeating Philadelphia in six games. Notably, it's the Flyers' sixth-consecutive Final loss since 1976. Blackhawks captain Jonathan Toews claims the Conn Smythe Trophy as playoff MVP. Flyers rookie Ville Leino sets a modern-day freshman record of nine points in the Cup Final and ties Dino Ciccarelli's mark of 21 points in one postseason.

Vancouver's Daniel and Henrik Sedin.

▲ 2010–11 Daniel Sedin wins the Art Ross Trophy a year after his twin brother Henrik claimed the award. The Sedins are not the first brothers to clinch NHL scoring titles, but they manage it in successive years with Vancouver. "Seeing what Hank did last year, I think we realized if we play the same way this year, and were consistent enough, we'd have a chance again this year," said Daniel. Henrik won the scoring title with a 29-83-112 record in 2009–10, Daniel had a 41-63-104 count.

▲ 2010 "The Big Chill at the Big House," played between the Michigan Wolverines and the Michigan State Spartans at Ann Arbor's Michigan Stadium, draws an official crowd of 104,173 fans, a world record turnout. With the wind chill factor, temperatures at the December 11 game range just above freezing. The Wolverines blank the Spartans 5–0.

The crash site of a Russian Yak-42 jet near Yaroslavl, on the Volga River.

▲ 2011 **The Lokomotiv hockey team disaster.** A Yakovlev Yak-42 charter flight carrying the roster and coaching staff of the KHL Lokomotiv Yaroslavl hockey club crashes during take-off near Yaroslavl, Russia. Forty-four of 45 people on board are killed, including 26 players—several of them former NHLers—and coach Brad McCrimmon. Poor training and pilot incompetence are to blame.

Tim Thomas with Patrice Bergeron.

▲ **2010–11** **Boston wins the Stanley Cup.** History was on Vancouver's side after zeroing the Bruins 1-0 in Game 1. In Cup Final history, all five previous Game 1 shutout winners went on to capture the Cup. But then Tuukka Rask-backup Tim Thomas tailors an historic postseason run, backstopping the Bruins to their first Cup since 1972, while setting NHL records in saves (798), shots faced (849) and saves in a Cup Final series (238).

Thomas plays clutch against Montreal, Philadelphia, Tampa Bay and Vancouver, winning a league record three Game 7s, netting a 4-3 OT win against Montreal in quarter-final play, a 1-0 shutout against the Lightning in the Conference Finals and then 4-0 versus the Canucks for the Cup. Not outdone, Boston skaters score 23 times in the Cup Final. Thomas, 37, becomes the oldest Conn Smythe MVP ever, giving up just eight goals in seven matches against Vancouver, the league's highest-scoring team.

New York Rangers' Derek Boogaard (right) fights Toronto's Colton Orr, 2010.

▲ **2011–12** During a four-month span in the off-season, former enforcers Derek Boogaard, Rick Rypien and Wade Belak die, leading to heightened awareness of brain injuries and post-career brain diseases associated with fighting. In some cases, like Boogaard and Bob Probert, subsequent examinations discover evidence of chronic traumatic encephalopathy (CTE), the degenerative disease from recurrent blows to the head.

2010–11
Mike Modano plays his last NHL game on May 10 in Detroit's 3-1 win against San Jose in Game 6 of the Stanley Cup Western Conference semifinals. Modano leaves the game the all-time goal-scoring and points leader among American-born players. Also retiring are future fellow Hall of Famers Peter Forsberg and Mark Recchi.

◄ **2011** **The World Junior Championship.** The biggest comeback or the most epic collapse by a team staged in U20 history, the gold medal game has Canada ahead with a 3-0 lead after two periods, only to surrender five unanswered goals in the final frame to Russia. It's Russia's first Junior title since 2003. USA defeats Sweden 4-2 for the bronze. Canada's Brayden Schenn is named the event's MVP.

Canada's Tyson Barrie looks on as Russia's Nikita Pivtsakin celebrates a third period goal in the gold medal game.

A Winnipeg homecoming for the Jets.

▲ 2011–12 **The Winnipeg Jets 2.0.** Seven years after True North Sports & Entertainment chairman Mark Chipman builds the 15,004-seat MTS Center, the Atlanta Thrashers are sold to his company for $170 million. During the inaugural game's opening ceremonies in October 2011, the atmosphere is far different than what greeted NHL boss Gary Bettman after protesters chanted "Bettman sucks!" 15 years earlier when the Jets relocated to Phoenix. In 1996, it was all anger and heartbreak, with teary farewells between players and fans in a collective bout of separation anxiety. This time Bettman is wildly cheered. The Jets are back "to right a wrong," said Bettman.

World Championship MVP Evgeni Malkin.

▲ 2012 **The World Championship.** Russia captures the gold medal by crushing Slovakia 6–2 in the May 20 final. Pavel Datsyuk and Alexander Semin each score three points and Evgeni Malkin is selected tournament MVP. For the second-straight year Canada finishes fifth, losing to Slovakia 4–3 in quarterfinal play. On the same day, USA loses 3–2 to Finland to finish seventh overall.

▼ 2012 **The Women's World Championship.** Canada finally dethrones three-time World Cup champion USA in a 5–4 overtime victory, courtesy of Caroline Ouellette's gold medal winner on April 14. Ouellette scores twice for three points in the finale.

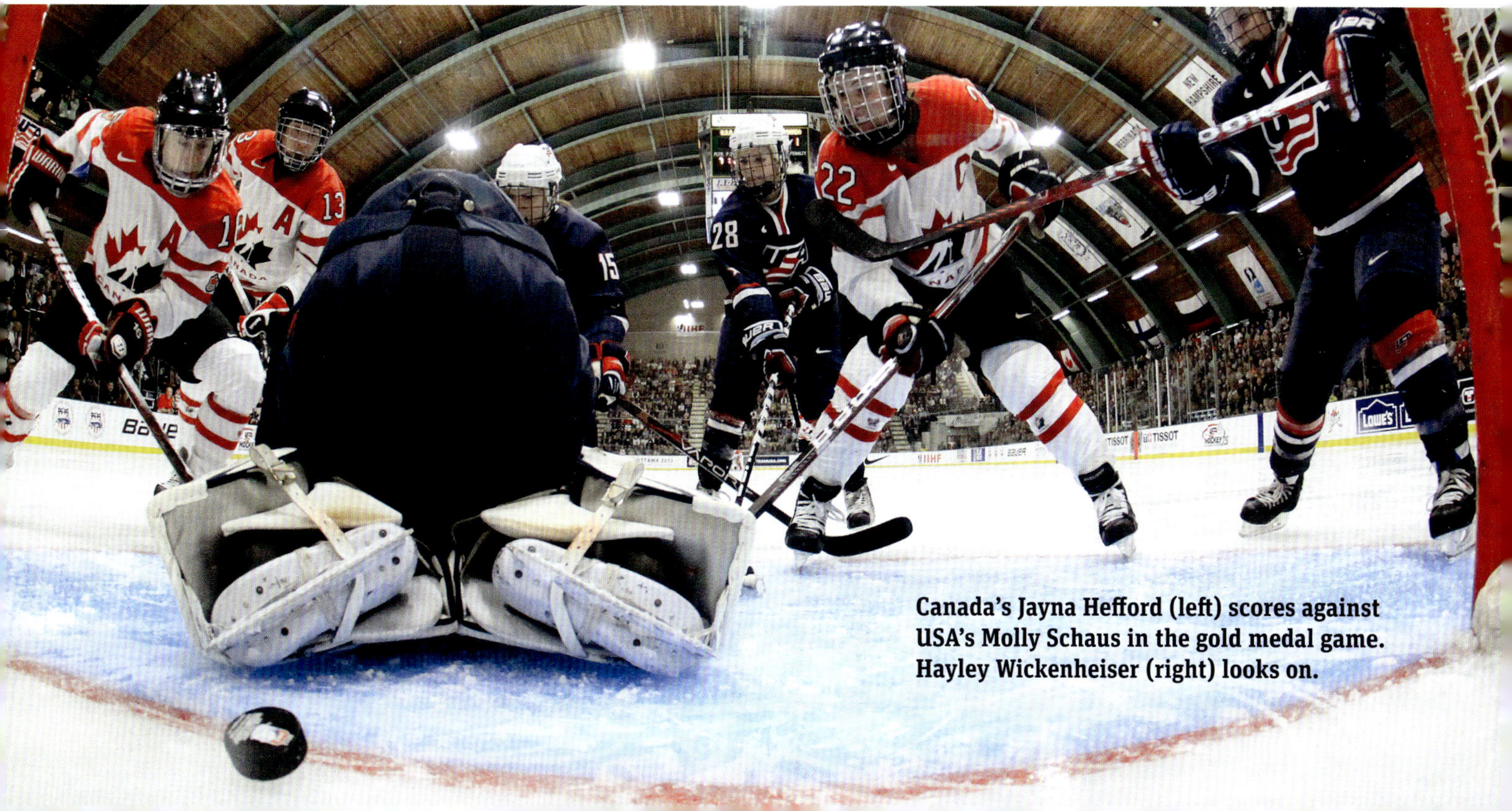

Canada's Jayna Hefford (left) scores against USA's Molly Schaus in the gold medal game. Hayley Wickenheiser (right) looks on.

Chris Pronger plays one of his last games.

▲ 2011–12 Chris Pronger plays his last NHL game on November 19, after suffering a serious eye injury on October 24. Limited to a season of just 13 games and facing post-concussion syndrome from multiple hits, the all-star defenseman steps down as Philadelphia captain—his playing career now likely over. With a contract that ran through to 2016–17, Pronger was technically an active player. But because he didn't play for three seasons, he was eligible and inducted into the Hockey Hall of Fame in 2015. Pronger officially retired in 2017, a Hart and Norris Trophy winner (2000), a Triple Gold Club member with Olympic (2002, 2010) and World Championship (1997) golds and a Stanley Cup with Anaheim (2007).

Conn Smythe Trophy winner Jonathan Quick.

▲ 2011–12 **The Los Angeles Kings win the Stanley Cup.** The powerhouse Kings lose only two games in three series, manhandling Vancouver, St. Louis and Phoenix before facing New Jersey in the Cup Final. Los Angeles proceeds to win three straight in two 2–1 overtimes and a 4–0 shutout. The Devils claw back two wins to make it a series, but the Kings respond with a 6–1 thumping to end it. Jonathan Quick is named playoff MVP, allowing only 28 goals for a .946 save percentage, as the Kings claim their first Cup.

Football fans during the NHL lockout.

▲ 2012–13 **The NHL lockout.** With the expiration of the league's CBA and negotiations at an impasse, franchise owners shut out players in Gary Bettman's third lockout. The labor dispute over revenue sharing, player contract limits and salary cap structure lasts until a new 10-year agreement is reached and ratified on January 9. The season is reduced to a 48-game schedule.

2012–13 **Martin St. Louis wins the Art Ross Trophy.** St. Louis, 37, becomes the oldest scoring leader, compiling a 17-43-60 total, three points better than teammate Steven Stamkos during the truncated 48-game season. It's St. Louis' second Art Ross and, with only 14 penalty minutes, his third Lady Byng.

P.K. Subban.

▲ 2012–13 **P.K. Subban wins the Norris Trophy.** Subban, the first Black player to claim the NHL's best defenseman award, scores 38 points in 42 games and is a plus-12 in his third full season with Montreal.

▲ 2013 **The World Championship.** Sweden becomes the first host country in 27 years to win gold on home ice, in a 5-1 victory against Switzerland. "To play in front of your home fans in your country and be able to win, that doesn't happen often, so that's pretty amazing," said Henrik Sedin. Henrik and brother Daniel each play the final four games after their Vancouver Canucks are eliminated in NHL playoff action. Henrik scores four goals and five assists and Daniel a goal and five assists in Sweden's championship.

Henrik Sedin scores against Denmark's Patrick Galbraith.

Dave Bolland.

◂ 2012-13

Chicago wins the Stanley Cup. Their second Cup in four years, the Blackhawks defeat Boston in six games. It's the first Cup Final between two Six Team Era clubs in 34 years. With Chicago ahead 3-2 in games, and down 2-1 to the Bruins with under two minutes to play in Game 6, the Blackhawks pull goal-tender Corey Crawford for the extra man. Nine seconds later, Bryan Bickell scores, tying it 2-2. Seventeen seconds after that, in the final minute of regulation, Dave Bolland notches the Cup winner at 19:01. Chicago's Patrick Kane captures the Conn Smythe Trophy as playoff MVP.

2012-13 Jarmo Kekalainen, a native of Finland, becomes the NHL's first European GM, running the Columbus Blue Jackets.

2013 The NHL shifts Canadian national broadcast rights from CBC to Rogers across numerous platforms for the next 12 seasons at a price of $5.2 billion. French-language broadcasts transfer to TVA Sports. *Hockey Night in Canada* continues on CBC.

2013-14 Aleksander Barkov becomes the youngest NHL goal scorer since the early 1940s when he pots a goal in his league debut in Florida's 3-2 win against Dallas on October 3. Barkov is 18 years and 31 days old.

Canada's Marie-Philip Poulin ties the gold medal game 2–2, scoring against USA's Jessie Vetter at 19:05 in regulation time.

Max Domi has a three-point night, as Canada's U20 squad defeats Russia 5–4 in the 2015 World Junior Championship final.

◂ 2014 Canada's Olympic comeback against USA. Marie-Philip Poulin earns her "Captain Clutch" reputation with Canada down 2–0 and 3:26 left in the gold medal match against USA. First, Brianne Jenner scores, making it 2–1. Then, USA comes agonizingly close to ending it, failing on a long shot that hits the post when Canada pulls goalie Shannon Szabados. Under a minute left in regulation, Poulin fires home the equalizer, 2–2. Into overtime, at 8:10, Poulin does it again, scoring the kill shot against Jessie Vetter. It's Canada's fourth consecutive Olympic win and the first ever decided in overtime. Teammates Hayley Wickenheiser, Jayna Hefford and Caroline Ouellette win their fourth Olympic gold medals, another first in women's hockey at the Winter Games.

◂ 2014 Canada's Olympic gold at Sochi. For the first time since 1928, Canada wins all of its games, allowing only three goals in six matches of competition, while shutting down USA 1–0 in the semifinals and Sweden 3–0 in the gold medal final. In the game Jonathan Toews, Sidney Crosby and Chris Kunitz each score their first goals of the tournament, as Canada's defensive core limits the Swedes to 24 shots on Carey Price. It's Canada's third gold medal in four Olympics. After winning bronze, Finland's six-time Olympian Teemu Selanne is named tournament MVP.

Canada's Carey Price makes a save against Sweden during gold medal play.

▸ 2013–14

Johnny Gaudreau, Nikita Kucherov and 2013 first overall pick Nathan MacKinnon make their NHL debuts. MacKinnon wins the Calder Trophy as top rookie with Colorado. On March 6, he breaks Wayne Gretzky's streak by an 18-year-old, registering a point in his 13th consecutive game, with a 5-13-18 scoring record. MacKinnon is the youngest player in league history (18 years, 224 days) to finish as rookie leader in goals, assists and points, scoring 24-39-63.

Colorado's Nathan MacKinnon clashes with Philadelphia's Michal Neuvirth.

Los Angeles' Alex Martinez and Kyle Clifford celebrate after Martinez beats New York Rangers goalie Henrik Lundqvist in Game 5 overtime to win the 2014 Stanley Cup.

Dallas' Jamie Benn collides into Edmonton's Ben Scrivens.

▲ 2014–15 **Jamie Benn wins the Art Ross Trophy.** The scoring race between Dallas' Benn and John Tavares of the Islanders plays out to the regular season's final agonizing seconds, with Tavares at 84 points and Benn at 83. Tavares records two points against Columbus in New York's 5–4 loss. But Benn scores a hat trick, his 86th point (to tie Tavares) into an empty net with 125 seconds remaining. Then, at 19:51, Benn earns a second assist on Cody Eakin's goal, as Dallas beats Nashville 4–1. Benn wins the NHL scoring title with just nine seconds left in the season.

Sidney Crosby and Alexander Ovechkin.

▲ 2015 **The World Championship.** Canada rules, winning all 10 tournament games, scoring 66 goals and allowing only 15. The Canadians dominate Russia in the gold medal final, outshooting them 37–12 in the 6–1 title match. Sidney Crosby joins the Triple Gold Club, its 26th member and first to captain a team to an Olympic gold medal, a World Championship title and a Stanley Cup.

Carey Price against Los Angeles.

▲ 2014–15 **Carey Price wins the Hart Trophy.** And the Vezina, Jennings and Pearson Trophies. Price carries a very average Montreal team to second overall in the NHL standings with 110 points, pacing the league in wins (44), goals-against average (1.96) and save percentage (.933). The Canadiens' best scorers are Max Pacioretty, ranked 21st overall (67 points), and Tomas Plekanec, 50th overall (60).

Nick Bjugstad scores against Washington's Braden Holtby to end the NHL's longest shootout.

▲ 2014–15 The NHL's longest shootout goes 20 rounds before Florida's Nick Bjugstad dekes out Washington's Braden Holtby to score the tiebreaker on December 16. It was Bjugstad's second attempt. Each team used all 18 skaters and started the shootout rotation over again. The Panthers tied the game five times after the Capitals had taken the lead. An NHL record 11 combined goals were scored. The shootout lasted 17:43.

2015 Chicago's Duncan Keith scores the Blackhawks' Stanley Cup winner against Tampa Bay's Ben Bishop.

RULE CHANGE

2015–16
Coaches can request video review of offsides or goaltender interference when a goal is scored. Teams play with three skaters and a goaltender in regular-season overtime.

▼ 2016
Finland dominates the U20 and U18 World Championship, winning both titles. In January, the Finns defeat Russia 4–3, on Kasperi Kapanen's overtime goal at 1:33, as World Junior champions. Three months later, the Finnish U18 team whips Sweden 6–1 for its gold medal World title.

2015 A selfie celebration. Hilary Knight celebrates USA's fifth title in the previous six tournaments following the 7–5 gold medal win against Canada at the Women's World Championship.

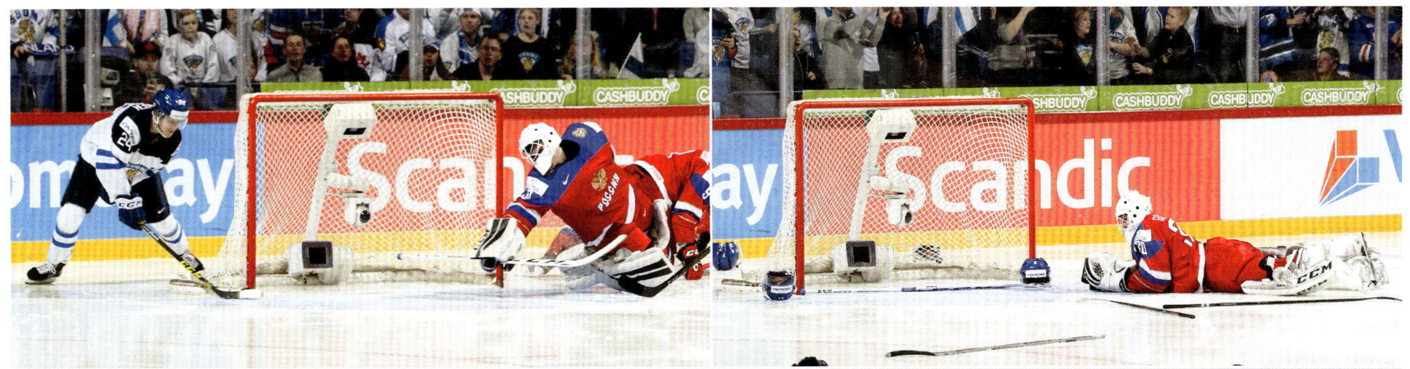

2016 Finland's Kasperi Kapanen scores the World Juniors' gold medal winner in overtime against Alexandar Georgiev of Russia; and the aftermath of Finnish gear littering the ice.

USA's Alex Carpenter (far left) scores 2016's 1–0 overtime gold medal winner against Emerance Maschmeyer of Canada. Meaghan Mikkelson (right) arrives too late.

▲ 2016 **The Women's World Championship.** USA once again owns Canada in the gold medal game, this time the heroics coming from the two Alexes. Alex Carpenter scores in the 1-0 overtime win, while Alex Rigsby stops 32 shots for the shutout. Hilary Knight sets the pace as tournament scoring leader to earn her second-straight MVP award.

Brad Marchand celebrates with Connor McDavid, Sam Reinhart and Matt Duchene.

▲ 2016 **The World Championship.** Canada shuts out Finland 2-0 in the final on goals by Connor McDavid and Matt Duchene. Cam Talbot earns the shutout with 16 saves. Patrick Laine, MVP at the World Juniors in January, makes the Worlds squad for Finland in May, again being named tournament MVP. That summer, Laine is selected second overall at the 2016 NHL draft.

Edmonton's Connor McDavid evades a check from Dallas' Johnny Oduya.

▲ 2015–16 Connor McDavid makes his debut on October 8 in Edmonton's 3-1 loss to St. Louis. McDavid plays 18:07 in 22 shifts and ends the night a minus-1. Nine days later, on October 17, Edmonton defeats Calgary 5-2, becoming the first NHL team to get goals from four different No. 1 draft picks, as McDavid (2015 draft) scores twice and Taylor Hall (2010), Ryan Nugent-Hopkins (2011) and Nail Yakupov (2012) each score once.

Chicago's Patrick Kane dodges past St. Louis defenseman Joel Edmundson.

▲ 2015–16 **Patrick Kane wins the Art Ross Trophy.** After winning three Stanley Cups with Chicago in 2010, 2013 and 2015 and the Conn Smythe Trophy as playoff MVP in 2013, Kane claims the NHL scoring title with a 46-60-106 total, 17 points ahead of Jamie Benn's 89. Kane is the first American-born scoring champion in the league's 99-year history.

2015–16 For the first time in NHL history, the majority of the league's players are not Canadian-born. In a two-week period in October, it's reported that 49.7 percent of the 680 players who played in games are born in Canada. And, by sheer coincidence, for only the second time in NHL history, none of the league's seven Canadian-based teams qualify for the playoffs.

2015–16 **The Stanley Cup.** Pittsburgh's journey to its fourth Stanley Cup Final went through the New York Rangers, Washington and Tampa Bay. Against first-time Cup Finalist San Jose, the Penguins are road warriors, notching pivotal wins in Games 4 and 6 at the Shark Tank in the six-game series. Pittsburgh captain Sidney Crosby is awarded the Conn Smythe Trophy as playoff MVP.

▸ 2016 Gordie Howe passes away on June 10. He was 88 years old. Howe competed as a top-10 scorer for an astonishing 21 consecutive NHL seasons. He won six Hart Trophies as league MVP. His greater legacy, however, may be as the most valuable player ever to the game.

Team Canada's Brad Marchand scores the tournament winner winner (off a pass from Patrice Bergeron) against Team Europe's Jaroslav Halak. World Cup of Hockey, 2016.

2016 **The World Cup of Hockey.** Canada, the Czech Republic, USA, Sweden, Finland, Russia and two all-star teams, Team North America and Team Europe, compete in the round-robin, with four teams advancing to the semifinals and the winners to the best-of-three final. Canada plays Team Europe for the title in September, winning both games 3-1 and 2-1, the tournament winner coming shorthanded from Brad Marchand with 43 seconds left in regulation to complete a perfect tournament run. Sidney Crosby scores three goals and seven assists as tournament MVP.

Henrik Lundqvist.

▲ 2017 **The World Championship.** Tre Kronor takes gold by winning a dramatic shootout against defending champions Canada. With the scored knotted 1-1 after 80 minutes of play, Sweden scores on two of its four shots, while Canada misses all four of its attempts against Henrik Lundqvist, who stones Mitch Marner, Ryan O'Reilly, Brayden Point and Nathan MacKinnon. William Nylander is named tournament MVP with seven goals and 14 points in 10 games, and a series-high plus-11. Russia wins the bronze medal, defeating Finland 5-3.

Auston Matthews scores his first NHL goal, 2016.

▲▼ 2016-17 Auston Matthews makes his NHL debut, scoring four times against Ottawa on October 12 to become the first modern player to do so. Only Harry Hyland and Joe Malone have scored more, and they, like Reg Noble, were both considered NHL rookies only because it was the league's first season of play.

Most Goals, Rookie, First NHL Game

Player	Season	Team	Date	Score	G	A	P
Harry Hyland	1917-18	Mtl Wanderers	12/19/1917	MTL 10 - TO 9	5	0	5
Joe Malone	1917-18	Mtl Canadiens	12/19/1917	MTL 7 - OTT 4	5	0	5
Reg Noble	1917-18	TO Arenas	12/19/1917	MTL 10 - TO 9	4	0	4
Auston Matthews	2016-17	TO Maple Leafs	10/12/2016	OTT 5 - TO 4 OT	4	0	4

Pittsburgh's Matt Murray stops Nashville's Colton Sissons, Game 4, Stanley Cup Final, 2017.

Most Points, Rookie, One Playoff Year*

Player	Team	Season	GP	G	A	P	PPG	SHG
Dino Ciccarelli	Minnesota	1980-81	19	14	7	21	5	0
Jake Guentzel	Pittsburgh	2016-17	25	13	8	21	1	1
Ville Leino	Philadelphia	2009-10	19	7	14	21	0	0

*Current to 2024-25

◄ 2016-17 Sidney Crosby captains Pittsburgh to the Penguins' second-consecutive Stanley Cup. Pittsburgh and Nashville split the first four games of the Cup Final, before Matt Murray stonewalls the Predators with back-to-back shutouts, 6-0 and 2-0, for the championship. Jake Guentzel ties Dino Ciccarelli's 21-point NHL record for most rookie playoff points. In an NHL first, two U.S.-born coaches, Mike Sullivan and Peter Laviolette, face off in Cup Final play.

2016–17 Within a month of each other, Columbus coach John Tortorella (December 18) and Nashville coach Peter Laviolette (January 22), become the first American-born NHL coaches to win their milestone 500th game.

2016–17 Rogers Place replaces Northlands Coliseum in Edmonton. The Oilers beat Calgary 7–4 in their first home game on October 12. The Detroit Red Wings play their final season at Joe Louis Arena before their move to Little Caesars Arena in October 2017.

Edmonton's Connor McDavid against Montreal's Antti Niemi.

▲ 2016–17 Connor McDavid wins the Art Ross Trophy. In his sophomore season, McDavid plays all 82 games and scores a 30-70-100 record on 251 shots and a plus-27, leading runners-up Sidney Crosby and Patrick Kane, each with 89 points.

RULE CHANGE

2017–18 The IIHF adopts several new rules, including matching NHL specifications for goal creases, use of electronic tablets by team staff on the bench and goalie penalties for covering the puck when they are able to play it.

2017–18 Adidas replaces Reebok as the supplier of all NHL team jerseys.

Germany's players react after their gold medal overtime defeat.

▲ 2018 The NHL-free Olympics in Pyeongchang, South Korea, guarantees an anything-can-happen tournament in which Germany goes on a stunning run for the gold medal against heavily favored Russia (who are officially the Olympic Athletes from Russia due to the IOC's penalty for doping violations). Players who have never played under such pressure bring the same intensity and pride-of-country to the competition. Canada beats the Czech Republic 6–4 for the bronze medal. In the gold medal game, Germany can taste victory, leading 3–2 with less than a minute in regulation play. But Russia scores the equalizer and then Kirill Kaprizov pots Russia's golden winner in OT. Germany stoically takes silver, their best showing in Olympic hockey history.

Team USA celebrates Olympic victory.

▲ 2018 In women's Olympic hockey, USA defeats Canada 3–2 in dramatic shootout fashion, as twin sisters Monique Lamoureux-Morando and Jocelyne Lamoureux-Davidson capture the spotlight for the Americans. Monique scores the game-tying goal, before Jocelyne clinches the gold medal on the final shootout goal of the game.

A memorial of the Humboldt bus crash in Saskatchewan.

▲ April 8, 2018 **The Humboldt Broncos bus crash.** Among the worst tragedies in Canadian sports history, 16 people are killed and another 13 injured when a semi-trailer truck fails to stop at a remote Saskatchewan highway intersection and collides with a coach bus carrying the Broncos to a playoff game in Nipawin. The trailer-truck driver receives concurrent sentences of eight years and five years.

Marc-André Fleury against the New York Rangers.

▲ 2017–18 The Vegas Golden Knights win 51 games, setting the NHL record for most wins by an expansion team in its debut season. GM George McPhee and coach Gerard Gallant picked shrewdly at the expansion draft, with better talent to choose from thanks to the league lowering the number of protected players on existing clubs. The Golden Knights became immediately competitive, acquiring some strong offensive players, top-four defensemen and goalie Marc-André Fleury, all working as a team that had something to prove before a new and vibrant fan base. The previous expansion team record was 33 wins by Anaheim and Florida in 1993–94.

Erik Karlsson.

▲ 2018 **The Erik Karlsson trade.** San Jose acquires two-time Norris Trophy–winner Karlsson and prospect Francis Perron from Ottawa in exchange for Josh Norris, Chris Tierney and others. With Norris Trophy–winner Brent Burns already on the back end, the trade is supposed to be San Jose's ticket to the Stanley Cup. Instead, one sixth-place overall finish the next year and then, in the shortened COVID-19 season, the once Cup-contending Sharks finish third worst, just ahead of their trade partner, the second-worst Senators. Norris later signs an eight-year, $63-million deal with Ottawa (followed by his March 2025 trade to Buffalo). In 2023, Pittsburgh deals Karlsson, who carries a diminishing annual value starting at $11.5 million through 2026–27.

Alexander Ovechkin.

▲ 2017–18 The Washington Capitals win their first Stanley Cup in franchise history, beating Columbus and defending champion Pittsburgh in two six-game series, then eliminating Tampa Bay in Game 7 of the Eastern Conference Final. Washington, in its 43rd season, faces the first-year Vegas Golden Knights in the Cup Final, capturing the Cup in five games. Danish-born Lars Eller scores the Cup clincher. Capitals captain Alexander Ovechkin is named playoff MVP.

2019 **"It doesn't feel real. It's absolutely incredible. I can't even explain. It feels like a video game we're in. It's what you dream of as a kid, posing with the Stanley Cup, getting to lift it."**

—St. Louis Blues center Brayden Schenn, on winning the 2019 Stanley Cup

2018–19 Alexander Ovechkin wins his eighth Maurice "Rocket" Richard Trophy, passing Bobby Hull's seven NHL titles as goal-scoring leader.

Kendall Coyne Schofield at the NHL All-Star Skills competitions, 2019.

▲ 2018–19 Kendall Coyne Schofield becomes the first woman to compete in the NHL All-Star Skills competition, entering the 2019 NHL Fastest Skater contest in place of Nathan MacKinnon. Coyne Schofield finishes eighth in a time of 14.346 seconds, less than a second off winner Connor McDavid's mark of 13.378.

Women's Worlds MVP Jenni Hiirikoski of Finland.

▲ 2019 **The Women's World Championship.** The Americans win their fifth-consecutive title after Amanda Kessel and Annie Pankowski score in the shootout against Finland. It marks the first time that any team other than Canada or USA wins the silver medal. Finland's Jenni Hiirikoski is awarded tournament MVP.

Stanley Cup playoff MVP Ryan O'Reilly.

▲ 2018–19 **The St. Louis Blues win the Stanley Cup.** St. Louis plays 26 of the maximum 28 games in four hard-fought series, defeating Winnipeg in six, Dallas in seven and San Jose in six before advancing to the Cup Final against Boston. Since 1939, in Cup Final action, Game 1 winners have won the Cup 77.2 percent (61 of 79 series) of the time. The Blues defy those odds after losing the first game 4-2.

As throughout the 2019 postseason, St. Louis travels well in the Final, winning three games away, including the 4-1 Cup clincher at TD Garden. Not one member of the Blues is a previous Cup champion. Forward Ryan O'Reilly, whose 23 points share the scoring lead with Boston's Brad Marchand, captures the Conn Smythe Trophy as playoff MVP.

Worlds MVP Mark Stone congratulates gold medalist Kevin Lankinen of Finland.

▲ 2019 **The World Championship.** Despite dressing 18 first-timers at the Worlds and being outshot 44-22 in the final, underdog Finland defeats Canada 3-1 to win the gold medal, its third championship. The Finns lose only two games, against Germany and USA. Russia takes the bronze in a shootout win against the Czech Republic. Sweden's William Nylander scores a tournament-high 18 points. Mark Stone of Canada is named tournament MVP.

▸ 2019-20 **"Awesome ... Once in a lifetime. I'll take it."**

—David Ayres, 42 years old, on becoming an emergency backup goalie (EBUG) in Carolina's 6–3 win against Toronto on February 22

▸ 2019-20 After Hurricanes goalies James Reimer and Petr Mrázek are injured, David Ayres, once a backup for the Toronto Marlies and a practice goalie with the Maple Leafs, enters the game with 8:41 left in the second period and Carolina holding a 3–1 lead. He wears No. 90 and Kasimir Kaskisuo's old Toronto Marlies helmet and pads. Ayres gives up goals on his first two shots but stops the next eight for the win. He's the first EBUG substitute with a credited win in NHL history and the oldest NHL netminder to win his regular-season debut. Following the game, Ayres is named first star. He gets to keep his game-worn jersey and game puck. His take-home: $500.

Edmonton's Leon Draisaitl against Calgary's Cam Talbot.

▴ 2019-20 The NHL pauses the season on March 12 due to the COVID-19 pandemic. Teams have played between 68 and 71 games. Boston leads the league with 100 points. Edmonton's Leon Draisaitl wins the Art Ross Trophy with 110 points in 71 games. On March 17 Ottawa becomes the first team to announce a positive player test for the virus.

2019 The Professional Women's Hockey Players Association (PWHPA) is founded in May to promote professional women's hockey. From 2019 to 2023, the non-profit organization coordinates a series of "exhibition seasons" known as the Dream Gap tours.

RULE CHANGE

2019-20 The NHL makes "Regulation Wins" the first tiebreaker for the regular-season standings. Video review is overhauled, giving referees the ability to review major/match penalties as well as what goal situations are subject to review/coach's challenges.

2019-20 On November 11, Sportsnet fires long-time *Hockey Night in Canada* commentator Don Cherry for inappropriate remarks about Canadian diversity.

2020 The World Championship, the Women's World Championship and the U18 World Championship are canceled due to the COVID-19 pandemic.

2019–20 Columbus' Joonas Korpisalo battles Andrei Vasilevskiy of Tampa Bay through regulation time and five overtime periods only to lose 3–2 on Brayden Point's game winner after 150:27 of play in Game 1 of Stanley Cup first-round action on August 11. Korpisalo registers an NHL-record 85 saves on 88 shots for a .966 save percentage. Vasilevskiy has 61 saves on 63 shots. Blue Jackets defenseman Seth Jones is a behemoth, playing 76 shifts to set his own modern NHL skater mark of 65:06 of ice time in a single playoff game.

One of 85 saves made by Columbus' Joonas Korpisalo against Tampa Bay on August 11, 2020. Korpisalo stops Anthony Cirelli, with Seth Jones picking up a holding call on the play.

Most Points by a Rookie Defenseman, One Playoff Year

Player	Team	Season	GP	G	A	P	PPG	SHG
Quinn Hughes	Vancouver	2019-20	17	2	14	16	1	0
Cale Makar	Colorado	2019-20	15	4	11	15	2	0
Glen Wesley	Boston	1987-88	23	6	8	14	4	1
Larry Goodenough	Philadelphia	1975-76	16	3	11	14	1	0
Al MacInnis	Calgary	1983-84	11	2	12	14	2	0

2020–21 The COVID-19 pandemic forces the NHL to reduce its regular season to 56 games. Play begins on January 13 and because of cross-border restrictions imposed by Canada, the league temporarily realigns all divisions, with seven Canadian teams playing in one division.

2019–20 The Stanley Cup playoffs are modified under COVID-19 pandemic restrictions, with 12 clubs from each conference playing in two "hub cities" at Toronto's Scotiabank Arena and Edmonton's Rogers Place. There are no spectators. Only essential staff are present. Qualifying rounds begin August 1, followed by the first and second playoff rounds and the Conference Finals and the Cup Final.

In Cup Final action at Rogers Place, Tampa Bay prevails in six games against Dallas, who play a record 27 games in the expanded playoff format. Brayden Point scores the Cup winner in Game 6's 2–0 victory. It's Point's league-leading 14th goal of the postseason. Nikita Kucherov assists and finishes with a playoff-high 34 points. Victor Hedman captures the Conn Smythe Trophy as the MVP.

Tampa Bay's Brayden Point scores on Dallas' Anton Khudobin.

Los Angeles' Jonathan Quick makes the save on Edmonton's Connor McDavid.

◂ 2020–21 Connor McDavid wins the Art Ross Trophy in the pandemic-shortened 56-game season. McDavid's 33-72-105 record bests Edmonton teammate and runner-up Leon Draisaitl by 21 points (31-53-84), who finishes 15 points ahead of Boston's Brad Marchand (29-40-69). McDavid is also named Hart Trophy recipient as regular-season MVP.

2020–21 Within a season of each other, NBC play-by-play announcer Mike Emrick and Pittsburgh Penguins radio play-by-play announcer Mike Lange retire from broadcasting. Emrick had a 47-year career and Lange was the voice of the Penguins for 46 seasons.

Quinton Byfield, Team OHL, Canada–Russia Series.

▴ 2020 **The NHL Entry Draft.** OHL Sudbury Wolves forward Quinton Byfield becomes the highest-selected Black player at the annual NHL draft, after being chosen second overall by Los Angeles. Originally scheduled in late June, the league's draft is conducted on October 6 and 7 at NHL Network Studios in Secaucus, New Jersey, due to the COVID-19 pandemic. Sixteen days later, the league announces that the Winter Classic and the All-Star Game have been postponed to the following season due to "ongoing uncertainty."

RULE CHANGE

2020–21
A player's skate doesn't have to be in contact with the blue line in order to be considered onside.

Marie-Philip Poulin and MVP Mélodie Daoust.

▴ 2021 **The Women's World Championship.** After having lost seven of its previous eight finals, Canada finally defeats USA 3-2 on a clutch goal by Marie-Philip Poulin at 7:22 of overtime. Canada wins all of its games and fields the top four scorers in the tournament. Scoring leader Mélodie Daoust is named MVP.

Alex Turcotte, Cole Caufield, Sam Colangelo, Hunter Skinner and Trevor Zegras.

◂ 2021 **The World Junior Championship.** Trevor Zegras figures in both goals, scoring a goal and an assist on Alex Turcotte's gold medal marker in USA's 2-0 victory against Canada. Spencer Knight records the shutout, stopping all 34 shots for the Americans. Due to the COVID-19 pandemic, all games were played behind closed doors without spectators at Edmonton's Rogers Place.

Tampa Bay's Andrei Vasilevskiy and Ryan McDonagh celebrate Stanley Cup victory.

▲ 2020–21 **The Stanley Cup playoffs.** Due to COVID-19, the NHL realigns the season into four divisions with the top four teams in each division making the playoffs. The divisional winners head to the Cup Semifinals and Final. Tampa Bay defeats Florida, Carolina and the Islanders before facing Montreal, the first Canadian team in the Final since Vancouver in 2011.

The Lightning strike quickly, winning their second-straight Cup in five games. Nikita Kucherov, who spent the regular season on the injury reserve list, leads all scorers with 32 points. Kucherov's return to playoff action exceeds Tampa Bay's salary cap by a reported $18 million. While some fans allege cap circumvention, the league determines no rules have been broken. Tampa goalie Andrei Vasilevskiy wins MVP honors.

NHL EXPANSION

2021–22 The NHL expands to 32 teams with the Seattle Kraken, as the league returns to a full 82-game schedule for the first time since 2018-19, the last season before the COVID-19 pandemic.

2020–21 Patrick Marleau becomes the all-time leader in NHL games played with his 1,768th game on April 19, breaking Gordie Howe's 41-year stretch. Two nights later, Marleau plays his 900th consecutive game, only the fourth player to reach that mark in NHL history. His 23-year career ends that season with a 566-631-1197 record in 1,779 games.

Luke Hughes (left) and his brothers Quinn and Jack, 2023.

▲ 2021 The Hughes brothers of Orlando, Florida, become the first American family in NHL history to have three siblings drafted in the first round. Quinn was selected seventh overall by Vancouver in 2018, Jack first overall by New Jersey in 2019 and Luke fourth overall by New Jersey in 2021.

There was little doubt of their promise as future stars. Their father, Jim Hughes, played with Providence College, was an assistant coach for the Boston Bruins and Director of Player Development for the Toronto Maple Leafs. Their mother, Ellen Weinberg-Hughes, a multi-sport athlete at the University of New Hampshire, played for the U.S. women's national hockey team and won a silver medal with Team USA at the 1992 Women's World Championship.

▶ 2021–22 **The Jack Eichel trade.** Second overall pick in the Connor McDavid sweepstakes at the 2015 NHL Draft, Eichel played most of six seasons with Buffalo before the Sabres moved him following a team medical dispute to repair a severe neck injury. The blockbuster deal sends Eichel and a 2023 third-round pick (Mathieu Cataford) to Vegas. Buffalo acquires Alex Tuch, Peyton Krebs, a 2022 first-round pick (Noah Ostlund) and a 2023 second-round pick (Riley Heidt). The Sabres have since struggled while the Golden Knights have won consistently, with Eichel's two-way game playing a key role by scoring a playoff-high 26 points in 22 games in Vegas' 2023 Stanley Cup.

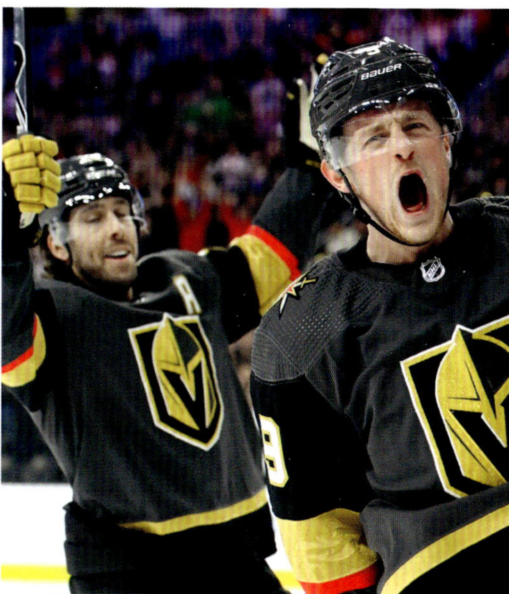

Vegas center Jack Eichel (front) and Chandler Stephenson celebrate Eichel's goal against Nashville.

Toronto's Auston Matthews scores his 59th goal of 2021–22 on Detroit goalie Alex Nedeljkovic.

▲ 2021–22 Auston Matthews wins the Maurice "Rocket" Richard Trophy as NHL goal-scoring leader in consecutive years, with 41 goals in 2020–21's pandemic-shortened season of 56 games and 60 goals in 2021–22, a first since Steven Stamkos' 60-goal performance with Tampa Bay in 2011–12. Connor McDavid wins his fourth Art Ross Trophy, scoring 44 goals and 123 points.

2022 Within a week, Quebec superstars Guy Lafleur and Mike Bossy pass away. Bossy, the record-holder of most consecutive 50-goal seasons (9) and a four-time Stanley Cup champion dies at age 65 on April 15. A week later, Lafleur, a five-time Cup champion, dies at age 70.

2021–22
Alexander Ovechkin scores his 275th power play goal on December 31, surpassing Dave Andreychuk's record to become the NHL's all-time leader on the man advantage. Late in the season, Ovechkin breaks Johnny Bucyk's record as the oldest 50-goal scorer at 36 years and 215 days of age.

2022
Ontario becomes the first Canadian province to expand its sports betting program, legalizing gambling from a controlled marketplace of virtual casinos and sportsbooks, permitting residents to wager anytime and from anywhere, beginning in April 2022. It becomes one of the largest iGaming markets in North America.

The Islanders' Zdeno Chara squeezes Toronto's Colin Blackwell into the net of Ilya Sorokin.

▲ 2021–22 Zdeno Chara sets the NHL record for most games by a defenseman in his 1,652nd game, a 4–3 New York Islanders shootout loss to San Jose on February 24. Chara, 6-feet, 9-inches, the tallest player in league history, ends his career as an Islander, but retires the following September, having signed a one-day contract with Boston so that he can retire as a Bruin. Chara, age 45, finishes his 24th NHL campaign with 1,680 games played. The previous games-played mark was held by Chris Chelios.

USA's Alex Cavallini stops Canada's Natalie Spooner.

▲ 2022 **The Olympic Games in Beijing, China.** Canada's women defeat Olympic defending-champion USA 3-2 in gold medal play before a pandemic-size crowd of 834 at Wukesong Sports Centre. Marie-Philip Poulin dominates again, scoring twice. Finland beats Switzerland 4–0 for the bronze medal.

Kent Johnson scores Canada's gold medal overtime winner against Finland's Juha Jatkola.

▲ 2022 The World Junior Championship. The IIHF postpones the Christmas–New Year's tournament citing health and safety concerns due to COVID-19 and reschedules the 19th World Juniors to August 9–20 at Rogers Place, Edmonton. Canada plays Finland in the 3–2 gold medal overtime thriller. The Finns had erased a 2–0 deficit with third period goals. But Canada's Kent Johnson scores on his own rebound at 3:20 of extra time. Tournament MVP Mason McTavish finishes first in goals (8) and points (17).

Finland's Teemu Hartikainen celebrates Sakari Manninen's gold medal overtime winner against Matt Tomkins of Canada.

▲ 2022 The World Championship. The IIHF suspends Russia and Belarus from competing following the Russian invasion of Ukraine. Austria and France take their place in the tournament. On home ice, Finland wins its fourth World title on Sakari Manninen's gold medal goal, defeating Canada 4–3 at 6:42 into overtime. Mikael Granlund has two goals and an assist. Finnish goalie Juho Olkinuora is named MVP.

► 2022 The Women's World Championship. Canada wins the Worlds, "battling it out," as captain Marie-Philip Poulin said, to defeat USA 2–1 in the gold medal match. The key was Canada's rock-solid defense against USA's potent offense. "We did it by blocking shots, killing penalties, the power play. We had to find other ways to win, and Ann-Renée Desbiens made a couple of saves to get the win." Brianne Jenner scores Canada's two goals and Desbiens stops everything while the Americans ice a sixth attacker for the final 2:39 of play. USA's Taylor Heise is the top scorer and MVP in this first year that the Women's Worlds is played during an Olympic year.

Colorado's Artturi Lehkonen scores the Stanley Cup winner against Tampa Bay's Andrei Vasilevskiy.

▲ 2021–22 The Stanley Cup. Colorado makes quick work of its opponents in postseason play, going 16-4 by downing Nashville 4-0 in games, St. Louis 4-2 and Edmonton 4-0 before finishing off Tampa Bay in six games of the Cup Final. Artturi Lehkonen scores the Cup clinching goal. Cale Makar is awarded the Conn Smythe Trophy as playoff MVP.

Canada's Ann-Renée Desbiens against USA's Amanda Kessel.

2022 "Soon as it happened, kind of relief."

—Alexander Ovechkin, in his best English, on scoring his 800th NHL goal, coming off a hat trick before an appreciative Chicago crowd at the United Center in Washington's 7-3 win against the Blackhawks on December 13.

Florida's Matthew Tkachuk crashes into Toronto goalie Joseph Woll, as Matthew Knies defends.

▲ **2022–23** **The Matthew Tkachuk-Jonathan Huberdeau trade.** After seven seasons, Tkachuk wants out of Calgary, his draft team in 2016. When he (and a 2025 conditional fourth-round pick) is dealt to Florida on July 22, the Flames get Huberdeau, MacKenzie Weegar and others. The sign-and-trade deal lands Tkachuk an eight-year contract worth $76 million. While Calgary gets a top point producer in Huberdeau and a top-six defenseman in Weegar, the Panthers with Tkachuk become Stanley Cup finalists in 2023 and Cup champions in 2024.

Mike Grier is introduced as San Jose's new GM, alongside assistant GM Joe Will (left) and Sharks president Jonathan Becher.

▲ **2022–23** San Jose's Mike Grier becomes the first Black NHL GM in July 2022. The Detroit native began his 14-year NHL playing career with Edmonton in 1996–97. He played on four teams, registering a 162-221-383 record in 1,060 games. Grier is also the first Black NHLer born and trained in America.

2023 **The World Championship.** Upsets dominate the tournament, with Latvia claiming its first IIHF medal after defeating USA 4-3 in overtime to finish third. Germany, on its own mission, reaches the final only for the third time and is dismissed by Canada 5-2 in the gold medal game. Samuel Blais scores twice, including the tournament winner. Well earned, Latvian goalie Arturs Silovs is awarded MVP honors.

◄▼ **2022–23** Phil Kessel plays 1,064 consecutive NHL games. Kessel doesn't miss a single regular-season game in 13 seasons, dating from his debut with Toronto in 2009–10 to his final days with Vegas and his third Stanley Cup in 2023. His record night comes on October 25 in his 990th-straight game, surpassing Keith Yandle's previous record. Not finished with hockey, as of 2024–25, Kessel has yet to sign again or officially retire.

Most Consecutive Games Played in NHL History

Player	Position	GP	Start -End Dates
Phil Kessel	Right wing	1,064	11/03/2009-04/13/2023
Keith Yandle	Defense	989	03/26/2009-03/29/2022
Doug Jarvis	Center	964	10/08/1975-10/10/1987
Garry Unger	Center	914	02/24/1968-12/21/1979

The Sportsbook

Given the sports fan's penchant for betting, odds were it was only a matter of time before federal, provincial and state governments legalized online gambling everywhere.

Now that it's readily available, and not just to betting consumers in the black and gray markets of bookies, criminals and offshore gambling sites, the best results would be greater fan engagement owing to a heightened betting experience, skyrocketing tax revenues (in the billions of dollars), more jobs and a "new innovation" economy.

What's mostly visible are the countless sportsbook ads, the disappointing celebrity endorsements and the flood of in-game interruptions that bombard viewers with point spread figures, the over/under and moneyline odds for live in-the-moment betting, often pitched by our most trusted hockey broadcasters.

This legitimization of gambling not only changes how fans participate in the viewing experience but how they regard sports in general. The psychology goes, if you have a financial stake in game results, player stats or related events, the emotional value and connection to gameplay is intensified. Fans become further invested in outcomes, which spike viewership and loyalty.

Of course, ever present are the greater public health concerns over gambling addiction, which can shatter lives and ruin jobs, friendships and families. For athletes, this new normalization offers the added temptation of betting on games themselves or "fixing" games, throwing into question the integrity of sporting events.

In more innocent times, gambling was commonplace, only less visible and without government backing. Game dispatches of the Montreal AAA's 1902 Stanley Cup victory against the Winnipeg Victorias reported "Betting is generally in favour of Montreal and in some cases big odds are offered. Quite a lot of money upon the game." During that decade, when industry titans in the rich mining and lumber towns of Northern Ontario were forming leagues and teams and splurging on ringers to win Stanley Cups, tens of thousands of dollars were routinely waged on matches.

In 1918, PCHA founder Frank Patrick told *The Globe*, "There is too much open gambling going on at the Toronto Arena on hockey matches." In Conn Smythe's time, organized gamblers famously congregated at the "bull ring" on the Church Street mezzanine of old Maple Leaf Gardens. The bull ring flourished because the ever-vigilant Smythe (who played the ponies himself) and the local constabulary likely turned a blind eye to its illicit activities. There are also the hockey stories of players who gambled, like Babe Pratt, Don Gallinger and Billy Taylor, among others more recently.

Gambling and professional sport is nothing new. For better or worse, sportsbooks are now a conspicuous, controversial and cautionary reality—an indicator of the state of hockey today.

Linus Ullmark and Jeremy Swayman celebrate another Bruins win.

◄▼ 2022–23 The Boston Bruins rampage through the NHL record books, establishing team marks for the fastest 100 points (in their 61st game) and fastest 50 wins (64th game). Their 63rd, 64th and 65th wins set single-season records for victories. Their 133rd point on April 11 surpasses the previous mark set 46 years earlier by Montreal in 1976-77.

In its abundance of wins, Boston becomes the first NHL team to feature both a 40-win goalie in Linus Ullmark (with a league best .938 save percentage and 1.89 goals-against average) and a 20-win goalie in Jeremy Swayman. Little good comes from it in the postseason. The Bruins fall in Round 1, losing 4-3 in games to eventual Stanley Cup finalist Florida.

Most Wins, One Season

Team	Season	GP	W	L	T	OT	P
Boston	2022-23	82	65	12	—	5	135
Detroit	1995-96	82	62	13	7	0	131
Tampa Bay	2018-19	82	62	16	—	4	128
Montreal	1976-77	80	60	8	12	0	132

The Islanders' Cal Clutterbuck checks Vancouver's Brad Hunt.

▲ 2022–23 Cal Clutterbuck records his 3,633rd hit, eclipsing Dustin Brown's record to become the all-time NHL leader in hits.

First-ever PWHL draft pick Taylor Heise (right) and former U.S. tennis icon and women's sport advocate Billie Jean King.

◄ 2023–24 The inaugural PWHL draft takes place on September 18. Minnesota wins the draft lottery and selects American Taylor Heise of the NCAA first overall. Jocelyne Larocque is the first Canadian drafted (second overall). Each team was allowed three free-agent signings prior to the lottery.

▲ 2023 Hilary Knight scores three goals in the 6–3 final against Canada to win USA's 10th World Championship in 2023. Knight, who wins her ninth title, becomes the first player to reach 100 career points at the IIHF tournament.

The Vegas Golden Knights, 2023 Stanley Cup champions.

▲ 2022–23 **The Stanley Cup.** After becoming Cup finalists in their inaugural season, Vegas wins the Stanley Cup in its sixth year, defeating Florida in five quick games. The Golden Knights show little mercy, amassing 26 goals to the Panthers' 12 markers. Reilly Smith scores the Cup clincher in Game 5's 9–3 beatdown by Vegas. Mark Stone becomes the first player in more than 100 years to notch a hat trick in a Cup-winning game, last accomplished by Babe Dye in 1922. Jonathan Marchessault is awarded the Conn Smythe Trophy as playoff MVP.

2023 Summer The U.S.-based Mark Walter Group acquires women's hockey's pro league, the Premier Hockey Federation, and partners with the Professional Women's Hockey Players Association to bring together the world's best players in one league, the PWHL, and one labor union, the Professional Women's Hockey League Players Association.

In its inaugural season the PWHL ices six teams in Montreal, Toronto, New York, Boston, Ottawa and St. Paul, Minnesota, in a 24-game schedule from January 1 to May 5. They compete for the Walter Cup, a sterling silver award named after the Walter family in honor of their philanthropic efforts as the league's financial patrons.

2023 **The Spengler Cup.** In what is the oldest European hockey tournament, Canada defeats Finnish team KalPa Kuopio 6-3 in a December 29 game played exactly 100 years after the first Spengler Cup game in 1923. In the final, Swiss team HC Davos beats Czechia's HC Dynamo Pardubice 5-3.

2023–24 Ella Shelton scores the first-ever goal in PWHL history as New York defeats Toronto in a 4–0 road win before a sellout crowd in Toronto on January 1.

2023–24 Former NHLer Adam Johnson of the Nottingham Panthers (of the UK's Elite Ice Hockey League) dies in a freak on-ice collision on October 28 when Sheffield Steeler Matt Petgrave's left skate blade cuts Johnson's throat, causing him to bleed out. Following the incident several NHLers begin wearing neck guards. The EIHL makes neck guards mandatory on January 1.

Gavin Brindley and Ryan Leonard.

▲ 2024 USA goes undefeated in seven games to capture its sixth gold medal at the World Junior Championship.

Canada's Danielle Serdachny scores the gold medal winner in overtime against USA's Aerin Frankel.

▲ 2024 **The Women's World Championship.** Canadian captain Marie-Philip Poulin scores twice and Danielle Serdachny pots the gold medal winner at 5:16 in overtime to defeat USA 6–5. American Laila Edwards is named tournament MVP.

2024 "I'm not going to sit here and complain about it ... Part of playoffs is trying to hurt every player on the other team ... People don't say that but that's just a fact of the game."

—Brad Marchand, on being injured in Game 3 of 2024's second round between Boston and Florida after taking a high hit from Panthers center Sam Bennett on May 10

World champion Czechia.

▲ 2024 **The World Championship.** For the first time in a decade, all three medalists are European teams, with Czechia taking its first gold medal in 14 years, Switzerland the silver and Sweden the bronze. David Pastrnak and David Kampf score third-period markers in Czechia's 2–0 gold victory. Swiss forward Kevin Fiala wins MVP status.

Corey Perry saluting Edmonton fans.

▲ 2023–24 Corey Perry reaches the Stanley Cup Final with a record five different franchises, winning his first and only Cup with Anaheim in 2006–07, losing four more times, as of 2023–24, with Dallas (2019–20), Montreal (2020–21), Tampa Bay (2021–22) and Edmonton (2023–24).

Kendall Coyne Schofield.

▲ 2023–24 Captain Kendall Coyne Schofield is first to lift the Walter Cup trophy after Minnesota beats Boston in a five-game series for the PWHL championship. The top four regular-season teams played a two-round best-of-five playoff to determine the champion.

◄ 2023–24 Nikita Kucherov wins the Art Ross Trophy. Selected 58th overall in the second round of the 2011 NHL Draft, Kucherov notches 44 goals and 144 points, four points ahead of Nathan MacKinnon's 51-goal and 140-point season. It's Kucherov's second Art Ross, after his first in 2018–19.

Tampa Bay's Nikita Kucherov.

The 2024 Stanley Cup champion Florida Panthers.

▲ **2023–24** **The Stanley Cup.** Florida wins its first Stanley Cup, defeating Edmonton in a classic seven-game Cup Final, with the Panthers winning the first three games and the Oilers claiming the next three to set up a one-and-done Game 7. The last time an NHL team went 0-3 in the first three games to force a seventh game in the Final was in 1945.

The finale was a nailbiter, won by the slimmest of margins, a 2-1 victory on a second-period goal by Florida forward Sam Reinhart. Of zero consolation, a devastated Connor McDavid gets the Conn Smythe Trophy as playoff MVP. The Edmonton captain nets 42 points, including a record-breaking 34 assists.

Seattle assistant coach Jessica Campbell.

▲ **2024–25** Jessica Campbell becomes the first woman to hold a bench position as an assistant NHL coach, promoted by the Seattle Kraken on July 3. After playing in the NCAA, the CWHL and on Canada's women's national team, Campbell spent two years as an assistant coach alongside Dan Bylsma of Seattle's AHL affiliate in Coachella Valley. When Bylsma was hired as head coach of the Kraken in May, Campbell came aboard to work on player development. "I'm humbled, obviously ... to be the first, but that's never really where my focus is. It's always on the work. It's on the impact. It's on the job," said Campbell.

2024–25 Pretrial hearings begin in November involving five pro players accused of sexually assaulting a woman in a London, Ontario, hotel, when they were Canadian team members at the 2018 World Junior Championship. In 2022, TSN blew open the case, reporting that Hockey Canada quietly settled a multimillion-dollar lawsuit by the alleged victim, using special internal funds to resolve sexual-assault cases. The trial began in April 2025.

2024–25 In a first for North America's four major leagues, Rogers Communications sells off a two-year NHL rights package of national Monday night games in Canada to Amazon's Prime Video service. Soon after, Rogers doubles-up 2014's original 12-year, $5.2-billion Canadian deal, which expires after 2025–26, to ink a new 12-year agreement, worth $11 billion. It ends in 2037–38.

2024–25 The NCAA approves rules that will permit players from the CHL (comprised of the WHL, OHA and QMJHL) to compete at U.S. colleges and universities—which effectively lifts the NCAA's long-established ban on CHL juniors playing in the NCAA.

2025 **"Thank you, Ilya Sorokin, for letting me score 895."**

—Alexander Ovechkin, on becoming the NHL's all-time goals leader

Alexander Ovechkin's celebratory bellyflop after his 895th NHL goal.

▲ **2024–25** **Alexander Ovechkin sets the all-time NHL goals mark.** Ovechkin becomes only the 10th NHL career leader in regular-season goals after surpassing Wayne Gretzky's 31-year reign of 894 goals on April 6, 2025. On a pass from Tom Watson, Ovechkin fires his historic marker with a wrist shot from the faceoff circle that eludes New York Islanders goalie Ilya Sorokin's blocker. The on-ice ceremony afterward features Gretzky, Gary Bettman, Ovechkin's family and an Ovechkin-Sorokin hug.

Ex-Leafs brawl with CRA

2024–25 The Canada Revenue Agency vs. Canadian professional sports. The dispute over tax bills worth millions between Canada's taxman and Toronto forward John Tavares garners new headlines after Patrick Marleau and Jake Muzzin file separate appeals to the CRA, each raising the same issue on their multi-million-dollar signing bonuses. Should they be taxed at 15 percent and not at the top income bracket, over 50 percent? Are their signing bonuses part of their employment income or an "inducement to sign an agreement," as per a Canada-U.S. tax treaty provision? The rulings could have huge ramifications for Canadian sports fans.

2024–25 "Can you guys pull this off? Can you really pull it off?"

—Gary Bettman, probing tech billionaire and NBA Utah Jazz owner Ryan Smith in February 2024 about relocating the plagued Phoenix Coyotes to Salt Lake City as the Utah Hockey Club for play in 2024–25. Smith answered a definitive yes: "We're here and we're ready."

Connor McDavid celebrates scoring the 4 Nations Face-Off tournament winner.

▲ 2025 "This wasn't a win for themselves, this was a win for 40-plus-million people."

—Team Canada coach Jon Cooper, on the prickly collision of sport and politics after his team defeated USA 3–2 in overtime at the NHL's 4 Nations Face-Off in February. The dramatic finish to the eight-day series between USA, Canada, Sweden and Finland unfolded under the menacing actions of U.S. President Donald Trump's tariff threats and his comments about Canada as America's 51st state. Connor McDavid scores the breathtaking tournament winner at 8:18 of OT.

Johnny Gaudreau and brother Matthew, 2014.

◄ 2024 NHL all-star Johnny Gaudreau, 31, and his brother Matthew, 29, are struck and killed by a drunk driver as they cycled on a rural road near their hometown in New Jersey. The tragedy occurred the evening before they were to serve as groomsmen at their sister Katie's wedding. The driver charged in their deaths had a blood-alcohol level of .087, above the .08 legal limit.

A longtime Calgary Flame and later Columbus Blue Jacket, Johnny Gaudreau was known as Johnny Hockey for his game speed and skill and his big-hearted, infectious enthusiasm. "There are few players in hockey history that matched his passion and love for the game of hockey," said former GM Brian Burke. His brother Matthew's career was spent entirely in the minors.

Gaudreau, selected 104th overall in 2011, had multiple 20-plus goal seasons and a career-best 40-goal season. A Hobey Baker Award winner in U.S. collegiate hockey, Gaudreau won 2017's Lady Byng Trophy for sportsmanship in NHL play.

2025 The World Junior Championship. USA wins back-to-back championships, defeating Finland 4–3 on Teddy Stiga's goal against Finnish goalie Petteri Rimpinen at 8:04 of OT. Canada fails to make the medal round for the second-straight year, to which Canadian forward Calum Ritchie said post-game: "It sucks."

Girl Power

Reneta Fast, Sarah Nurse, Natalie Spooner and Mélodie Daoust, 2021.

Megan Bozek, Brianna Decker, Kacey Bellamy, Amanda Kessel and Melissa Samoskevich, 2019.

If there were any doubts about whether the PWHL changed the way people think about their game and its arrival, those misgivings eroded considerably following the Montreal–Toronto match at Scotiabank Arena on February 16, 2024. Tickets sold out immediately. The crowd of 19,285 shattered women's attendance records. In her description of the Battle on Bay Street between the rival hockey cities, *Globe and Mail* sports writer Rachel Brady witnessed something that went beyond just a one-off curiosity moment in sport.

"I saw rows of girls," wrote Brady, "in their team jerseys, a sea of bright-coloured minor-hockey crests, rainbow flags, dads and daughters, couples in matching Toronto jerseys, and groups of older women sporting their faded, decades-old hockey jackets and beer-league sweaters. Suites were spotted with VIPs, from sports executives to NHL players and Olympic medalists."

The night was about parity and equality—now a more attainable right that had been waged by a small army of hockey pioneers from generation to generation during more than a century of play and gender discrimination.

Women's hockey had rarely ever qualified as "real" sport. And, certainly, never big-league sport.

Trailblazers like Albertine Lapensée, Hilda Ranscombe and the great Bobbie Rosenfeld were admonished for their competitive spirit and pluck, not only by game fans and that era's tsk-tsk-ing homebodies but by the likes of misogynistic 1930s columnist Andy Lytle, who wouldn't have believed his eyes at the magnitude of the Battle on Bay Street's spectacle.

Everyone from the sacred to the profane had a voice in the "novelty" of women in sport. Little changed until the first world competitions in 1987, which inspired major tournaments in Europe and Asia and the 1990 IIHF-sanctioned Women's World Championship.

Olympic recognition followed in 1998, triggering new corporate and government assistance while creating top-level competitive opportunities for Canadians, Americans and the many national start-up squads overseas.

Typically marginalized, those like Hayley Wickenheiser and Kendall Coyne Schofield grew up playing at one time or another on boys' teams and, later, even men's pro teams to spike their compete levels. This history runs deep, perhaps most famously storied by Abby Hoffman, the nine-year old Toronto girl who cropped her hair and geared up at home to secretly play on boys' teams. She caught world attention when Abby, really Abigail, was invited to play in her league's all-star game in 1956 and league officials asked for her birth certificate.

After years of unsuccessful women's hockey leagues, the PWHL should tip the cultural struggle to less gender bias and give women the opportunity to take full control of their own experience and, importantly, earn a living playing hockey.

Glossary

AAA (Montreal) Amateur Athletic Association
AAHL American Amateur Hockey League
AHA American Hockey Association
AHAC Amateur Hockey Association of Canada
AHL American Hockey League
CAHA Canadian Amateur Hockey Association
CAHL Canadian Amateur Hockey League
CBC Canadian Broadcasting Corporation
CHL Canadian Hockey League
CRA Canada Revenue Agency
COWHL Central Ontario Women's Hockey League
CWHL Canadian Women's Hockey League
ECAHA Eastern Canada Amateur Hockey Association
ECHA Eastern Canada Hockey Association
ECHL East Coast Hockey League
EHL Eastern Hockey League
EIHL Elite Ice Hockey League
FAHL Federal Amateur Hockey League
GTHL Greater Toronto Hockey League
HNIC *Hockey Night in Canada*
IAHL International-American Hockey League
IHL International Hockey League
IIHF International Ice Hockey Federation
IOC International Olympic Committee
KHL Kontinental Hockey League
KLM line Vladimir Krutov, Igor Larionov and Sergei Makarov
LCB line Reggie Leach, Bobby Clarke and Bill Barber
LIHG Ligue Internationale de Hockey sur Glace
MHL Manitoba Hockey League
MLG Maple Leaf Gardens
MLSE Maple Leaf Sports & Entertainment
MSG Madison Square Garden
NBA National Basketball Association
NBC National Broadcasting Corporation
NCAA National Collegiate Athletic Association
NHA National Hockey Association
NHL National Hockey League
NHLPA National Hockey League Players' Association
OHA Ontario Hockey Association
OHL Ontario Hockey League
OPHL Ontario Professional Hockey League
OSAHL Okanagan Senior Amateur Hockey League
PA Players' Association (as in NHLPA)
PCHA Pacific Coast Hockey Association
PCHL Pacific Coast Hockey League
PHF Premier Hockey Federation
PWHL Professional Women's Hockey League
PWHLPA Professional Women's Hockey League Players Association
PWHPA Professional Women's Hockey Players Association
QMJHL Quebec (Major) Maritimes Junior Hockey League
QSHL Quebec Senior Hockey League
SI *Sports Illustrated*
USAHA United States Amateur Hockey Association
USHL United States Hockey League
WHA World Hockey Association
WCHL Western Canada Hockey League
WHL Western Hockey League
WPHL Western Pennsylvania Hockey League

Some of these initials could apply to different leagues of the same name in different eras. Image: Boston Garden, ca. 1935–1955

Acknowledgments

At the time it seemed like a fairly straightforward idea. Tell the story of hockey in a timeline format to celebrate the 150th anniversary of the first organized indoor game. A significant milestone, some historians even labeled that historic match, played at the Victoria Skating Rink in Montreal on March 3, 1875, the "big bang" moment of game history.

Anything but straightforward, the story took on another face in our fiery trials to bring the evolution of play to life. The project required a comprehensive and objective presentation of images that would reflect the full expression of a sometimes-unhinged game. The book had to be, first, a visual spectacle.

The great challenge was bringing verve and context onto the two-dimensional space of the printed page. Without question, the book would eat up a lot of imagery—anywhere from five to 10 pictures per page spread. The style of writing had to be simple, in a just-the-facts composition to frame the story in an accessible light. Text, typeface and picture had to work in unison like cogs and springs of a timepiece, though the words would act mostly as a support mechanism.

It meant finding a talented graphic designer with vision and plenty of patience and resolve to work within what this book's designer calls "the constraints of geometry," in order to package everything without it looking like chaos. The writer had to trim the game's story of its circumlocution. (See what I mean.) The fact-checker must be a real hockey historian, conversant in each of the eras of competitive play dating back 150 years and earlier.

The managing editor, as the organizational chief, would have to perform like a chariot driver working to keep her creative team of wily Berber horses from charging off in all directions. It was an all-hands-on-deck commitment. The publisher needed to be the best fit. One who not only recognized a good book idea at the right time, but believed in the work strongly enough to bear the costs of a 600-picture book.

That's the surface and known stuff. The subtleties of bringing this book home became the iceberg below the watermark. It really meant a tireless effort to secure the high-resolution imagery and the dogged detective work to obtain the photo rights. It meant working the text into the "historical present" to elevate old reports into meaningful stories for today's fan, holding the line on the limited budget, keeping the multiple design do-overs to a minimum, maintaining the house style (is it cup or Cup?), laboring over the cover layout and imagery to represent all of hockey history and, finally, keeping the crazy contained while blowing through deadlines.

What was supposed to be six months of work turned into 16 months of inspired creation, which says much about how everyone enjoyed working on this project. Really. So thank you to graphic designer Gareth Lind, for bringing this wild idea to life and extracting the gold from the gravel to make the imagery of hockey pop so wonderfully in print. Thank you to Firefly Books managing editor Julie Takasaki, who saved the day so often. And for her limitless contact list. Thank you to historian Jean-Patrice Martel, for saying "wrong" when I was, ahem, wrong. Thank you to proofreader Ronnie Shuker for his hockey sense and commitment to proper grammar. Thank you to Firefly Books design manager Hartley Millson and editorial and production intern Payton Flood for removing dust and scratches on old images and ensuring color quality throughout the all-important printing process. And thank you to Firefly Books publisher Lionel Koffler for his encouragement and valued support.

I would also like to thank Craig Campbell, Phil Pritchard and all the contributing photographers at the Hockey Hall of Fame. This book would not have been possible without their concerted efforts. Images on Ice, the Hall's thriving image bank, is responsible for hundreds of pictures on these pages. Those like Howie Morenz, Maurice Richard and Wayne Gretzky are the historical backbone of this book.

Thank you to the commercial image agencies who also played such an important role, including Getty, Canadian Press Images, Associated Press, Alamy and Icon Sportswire. Special thanks to Andrea Gordon of CP for all her help and patience.

Thank you to the following individuals, libraries, archives and museums for their generous support: Nancy Fay and Margaret Couper of Library and Archives Canada and Jacqueline Vincent of Chislehurst Digitization Inc. Images of early Canadian hockey courtesy of Library and Archives Canada.

Photos of early Boston hockey courtesy of the Boston Public Library, Leslie Jones Collection.

Early painting and hockey skate advertisement courtesy of the Nova Scotia Archives.

Lena Beliveau of the Royal Military College of Canada. Image of the 1886 RMC varsity team courtesy of the Royal Military College.

David S. Eskenazi. Images of Bernie Morris and the Seattle Metropolitans courtesy of David S. Eskenazi.

Kimberly McGarr. Photos of the early Montreal hockey and the Richard Riot courtesy of the Bibliothèque et Archives nationales du Québec,

Addison Oberg. Photo of the 1961 Smoke Eaters courtesy of the Trail Historical Society.

Bruce Jessop. Photo of Czechoslovakia's 1969 win against the Soviets courtesy of International Hockey Archives, © Photo: International Hockey Archives: Rolle Rygin.

Katie Tanner. Photo of John Paris, Jr. courtesy of the Nova Scotia Sports Hall of Fame.

Jason Beck. Photo of the 1955 Penticton Vees courtesy of the British Columbia Sports Hall of Fame.

Christian Vachon. Images of early hockey in Montreal courtesy of the McCord Stewart Museum.

Shannon Baxter. Images of early hockey in Nova Scotia courtesy of the Dartmouth Heritage Museum.

Larry Paquette of the Original Hockey Hall of Fame and Lisa Gervais of Queens University Archives. Image of John Harty courtesy of Queen's University Archives.

Noémie Provencher and Marianne Podilchuk of Le club de hockey Canadien. Images of Jean Béliveau's contract signing and Elmer Lach courtesy of Le club de hockey Canadien Inc.

Mitchell Norenberg of the Edmonton Historical Board, City of Edmonton Archives. Image of a ladies hockey team in Alberta courtesy of the City of Edmonton Archives.

Vancouver Public Library. Image of the Denman Street Arena courtesy of the Vancouver Public Library.

Image of the 228th Battalion junior squad courtesy of the Discovery North Bay Museum.

Elizabeth Johnson. Image of the Edmonton Rustlers courtesy of the Provincial Archives of Alberta.

Matthew Gourlie. Image of Fred Sasakamoose courtesy of the Saskatchewan Sports Hall of Fame.

Christa Dix and Sophie Adams of the Griffin Museum of Photography. Image of Boston Garden courtesy of Copyright © Arthur Griffin Archive.

Emma Baril of CBC. Image of Danny Gallivan and René Lecavalier courtesy of the Canadian Broadcasting Corporation. And Rob Purchase at Sportsnet, Rogers Sports and Media.

Don Pillar and Aubrey Ferguson. Image of Bee Hive Corn Syrup promotion courtesy of the St. Lawrence Starch Company.

Marc Durand, author of *La Coupe à Québec*: *Les Bulldogs et la naissance du hockey*. Images of the Quebec hockey courtesy of the Ernie Fitzsimmons Collection.

Lynda Baril, author of *Les Glorieuses: plus de cent ans de hockey féminin au Québec*. Image of Isobel Stanley, 1889, courtesy of the author.

Kevin Lennon of Trillium Corporate Communications. Image of Paul Henderson celebrating his winning goal at the 1972 Summit Series courtesy of Frank Lennon's estate.

And thank you to these other institutions and individuals for their valued support:

The Yale University Art Gallery, Harvard College Library (*Wide Awake* magazine), canadiana.ca, Wikimedia Commons, Toronto Public Library, Library of Congress, Canada Post, Sweden Post Office, European researcher Patrick Houda and indexer Katie Weekes for her creative and administrative assistance.

Thank you to the following newspapers and magazines for their research materials and headlines, including the *Montreal (Daily) Star*, *Montreal Gazette*, *Montreal Daily Witness*, *Toronto Star*, *Canadian Magazine*, *Ottawa Citizen*, *Winnipeg (Manitoba) Free Press*, *Globe and Mail*, *Pittsburgh Daily Post*, *Spalding Ice Hockey and Ice Polo Guide*, *Yukon World*, *La Presse*, *Oregon Daily Journal*, *Pittsburgh Press*, *The Hockey Hour*, *New York Times*, *The Hockey News*, *Chicago Tribune*, *Boston Globe* and *Detroit Free Press*.

Thank you to the following artists for their continued support:

Aislin (Terry Mosher). Cartoon of the NHL-WHA merger, originally published in 1977, courtesy of the artist and the *Montreal Gazette*.

Bruce MacKinnon. Illustration of Sidney Crosby, originally published in February 2014, courtesy of the artist and the *Chronicle Herald*, Halifax.

Arthur Racey. Editorial cartoons of hockey courtesy of the Arthur Racey estate, the *Montreal Star* and the McCord Stewart Museum.

Lou Skuce. Cartoon of hockey, originally published in November 1914, courtesy of the *Toronto Sunday World*.

Jimmy Thompson. Sports cartoon of Conn Smythe, originally published in October 1930, courtesy of the *Toronto Star*.

This book's Citations and Notes is available at picturingthegame.ca/hhof-timeline.

—Don Weekes, May 2025

Photo Credits

Photographer Nat Turofsky with Toronto's Harry Watson, Bill Ezinicki and John McCormack in the Maple Leafs dressing room, 1940s.

Boston Public Library (Estate of Leslie Jones): p. 5 (game play), 8 (dressing room), 65 (Conacher), 73 (game), 76 (Hill)

Yale University Art Gallery: p. 10 (lacrosse)

Nova Scotia Sports Hall of Fame: p. 11 (Starr ad), 156 (Paris)

Wikimedia Commons: p. 12 (Franklin, Mi'kmaq), 18 (ice machine), 72 (Rivulettes), 110 (Sterner)

The Collection of the Dartmouth Heritage Museum: p. 12 (laborers), 13 (Forbes), 23 (Chebuctos), 24 (skates)

Alamy Stock Photo

History and Art Collection/Alamy Stock Photo: p. 12 (Quebec rink)
Science History Images/Alamy Stock Photo: p. 22 (Wright)
Historic Collection/Alamy Stock Photo: p. 35 (Dawson)
Dragan Ilic/Alamy Stock Photo: p. 125 (postage)
Nova Scotia Archives: p. 13 (Acme ad), 14 (curlers)
Bibliothèque et Archives nationales du Quebec (BAnQ): p. 13 (Victoria Rink), 20 (poster), 33 (arena), 95 (street riot, protestors)

Canadian Illustrated News: p. 14 (lacrosse)

McCord Museum: p. 14 (lacrosse), 16 (Victoria Rink), 19 (trophy, McGill), 28 (Victoria Rink), 29 (St. Mary's, Victorias), 33 (Victorias), 49 (Blueshirts), 53 (Morenz), 54 (fire), 63 (arena)

Anonymous: p. 15 (Cigars)

Montreal Gazette: p. 17 (game report), 18 (rules), 33 (arena ad), 40 (game report), 56 (game report), 83 (stat box)

Marc Durand, La Coupe du Hockey: p. 18 (Miller), 29 (Quebec HC), 47 (Bulldogs)

Library and Archives Canada

Library and Archives Canada: p. 19 (Montreal Victorias), 58 (Forbes), (Hockey Hour), 66 (Vézina/Hockey Hour)
J.E. Livernois / Library and Archives Canada / PA-024066: p. 19 (arena)
Alexander Henderson / Library and Archives Canada / C-081683: p. 21 (McGill)
Steel & Wing / Library and Archives Canada / C-079304: p. 24 (Victorias)
George Arthur Emerson Chapman / Library and Archives Canada / PA-203558: p. 43 (arena)
Rice Studios / Library and Archives Canada / C-019274: p. 63 (Byng)

Frank Lennon/Toronto Star / Library and Archives Canada / e008440339: p. 126 (Henderson)

Wide Awake Magazine: p. 20 (outdoor play)

Queen's University Archive (with permission from Larry Paquette, Original Hockey Hall of Fame): p. 28 (Harty)

The Mail and Empire: p. 22 (curling sketch)

Lynda Baril Collection: p. 23 (Lady Stanley)

Royal Military College of Canada: p. 21 (team)

Montreal Star: p. 28 (McCulloch), 30 (report), 31 (AAHL), 32 (Shamrocks), 34 (goal nets), 35 (women, Shamrocks), 38 (cartoon), 40 (cartoon), 42 (arena ad), 43 (sketches), 45 (cartoon), 56 (Malone report)

Canadian Magazine: p. 30 (player sketch)

Montreal Daily Witness: p. 31 (sketches)

Library of Congress, LCCN 2001696502: p. 31 (arena)

Spalding Ice Hockey and Ice Polo Guide: p. 32 (covers)

Toronto Saturday Night: p. 32 (sketches)

Hockey: Canada's Royal Winter Game: p. 34 (pond hockey, woman)

Manitoba/Winnipeg Free Press: p. 36 (Cup sketch/headline, game sketch)

The Globe: p. 36 (McKay)

Toronto Star: p. 42 (cartoon), 66, (headline), 71 (illustration)

How to Play Hockey by Percy LeSueur: p. 45 (cover)

City of Edmonton Archives EA-500-213: p. 46 (team)

La Presse: p. 46 (newspaper), 57 (Canadiens), 60 (Morenz/Joliat/ Gagnon)

Vancouver Public Library, Special Collections, VPL 6549: p. 47 (arena)

Discovery North Bay Museum: p. 49 (228th Battalion)

David S. Eskenazi: p. 50 (Morris), 56 (Metropolitans)

Oregon Daily Journal: p. 58 (Johnson)

Toronto Sunday World: p. 64 (cartoon)

Pittsburgh Press: p. 65 (game report)

Canada Post: p. 68 (postage)

Provincial Archives of Alberta: p. 72 (Rustlers)

Getty

John G. Zimmerman/Getty Images: p. 80 (Plante)
SI Cover/Getty Images: p. 98 (Béliveau)
Bettmann/Getty Images: p. 99 (Lindsay), 103 (Plante)
Walter Iooss Jr./Getty Images: p. 112 (Hull)
Tony Triolo/Getty Images: p. 114 (Orr)
Heinz Kluetmeier/Getty Images: p. 134 (Olympics)
B Bennett/Getty Images: p. 144 (Lemieux/Gretzky)
Steve Babineau/Getty Images: p. 148 (Stastny)
David E. Klutho/Getty Images: p. 149 (Lemieux/Casey)
Donaldson Collection/Getty Images: p. 166 (Wheaties)
Richard T Gagnon/Getty Images: p. 216 (Gaudreau)
Maddie Meyer/Getty Images: p. 216 (4 Nations)

The Hockey News: p. 87 (cover)

Associated Press

AP Photo/J. Walter Green: p. 87 (Olympics)
AP Photo: p. 109 (Howe), 143 (Piestany)
AP Photo/Sal Veder: p. 122 (Orr/ Esposito)
AP Photo/Chris O'Meara: p. 153 (Rhéaume)
AP Photo/Doug Kanter: p. 156 (Whitten)
AP Photo/Eric Draper: p. 157 (Gretzky)
AP Photo/Dan Loh: p. 161 (Foxtrax)
AP Photo/Rick Bowmer: p. 160 (rat trick)
AP Photo/Rusty Kennedy: p. 163 (Vernon)
AP Photo/Carlos Osorio: p. 164 (Shanahan), 189 (Michigan)
AP Photo/Keith Srakocic: p. 166 (Lemieux)
AP Photo/Gene Puskar: p. 167 (Hull/Hasek), 181 (Sunohara), 185 (Detroit)
AP Photo/Dusan Vranic: p. 168 (Stepanek/Sekeras)
AP Photo/John Bazemore: p. 169 (Kovalchuk/NHL)
AP Photo/Charles Krupa: p. 173 (Devils)
AP Photo/Ed Betz: p. 175 (Boucher)
AP Photo/Steve Nesius: p. 180 (Tampa)
AP Photo/George Widman: p. 181 (Ovechkin)
AP Photo/John Marshall Mantel: p. 181 (Staal)
AP Photo/Elsa: p. 182 (Sweden)
AP Photo/Ivan Sekretarev: p. 182 (Red Square)
AP Photo/Mark Avery: p. 184 (Anaheim)
AP Photo/Tom Hevezi: p. 184 (London)
AP Photo/Paul Sancya: p. 186 (Malkin)
AP Photo/Julie Jacobson: p. 187 (Szabados)
AP Photo/Chris O'Meara: p. 187 (Crosby)
AP Photo/Keith Srakocic: p. 188 (Savard)
AP Photo/Matt Slocum: p. 188 (Byfuglien), 195 (MacKinnon)
AP Photo/Misha Japaridze: p. 189 (plane crash)
AP Photo/Julio Cortez: p. 194 (Price), 201 (Germany)
AP Photo/Mark J. Terrill: p. 195 (Kings)
AP Photo/Alan Diaz: p. 196 (Bjugstad)
AP Photo/Nam Y. Huh: p. 197 (Keith)
AP Photo/LM Otero: p. 198 (McDavid)
AP Photo/Mark Humphrey: p. 200 (Murray)
AP Photo/John Locher: p. 202 (Ovechkin)
AP Photo/Jeff Chiu: p. 203 (Schofield), 210 (Grier)
AP Photo/Phelan Ebenhack: p. 207 (Tampa), 209 (Lehkonen)
AP Photo/David Becker: p. 207 (Eichel)
AP Photo/Godofredo A. Vasquez: p. 210 (Kessel)

Canadian Press

CP Photo/COC: p. 91 (Mercurys)
The Canadian Press/Doug Ball: p. 130 (Gretzky)
The Canadian Press/Bill Grimshaw: p. 137 (Soviets), 145 (McDonald)
CP/Dave Buston: p. 138 (Gretzky), 146 (Gretzky)
CP Photo/Macdougall: p. 140 (Tonelli)
The Canadian Press: p. 142 (brawl)
The Canadian Press/Frank Gunn: p. 148 (Yuen), 204 (Ayres), 205 (Korpisalo), 208 (Matthews, Chara), 210 (Tkachuk)
The Canadian Press/Jacques Boissinot: p. 158 (Robitaille), 183 (Toews)

CP Photo/Kevin Udahl: p. 165 (Kennedy)
CP Photo/Paul Chiasson: p. 166 (Hasek), 176 (fan sign), 177 (Brière), 182 (Ward)
CP Photo/Jeff McIntosh: p. 169 (Tootoo)
CP Photo/Chuck Stoody: p. 169 (Brashear), 174 (Moore), 180 (Thornton)
CP Photo/Ryan Remiorz: p. 170 (Avalanche), 171 (Slovakia), 172 (Lidstrom), 202 (Humboldt), 208 (Olympics)
CP Photo/COC/Andre Forget: p. 170 (Kariya), p. 171 (Fleury)
CP Photo/Tom Hanson: p. 171 (Hefford), 174 (Theodore)
CP Photo/Kevin Frayer: p. 173 (Lemieux/McCabe)
The Canadian Press/Graham Hughes: p. 178 (Ovechkin, Poulin)
The Canadian Press/Jason Franson: p. 178 (McDavid), 196 (Benn), 205 (Point), 206 (Quick/McDavid), 211 (arena), 214 (Perry)
The Canadian Press/Darryl Dyck: p. 189 (Sedins), 212 (Clutterbuck)
The Canadian Press/Jonathan Hayward: p. 190 (Thomas)
The Canadian Press/John Woods: p. 191 (Jets), 215 (Campbell)
The Canadian Press/Dave Chidley: p. 192 (lockout)
The Canadian Press/Nathan Denette: p. 199 (World Cup), 215 (Florida)
The Canadian Press/Sean Kilpatrick: p. 200 (Matthews)
Lehtikuva/Vesa Moilanen: p. 201 (USA)
The Canadian Press/Ethan Cairns: p. 207 (Hughes)
The Canadian Press/Spencer Colby: p. 212 (draft/Heise)

Icon Sportswire

Icon Sportswire: p. 184 (Afinogenov)
Tony Ding/Icon Sportswire: p. 186 (Crosby)
Christopher Szagola/Icon Sportswire: p. 186 (Brodeur)
Mingo Nesmith/Icon Sportswire: p. 186 (Weekes), 214 (Schofield)
Anson Hung/Icon Sportswire: p. 190 (Boogaard)
Andy Mead/YCJ/Icon Sportswire: p. 192 (Pronger)
Shelly Castellano/Icon Sportswire: p. 192 (Quick)
Bill Streicher/Icon Sportswire: p. 192 (Subban)
Michael Tureski/Icon Sportswire: p. 193 (Bollard)
Daniel A. Anderson/Zuma Press/ Icon Sportswire: p. 194 (Poulin)
Minas Panagiotakis/Icon Sportswire: p. 196 (Price)
Robin Alam/Icon Sportswire: p. 198 (Kane)
Vincent Ethier/Icon Sportswire: p. 201 (McDavid)
Greg Thompson/Icon Sportswire: p. 202 (Karlsson)
Joshua Sarner/Icon Sportswire: p. 202 (Fleury)
Brett Holmes/Icon Sportswire: p. 204 (Draisaitl)
John Cordes/Icon Sportswire: p. 212 (Bruins)
Jeff Speer/Icon Sportswire: p. 213 (Vegas)
Fred Kfoury III/Icon Sportswire: p. 214 (Kucherov)
Andrew Mordzynski/Icon Sportswire: p. 215 (Ovechkin)

David Bier/Le club de hockey Canadien Inc.: p. 92 (Lach), 93 (Béliveau)

St. Lawrence Starch Company: p. 93 (ad)

Saskatchewan Sports Hall of Fame: p. 94 (Sasakamoose)

BC Sports Hall of Fame: p. 96 (world cups)

Trail Historical Society: p. 106 (game play)

© Photo: International Hockey Archives: Rolle Rygin: p. 119 (Czechs beat Soviets)

CBC Still Photo Collection: p. 118 (Gallivan/Lecavalier)

Terry Mosher/Aislin: p. 126 (cartoon)

Bruce MacKinnon/Chronicle Herald, Halifax: p. 179 (Crosby)

Swedish Post Office: p. 157 (postage)

Griffin Museum, Copyright © Arthur Griffin Archive: p. 218 (arena)

Don Weekes Collection: p. 9 (kids' game)

Hockey Hall of Fame

Hockey Hall of Fame Archives: p. 15 (Creighton), 22 (Paton), 23 (Stanley), 24 (Rebels), 26 (Taylor), 27 (ring), 28 (AAA), 30 (Victorias), 32 (Trihey), 36 (Wellingtons), 37 (Portage), 39 (Klondikers), 40 (Phillips, Smith), 42 (Thistles), 43 (Lalonde), 44 (LeSueur, stick, Renfrew), 45 (Montagu), 46 (Lalonde, Baker), 47 (Cleghorn, Maxwell), 48 (L. Patrick, F. Patrick, Rangers), 49 (crest), 50 (Irvin, Millionaires), 52 (Seattle), 54 (Livingstone, Malone), 55 (Arenas, Noble, Hall), 56 (Fredrickson), 57 (Falcons, Darragh, crest), 58 (Broadbent), 60 (Nighbor, Gerard), 61 (Morenz), 62 (Vézina, Adams), 63 (Cougars), 65 (Bread Line), 66 (Connell, Lehman), 69 (Olympics), 70 (Thompson), 72 (Noble, Shore), 73 (Gardiner, Bailey/Shore), 74 (Olympics), 75 (Blackhawks), 76 (jersey), 77 (Hot Stove League), 78 (Anderson), 85 (Pulford, Turner), 94 (Soviets), 96 (Zamboni), 97 (Soviets), 105 (Olympics, Howe), 107 (McGimsie), 110 (Sawchuk/ Bower), 119 (Hull), 127 (Flyers),129 (Sjoberg), 131 (Bossy), 132 (Lafleur), 135 (Gretzky), 144 (Hull)
Le Studio de Hockey/Hockey Hall of Fame: p. 25 (Stanley Cup), 33 (Bowie), 37 (Gibson), 41 (Silver Seven), 42 (Stuart), 48 (Rangers), 51 (Calder), 57 (arena), 60 (Clancy), 63 (Tigers), 64 (Amerks), 66 (Denneny), 68 (Patrick, Ross net), 69 (Bruins), 70 (Dynamite Line, Johnson), 74 (Smith, Blake),75 (memorial), 76 (Red Wings), 77 (Kraut Line), 78 (LoPresti), 82 (Amerks, McAuley), 83 (Durnan, Gorman), 85 (Hollett, Campbell), 86 (Howe), 87 (Durnan/Broda), 88 (Production Line), 89 (Lindsay), 90 (Barilko), 91 (Mosienko, Sawchuk), 94 (Norris), 106 (Chicago), 117 (Plante/Hall), 125 (Cheevers), 130 (Sittler/Dzurilla), 133 (Orr)
Imperial Oil/Turofsky Collection — Hockey Hall of Fame: p. 38 (Waghorne), 58 (Dye), 62 (Watson), 65 (Cleghorn), 67 (Smythe), 69 (Hainsworth), 71 (Leafs), 74 (Bruneteau), 75 (Horner), 76 (Brimsek), 77 (dressing room), 78 (Richard, Cowley, Day), 79 (Ross), 82 (Guidolin, Patrick), 83 (Kennedy), 84 (Richard, Punch Line, Schriner), 85 (Rayner), 86 (Toronto, Clapper), 87 (Bentleys, Kwong), 88 (Leafs), 89 (Sawchuk, Howe), 90 (Howe), 91 (Broda), 92 (Richard, Worsley), 93 (McNeil), 96 (Blake), 100 (Mahovlich), 102 (Storey, Plante), 105 (Kelly, Toppazzini), 106 (Toronto), 107 (Adams), 108 (Hall, Bauer), 109 (penalty box), 128 (Horton)
James Rice/Hockey Hall of Fame: p. 54 (Benedict), 64 (Stewart), 70 (Benedict)
Michael Sr. Burns/Hockey Hall of Fame: p. 59 (Hewitt), 71 (clock), 88 (Quackenbush), 93 (Rollins), 98 (Fontinato), 100 (Richard), 101 (Hall, Dunlop, Broden), 102 (Bower), 107 (Harvey), 110 (Horton)
Studio Alain Brouillard/Hockey Hall of Fame: p. 81 (Howe), 104 (Horvath), 111 (Béliveau)
Dave Sandford/Hockey Hall of Fame: p. 62 (skates), 136 (Cherry/MacLean), 150 (Stevens), 154 (Sundin, Hasek, Forsberg), 155 (Larionov), 157 (Modano), 158 (Sundin, Jagr), 161 (Nieuwendyk), 164 (Hasek), 165 (Konstantinov), 167 (Gretzky), 168 (Ricci, Stevens), 206 (Byfield)
Louis Jacques/Hockey Hall of Fame: p. 89 (Durnan)
Craig Campbell/Hockey Hall of Fame: p. 92 (TV booklet), 153 (Bettman), 203 (O'Reilly)
Graphic Artists/Hockey Hall of Fame: p. 98 (Mikita), 108 (Ferguson/Sawchuk, Toronto), 110 (Hull/Mikita), 111 (Crozier), 113 (Orr), 116, (Eagleson), 117 (Esposito, Worsley), 120 (Savard), 124 (Bowman), 125 (Ballard), 127 (Salming), 133 (Gretzky, Mahovlich)
Lewis Portnoy/Hockey Hall of Fame: p. 101 (Bucyk), 113 (Esposito), 116 (Cheevers), 120 (Orr, Esposito), 122 (Perreault), 129 (Dionne, Sittler), 130 (Orr), 137 (Trottier), 139 (Park), 163 (Salming)
James McCarthy/Hockey Hall of Fame: p. 104 (Bathgate), 100 (O'Ree)
Macdonald Stewart/Hockey Hall of Fame: p. 104 (Montreal)
Frank Prazak/Hockey Hall of Fame: p. 109 (Worsley), 111 (Pilote), 112 (Toronto), 113 (Giacomin), 117 (Orr/Sinden), 121 (Sawchuk, Green), 122 (Dryden), 124 (Lafleur), 128 (Bruins)
Paul Bereswill/Hockey Hall of Fame: p. 115 (Gretzky), 128 (Potvin), 132 (Gainey, Neilson), 135 (Goring), 136 (Stastnys, Gretzky action, Gretzky), 138 (Barrasso, brawl), 139 (Lemieux, Oilers), 140 (Lindbergh), 141 (Coffey/ Hayward, Cup celebration), 142 (Hextall), 143 (Neely, Hextall), 144 (Lemieux), 145 (Gretzky, MacInnis), 150 (Francis, Belfour), 151 (Bowman, Johnson, Falloon), 152 (Lindros, fans), 153 (Roy), 158 (Loob), 162 (Roy), 163 (MacTavish), 172 (Trottier), 173 (Fuhr), 177 (Larionov)
O-Pee-Chee/Hockey Hall of Fame: p. 116 (Masterton), 127 (Howes)
Steven Goldstein/Hockey Hall of Fame: p. 116 (Berenson), 131 (Robinson/Savard), 133 (Trottier)
Dimaggio Kalish/Hockey Hall of Fame: p. 121 (Clarke)
Fred Keenan/Hockey Hall of Fame: p. 123 (Orr)
Robert Shaver/Hockey Hall of Fame: p. 124 (Shack/Ehman), 133 (Howe), 138 (Langway), 140 (Williams)
Matthew Manor/Hockey Hall of Fame: p. 124 (gloves), 159 (Bettman), 161 (Smyth), 174 (St. Louis), 175 (Hull), 185 (Clarkson), 199 (skates)
Jack Mecca/Hockey Hall of Fame: p. 132 (Lambert), 135 (Quinn)
Peter S. Mecca/Hockey Hall of Fame: p. 135 (Bossy)
James Lipa/Hockey Hall of Fame: p. 137 (Tretiak/Robinson), 146 (Sundin)
Howie Borrow/Hockey Hall of Fame: p. 140 (Sutters)
Doug MacLellan/Hockey Hall of Fame: p. 147 (Fedorov), 156 (Messier, Fedorov), 162 (Avalanche), 160 (Stevens), 164 (Chelios)
Chris Relke/Hockey Hall of Fame: p. 152 (Selanne), 154 (Bure), 157 (Fans), 165 (Bure), 176 (Granato), 177 (MacInnis)
Graig Abel/ Hockey Hall of Fame: p. 154 (Lidstrom), 183 (Crosby), 188 (James/Granato/Ruggiero)
Andy Devlin/Hockey Hall of Fame: p. 161 (Yzerman)
Al Smith/Hockey Hall of Fame: p.171 (Iginla)
Phillip MacCallum/Hockey Hall of Fame: p. 172 (Martin)
John Holmberg/Hockey Hall of Fame: p. 176 (Canada)

International Ice Hockey Federation

Andrea Leigh Cardin/IIHF: p. 2–3 (team), 214 (Czechia), 209 (Desbiens)
Andre Ringuette/IIHF: p. 6–7 (game), 177 (Ruggiero), 191 (Malkin), 193 (Sedin), 196 (Crosby/Ovechkin), 197 (Knight, Kapanen), 198 (Carpenter, Marchand), 200 (Lundqvist), 203 (Hiirikoski), 209 (Hartikainen), 213 (Serdachny), 217 (Canada, USA)
Jana Chytilova/IIHF: p. 129 (Tretiak), 146 (Tretiak)
Jukka Rautio/IIHF: p. 154 (Selanne), 169 (Kovalchuk Europe), 173 (Wickenheiser), 175 (Doan)
Matthew Manor/IIHF: p. 185 (Radulov), 190 (Barrie)
Dave Sandford/IIHF: p. 191 (Hefford)
Richard Wolowicz/IIHF: p. 194 (Domi)
Matt Zambonin/IIHF: p. 203 (Stone/Lankinen), 206 (Poulin/ Daoust, Turcotte), 212 (Knight), 213 (Brindley)
Chris Tanouye/IIHF: 209 (Johnson)

Headlines courtesy of: *Boston Globe*, *Chicago Tribune*, *Detroit Free Press*, *Montreal Gazette*, *Montreal (Daily) Star*, *New York Times*, *Ottawa Citizen*, *Pittsburgh Daily Post*, *Toronto (Daily) Star*, *Trail Daily Times*, *Winnipeg (Manitoba) Free Press*, *Yukon World*

Index

This is an index of individuals and arenas.
Bold entries indicate photographs.